Advance praise for *Learning Under the Influence of Language and Literature*

I'd like to give *Learning Under the Influence of Language and Literature* as a gift to every teacher I know. Laminack and Wadsworth's vision is simple yet brilliant: to read aloud across the day. Be sure to read with a pen in hand as they give us an extensive collection of book titles and annotations from which to design a daily read-aloud blueprint. Every teacher's voice can now release the art and magic of children's literature into the classroom.

—Georgia Heard

By sharing their favorite books for reading aloud at different times of the day for a variety of purposes, Lester and Reba create new possibilities for classrooms and for children's lives. Their passion for story and unmatched talent for discovering the best books add new riches to the legacy of read-alouds.

Kathy G. Short
University of Arizona

# Learning Under the Influence of
# Language and Literature

## Making the Most of Read-Alouds
## Across the Day

Lester L. Laminack
Reba M. Wadsworth

HEINEMANN
*Portsmouth, NH*

**Heinemann**
A division of Reed Elsevier Inc.
361 Hanover Street
Portsmouth, NH 03801–3912
www.heinemann.com

*Offices and agents throughout the world*

**Library of Congress Cataloging-in-Publication Data**
Laminack, Lester L., 1956–
    Learning under the influence of language and literature : making the
most of read-alouds across the day / Lester L. Laminack, Reba M.
Wadsworth.
        p.   cm.
    Includes bibliographical references and index.
    ISBN 0-325-00822-1
    1. Oral reading.    I. Wadsworth, Reba M.    II. Title.
LB1573.5.L346 2006
372.45′2—dc22                                        2005029379

*Editor: Lois Bridges*
*Production: Elizabeth Valway*
*Cover and interior design: Joyce Weston*
*Composition: Technologies 'N Typography, Inc.*
*Manufacturing: Steve Bernier*

Printed in the United States of America on acid-free paper
10  09  08  07  06  RRD  1  2  3  4  5

# Contents

# Acknowledgments

$A$CKNOWLEDGMENTS are a tricky thing. There is always the risk of leaving out someone who has been profoundly important in the journey. There is also the risk of creating a laundry list so long and tedious that no one really reads it or cares. So we begin this task with those concerns. First, we wish to acknowledge those folks to whom we share a debt of gratitude. We gratefully acknowledge our tireless editor, trusted friend, and "goddess of goodness," Lois Bridges. Lois was there for us from the first mention of this idea to the last drop of ink on the very last page. She was our lighthouse, our fortress, our guardian, and our guide. The journey would have been much less of a joy without her. So to Lois-the-goddess-Bridges, goes our first and most heartfelt thanks.

During the summer of 2003, a group of dedicated book lovers, the original BBB's (Books, Beach, and Beverages), met in Gulf Shores, Alabama for a long weekend to explore new books. Those hours of reading, discussing, and celebrating over three hundred new treasures planted seeds that would eventually grow into a book proposal for Lois Bridges. To each of these friends: Christy Johnson, Kristi Adams, Mary Kay Hodges, Pat Mathis, Nancy Johnson, Sara Jane Tarter, and Georgina Pipes, we say thank you for those joyous hours together. We hope you find this book useful in your work with children.

And, of course, each of us has individuals to acknowledge. We'll begin with Lester.

I am one of those fortunate few who has the opportunity to spend a great deal of time in schools and classrooms across the nation. I love those moments when children make connections and see themselves as fully worthy and smart human beings. I cherish those moments when I get to be part of that and I gratefully acknowledge all the many children and teachers around the country who have played a role in shaping my vision of the many ways picture books can be a viable part of the instructional day.

There are a few very special folks that I feel compelled to mention. First, I wish to acknowledge the family of teachers and students at Woodmeade Elementary in Decatur, Alabama who always welcome me as one of their own and allow me to learn alongside them each time I visit. I want to also acknowledge the friends and colleagues in the St. Paul/Minneapolis area who have supported my work with care and stretched my thinking with each visit: Georgia Loughren, Sharon Androff, Kathy Quick, Patti Green, and Ann Griffin among the many others with whom I have been privileged to teach and learn. Thanks also to my dear friends and colleagues at Country Hills Elementary in Coral Springs, Florida, especially Barb Gratsch whose uncompromising standards about what is right for children is a beacon for us all. Thanks to the folks of Washington County Schools, Tennessee especially my dear friend Karla Kyte who leads a district with heart and wisdom and unfailing courage to stand up for children. And my heartfelt thanks to the V.I.E.W. team in the Lakota School District in Ohio, you folks have vision and, more importantly, the strength to see it through.

I gratefully acknowledge the influence of Mem Fox, a dear friend and tireless advocate for literacy. Your enthusiasm, your passionate advocacy for children and the power of reading aloud have been an inspiration to me through the years. Each time I hold a book in my left hand and stand before an audience of any age, I hear your careful attention to pacing, tone, intensity, and mood. Each time I read aloud I hear the drama in your voice and I see your expressive face.

I owe much to my colleagues at Western Carolina University for twenty-three years of conversation around books and literacy education. I offer a special thanks to Barbara Bell who steadfastly stands for her beliefs and is forever on the lookout for another good book. And also to Terry Rose who consistently and gently reminds me that my beloved picture books can be very useful resources as children develop essential understandings in mathematics. The two of you make me smarter; more importantly, you let me be myself and you make me laugh.

A truckload of thanks (that's a southern thing) goes to my dear friend Katie Ray for all the many, many hours of thoughtful conversation around picture books and the teaching of writing. I grow each time I am in your audience. I delight in the opportunity to share your company and your thinking.

I cannot fail to acknowledge the influence of Jeannette Davis of R.L. Bryan Books in Columbia, SC. You have been a steadfast friend and a tremendous resource over the years to help me stay abreast of new titles. You are one of the most knowledgeable book people I have ever known. In addition, I would like to acknowledge your colleague (now retired) Joan Stevenson who has the most amazing network of book folks you can imagine. "Aunt Joan" has been there through thick and thin. Thanks to the two of you for all your support.

Clearly, I owe a great debt of gratitude to my wife Glenda who has been my fervent supporter for thirty-one years. In typical fashion you offered unfailing support throughout this project. You were always there in your quiet way, waiting for those moments when I needed to sit on the porch with a glass of wine and get away from work, or take a walk to clear my head, or just drop the top and cruise over the parkway. Thank you, dear one, for the space to follow this passion.

To my son, Zachary I am grateful for your zest for life, your giving spirit, your commitment to your own writing life, and for the many, many stories we shared when you were younger. Your willingness to listen, your eagerness for one more story only intensified the passion for books that has led to this project so many years later. You are a living example of the power of story in the lives of children. I eagerly await the day I hold your first novel in my hand. I know that day is coming.

Last, but certainly not least, I wish to acknowledge Reba Wadsworth, a trusted friend, a passionate "bookaholic," and an outstanding educator. I have had the pleasure and privilege of working in some of the finest schools in the country, but I have never met a principal who more clearly demonstrates the notion of putting children first in every decision, every day, in every way. A project like this one has the potential of becoming an unwieldy and daunting task. However, the daily phone conversations and the steady stream of email keeping communication open and flowing have made this project a joyous and productive adventure. At times I have felt as if we were Lewis and Clark moving in search of one more bookstore, one more book—just one more book with a focus on friendship, another angle on civil rights, or a book that could be a model for making smooth transitions between ideas. It has been a delightful journey. I cannot think of another person who could be more passionate about finding good books and getting them into the hands of children and their teachers. I cannot think of another person with whom I could have written this book. You have pushed my thinking and stretched my understanding. You have led me to new connections within and between books. You have fueled my passion for this work when the flames were dwindling and I was near the end of my rope. I am proud to coauthor this project with you, but most of all I am honored to call you a trusted and dear, dear friend.

And now Reba wishes to acknowledge the following:

All the months of long hours spent on this book have been a glorious experience filled with surprises as we discovered many new and wonderful books that belong in the hands of others. Having had Lester as a writing partner has been a dream come true for me because he never tired of the hunt—the hunt for just the right word or one more delicious book. Phone call after phone call (he in North Carolina with me in Alabama), email after email, hour after hour, his excitement and energy never wavered. Ten years ago, when I first met and heard him read aloud at a Mid-South Reading and Writing Institute in Birmingham, AL, I became captivated by his talent, his enthusiasm, and amazing ability to mesmerize an audience with the cadence of his voice as he put the language of a breathtaking picture book into the air. Since that time my respect for him has only increased as I have come to appreciate that whether he is in front of thousands of teachers at a national conference or a single classroom of children at Woodmeade Elementary, he is the consummate educator, author, and friend.

There are many others whose work has had profound influence on my professional life. Every phase of my career has been greatly shaped and guided by the work and wisdom of Ralph Peterson, Dick Allington, Lucy Calkins, Lester Laminack, and Maryann Manning. This project would never have entered the realm of my thinking had I not first read their books and worked under the influence of their thinking. Ralph Peterson helped me realize the importance of building a supportive learning community for children—a learning community that works to establish traditions and customs just as we do in our families. Dick Allington for his life's work in researching exemplary reading practices that moved beyond the narrow thinking that skill and drill equaled strategies; instead his work moved me toward the reality that if we want our children to be fluent readers they must spend extensive time reading authentic materials. Lucy Calkins for making us smarter as teachers of writing by simply following the writing workshop framework she has helped to delineate. Her work with children and teachers over the years has provided the research that helped me dream large about the importance of providing young writers with the time to write in a classroom community that values good literature—literature to fill their heads and writing hearts with possibilities. And once again to Lester, a gifted human being, for constantly filling my head with the potential that good children's literature offers to every classroom regardless of age, gender, race, or background. And lastly, my personal and professional thanks goes to my mentor Maryann Manning, professor at the University of Alabama in Birmingham, who initially introduced me to the thinking of each of these educators and thus played a pivotal and critical role in my professional life. Thank you, my friend, for your generosity, your continuous support, and above all, your wise counsel.

The acknowledgments would not be complete without the recognition of the teachers at Woodmeade Elementary School in Decatur, Alabama. Each day when I walk the halls and visit classrooms, I am profoundly thankful for the work I observe from the educators who fill those classrooms with ceaseless energy and commitment to excellence. I am filled with respect for them and for their accomplishments. They are talented educators who inspire me to greater heights as I watch them work with children, listen to them read aloud, and hold deep conversations about books with children. I am in awe that they let no obstacle interfere for long with their work in doing what is right for children. I would not have been able to complete this book with the joy and passion I hold if it were not for their steadfast devotion to the children we serve.

It goes without saying that it would not have been possible to accomplish something of this magnitude without the additional support my family has provided. Each of them has worked daily to make up for my absence out of the family circle by weaving an even stronger fabric that kept my daily life on track. Their love and understanding regardless of my agenda made everything possible. To my mom and biggest cheerleader I thank you for serving as a strong role model to show me that most things are possible if I only believe and work hard enough. Your life has helped me stay true to my ideals. I know of no one who can see through a dense forest to see the single loveliness of a tree better than you. I know this work will bring you great joy and that pleases me. To Christy, a collaborator who never tires of "kidtalking," a fellow educator who works to build a stronger knowledge base and above all an adorable daughter who is everything I could have dreamed of. I thank you for simply shelving book after book for me in hopes of bringing a semblance of order to my life long after I had given up and settled with the lopsided stacks. I celebrate your love of great literature and deeply held belief that stories are essential in the lives of children. To Jim, my son-in-law, I thank you for all the wonderful Saturday morning (Waffle House) breakfasts we shared throughout the last thirteen months and for showing interest in this writing project. Thank you for becoming a cherished member of our family. And to Mike, a husband-for-all-seasons, I thank you for your encouragement when my plate seemed too full to dream. You have always been the support who encouraged me to seek the truth and to always know that at the end of the day that truth and integrity were essential to wholeness. My contentment comes from those elements you've taught me so well. Thank you for your love. But lastly, I want to acknowledge the memory of my darling son, Brad, who left my life far too early but whose sixteen short years on this earth gave me tremendous joy and left me far better than I would have been without ever having experienced them. His very large footprint can be seen in my life as clearly as if he walked on my heart yesterday. To him, my life's work with children is dedicated.

# Introduction

W E'RE BETTING that you can recall at least one teacher who had the power to whisk you away on the written word. It may have been an elementary teacher who read from a favorite chapter book every day right after lunch or perhaps she shared a new picture book every day and took the time to examine the art with you. It may have been a teacher in junior high or middle school who so admired poetry that he simply couldn't imagine a day passing without putting poetry in the air. Or maybe you had a high school teacher who so loved the sound of language that she "took valuable time" from each period to share a short piece only to comment on the artful writing.

We're betting you are like us and can recall that feeling of drifting away, pulling farther and farther from the shores of reality on the tide of language crafted by an artful writer and played on the voice of a talented and passionate reader. We are betting you, like us, can trace your love of language to the music in the voice of at least one significant adult who took the time to make the sounds of written language a part of the legacy he or she wanted to leave with you.

Lester can trace that legacy all the way back to his preschool years. As Lester pointed out while at Hamline University (2002): "I was an onlooker, a lusting voyeur. I sat perched on the wide arm of that oversized chair looking over the shoulder of my brother. He sat next to my mother, open book spread across his lap. He was in first grade, I was going on five and I was in awe. I watched in amazement as my brother placed his finger under a word and it spilled forth from his mouth filling the air with sounds.

"I listened to the music of that rhythmic language—'I do not like them, Sam-I-am. I do not like green eggs and ham.' . . . 'One fish, two fish, red fish, blue fish.' . . . 'The sun did not shine. It was too wet to play. So we sat in the house all that cold, wet day.'

"It was that music that I carried with me around our upstairs apartment. I walked about chanting, 'I do not like them here or there. I do not like them anywhere. I do not like green eggs and ham. I do not like them, Sam-I-am.'

"I was an onlooker, an eavesdropper longing to join the magical club of readers. I wanted to place my finger under a word, just so, and have those words spilling forth from my mouth. I wanted to sit in the big chair next to my mother with a book spread across my lap. I wanted to make the music that was somehow trapped on the page waiting for the touch of a magic finger. I wanted that finger to be mine.

"I listened and watched every evening. I carried the music everywhere chanting the memorable language that continued to resonate long after.

"I did, of course, hold the books and lick the tip of my index finger before carefully turning each page. I did chant the music as I touched the words and I did believe with the faith of a child that I had found that magic.

"Then I went to first grade. I met Dick and Jane. I met Spot. I met Sally. I met Puff—'See Dick. See Jane.' 'Run Spot.' 'Oh, Sally!' 'Get down Puff.' I sat in small circles as we took turns telling everyone to 'Look,' or 'Get down' or 'Run, run, run.' We took turns saying those words, touching them with our fingers, but the music was gone. There was no memorable language. Nothing would resonate long after. I did not walk about chanting, 'Oh Sally. Look, look, look.' 'Get down Puff, get down.' I did not want to read. I wanted to 'Run, run, run!'

"I did, of course, learn to read. As I recall that was neither a remarkable event nor a struggle. Just another occurrence in the journey called childhood.

"The remarkable thing is that I did not long to read. Somehow the magic and the music had vanished. I was in third grade before I even heard the music again. And when I did, it played on the slow-paced, deep and smooth, southern voice of Mrs. Hand, our school librarian.

"It was in the library, once each week. It started with *Uncle Remus Tales* and moved to weekly adventures with Henry and Violet and Jesse and Benny as they struggled to survive in that old boxcar with their adopted dog, Watch. I longed to be Henry, the brave leader. I longed to dam up the stream and make a pool that doubled as the refrigerator. I could taste the cold milk and feel the crack in Benny's cherished pink cup as I drank with him."

It was Mrs. Hand who revived the music I longed to hear. And I continued to cherish the sound of it.[1] I can still hear her voice. Strong and smooth—a little richer than most women I knew then—like thick velvet. It's a quiet voice that can come alive when Brer Rabbit begs his captor, "Please, whatever you do, don't

1. The rest of this paragraph and the next are from Lester L. Laminack, "Living Language: The Art of Reading Aloud," *Teaching K–8*, Sept. 2000.

throw me in that briar patch!" It's a compelling voice that pulls you along like a current running downstream through a story. Even now, if I will quiet myself and listen, I can hear her voice and I am carried away by that same current. I am hiding away with Henry and Jesse and Violet and Benny in an old boxcar. I wash the dishes, including little Benny's treasured pink cup, in the waterfall. I help care for Watch when he has a thorn in his paw and I cheer for Henry when he brings milk and food home to the boxcar.

I can smell the library in the elementary school where I was a student. I can feel the cool hard surface of the wooden chair I sat on and the table where I rested my head on my folded arms. I can see Mrs. Hand, our librarian, in her special spot holding a book she obviously treasures as she looks from the page to our eyes knowing that she was working her magic with that voice. She was casting a spell and she knew it, a spell that would last a lifetime.

Although I had the power to take hold of that sound with my ear, I still could not echo it with my voice. That would come in a few more years.[2]

In the fifth grade my family moved to Key West. It was supposed to be a short stay, so we rented a furnished place. It had no television. The weather was warm and pleasant even in the fall evenings and filling the time outdoors with my brother and friends was no challenge. But the night, the dark and quiet night, was another thing altogether. We played cards and board games, but that grew old quickly. I resorted to reading a book at my mother's suggestion. We bought a copy of the *Wizard of Oz*. It took only a few pages before I was hearing the music, the rhythm of the story, the voices of the characters and finding myself living among Dorothy, the Tin Man, the Cowardly Lion, and the Scarecrow. I was marching down the yellow brick road, I kept watch for that wicked, wicked witch and I feared—even in my dreams—those flying monkeys. You see, I had found it. And once you do, it is yours forever.

It was that voice, and I am sure of this, that led me to believe there was something worth the effort in a chapter book. It was that voice that showed me print could have life in the hands of one who loved words and language and stories. I didn't, of course, realize all this at the time. No that came years later, long after Mrs. Hand had retired and unfortunately even after her death. That insight came in layers over the years. It started when I began reading aloud, first to my own students in first grade and later for my son and then for teachers in workshops and for my college students and in schools where I've been invited (like a storyteller)

2. From Lester L. Laminack, Hamline University Magalog.

to come read aloud to groups of children. I began to realize that people of all ages love to be caught up in that current, love to be swept away from the banks of onlooking and carried through the flow of a story to another place and time. That's when I began to pay attention to how that happens.

I realize now that Mrs. Hand was a master at the art of reading aloud. She not only brought life to stories; she was a living demonstration of the art itself. Without even knowing it we sat in her spell and became her apprentices. I realize now that my love of words and language and stories has one of its roots tapping into that history, pulling life-sustaining energy from the demonstrations of a single librarian, Mrs. Hand.

The legacy of story, the legacy of the rhythm and music of language is a most powerful force in the lives of readers and writers. There is a flow, a current in the language of literature that will resonate long after the book is closed. It is on that current that we move our oral and written language forward as literate beings. We challenge each of you to consider the legacy you are leaving with your students. Will the sounds of language resonate long after they leave you? Will artful language find its way to the voices of your students' spoken words and written works? Will your voice echo in their ears when they open a book and read it cold?[3]

It's unfortunate, but many teachers feel they don't have time for reading aloud or that reading aloud is a treat for students when they have finished their work or as a transition right after lunch, or on rainy days when the kids are trapped indoors. We hope to convince you that reading aloud is not a luxury or a treat, but that it is essential to the literate lives of students. Lester is fond of saying that if he were in charge of the world (that's a scary thought isn't it), teachers would read aloud as many as six times every day. We know that sounds like a lot of time taken from other things; hold on and we'll try to lay out a plan of action that may make it more manageable than you first imagine.

First, it is important to think of each as *an opportunity* to layer another read-aloud experience into your day. It is important to also remember that each time you seize an opportunity to read aloud during the day, it is an instructional act. Finally, remember that each of the opportunities to read aloud is deliberate and carefully planned; they are not simply to fill time, entertain, or reward behavior. For now, we'll briefly outline the focus of the six opportunities for reading aloud. Then, throughout the chapters, we'll flesh them out one at a time and

3. From Lester L. Laminack, "Living Language: The Art of Reading Aloud," *Teaching K–8*, Sept. 2000.

include annotated lists of books we have found to be especially effective for each opportunity.

## ■ *Reading Aloud Across the Day and Throughout the Curriculum*

The first opportunity for reading aloud is at the beginning of the day. The very first thing we do as a class is to gather for a read-aloud. The focus of this reading is building community and needs to include books that feature characters learning to recognize that our similarities as human beings are more powerful than the outward and individual differences that set us apart. This segment should also include books that help each of us be more caring and supportive as we learn to participate as members of a developing community within the classroom.

The second opportunity for reading aloud is to simply put the sound of written language in the air. This reading time features books or other selections with lyrical language, poetic prose, striking imagery, rich description, alliteration, assonance and consonance, playfulness, puns, humor, rhyming, and rhythm. This read-aloud could easily be done as a transition between two events in the daily routine. If you and your students need a few minutes to put things away, refocus, and gather new things—there will always be that stagnant in-between time. Think of this read-aloud as the hinge between two segments in your day. If it is done daily, students will come to understand they must make the transition quietly and quickly in order to hear the story. It is also a nice way to establish a time frame for transitions—everyone should be ready when the book is closed. One more thing: When all minds are traveling along the current of the story, all minds are together in the moment. So, as you close the book, you will have everyone's attention to make any transitional comments about the language before moving on into the next segment of your daily routine.

The third opportunity for reading aloud can serve the same purpose, sharing the same focus, but features poetry exclusively. We are concerned that poetry gets slighted in the curriculum and in the classroom. Even though children's publishers are paying more attention to poetry, we are not seeing the amount of time devoted to it increasing—at least not in the schools and classrooms we have been able to visit and work with. So it is with this in mind that we encourage you to make time for poets and poetry every day. In Chapter 4, we flesh out a plan for using poetry across the week and offer a list of poetry collections and anthologies that will be useful for this read-aloud opportunity.

The fourth opportunity for reading aloud should support the writing workshop. This is not to be done in place of the writing workshop, rather it should extend or scaffold work done in minilessons or when conferring. This read-aloud opportunity needs to feature text selections that are already familiar to the community of learners—texts previously shared in one of the other read-alouds. The purpose is to immerse writers in demonstrations of well-crafted written language. Read-alouds here should feature moves made by other writers to show potential, to extend invitations, to encourage exploration, and to lead the writers in our community toward new options within their own work. Material shared most likely will feature selected segments from the second, third, and sixth opportunities for read-alouds as well as short pieces from newspapers, magazines, and so on. It is essential to note that this read-aloud features segments and not whole texts. We find this works well as a way of refocusing learners right after lunch.

The fifth opportunity for reading aloud should be part of a content area. For example, during a unit of study focused on the civil rights movement in the United States, we would start every class period with a carefully selected picture book. Chapter 6 provides an in-depth look at a specific collection of picture books selected to support a study of civil rights. The collection detailed there will extend the content presented in any textbook, layer in vocabulary, and help students develop a visual image of events from that period in history. We use this more thorough collection as an example of what can be done for any topic in the curriculum. Then, to support other areas of the curriculum, we have put together several other collections of picture books that are featured in our book, *Building Bridges Across the Curriculum with Picture Books and Read-Alouds* (2006, Heinemann). While we recognize that the lists aren't exhaustive, they do provide a demonstration of the potential held within a carefully selected collection of picture books.

The sixth and final opportunity for reading aloud comes at the absolute end of every day. If time is needed to put the room in order and gather book bags and jackets, then these tasks should be completed before this final read-aloud. The focus of this selection should be on leading students toward sustaining a story in their minds and features a well-chosen chapter book, even with the youngest children. The goal is to have students leave school creating images of the events in the ongoing story, to have that language linger in their minds, and to have them thinking throughout the evening about the lives of the characters and what may happen tomorrow. Then, if we are lucky and use our voices well, we will have them begging for just one more chapter.

Well, there you have it and we can already hear some of you out there mumbling something under your breath about how much time this will take and how you don't have enough time already to meet the demands of the day. Consider this: Time is like a budget; as teachers, we live on a "fixed income" when it comes to time. We have only so much and know we will not get any more. When creating a budget, most of us set priorities and make tough decisions. We decide where to put our resources on the basis of what we value and consider most essential. The six read-aloud opportunities will consume some portion of our budgeted time; there is no question about that. The question we beg you to consider is the value of reading aloud to your students. Will the investment of valuable time pay off in other ways? Hang on—as we move through the chapters, we will address the time investment and the payoff for each read-aloud.

# *Learning Under the Influence of*
# Language and Literature

# 1

## *What Difference Does Reading Aloud Make?*

*D*OES READING ALOUD to students make a difference? Oh, you bet it does. When we read aloud to children, we fill the air and their ears with the sound of language. Reading aloud to students (of all ages) invites them to make meaning, create images, and linger with language—become infatuated with words and simply fall into a story. Engaging as active listeners expands their vocabularies and broadens their understandings of the world around them. In fact, the benefits of reading aloud to children may be the one aspect of literacy learning that most literacy educators agree on. The following are some of the many benefits of reading aloud to children on a consistent and predictable basis.

**Reading Aloud**

- Provides models of language in use
- Builds interest in language
- Increases awareness of words
- Builds vocabulary
- Aids in the development of new insights and understandings
- Extends and layers on existing knowledge
- Aids in overall comprehension
- Creates a risk-free zone in which all listeners have more equal access to knowledge
- Has the potential to spark a love of reading
- Can have a positive influence on reading attitudes
- Provides models of fluent reading

- Provides a living demonstration of the act of reading
- Can model how readers think in the process of reading
- Demonstrates the nature and purpose of reading
- Shows the range of topics, styles, and genres available in written language
- Helps develop tastes in reading and in selecting literature
- Improves listening skills
- Aids in the development of imagery
- Offers multiple perspectives
- Broadens a listener's worldview
- Makes the rhythms of written language familiar
- Provides demonstrations of the various ways stories can be developed

According to X. J. Kennedy and Dorothy M. Kennedy (1999):

> There is a close correlation between a child's reading skills and whether that child enjoys books instead of television shows as bedtime rewards. You can do children a great service by reading to them every day, even for fifteen minutes. And why stop after they've learned how to read for themselves? Even for readers, hearing language read aloud continues to nourish literacy. (158)

As teachers, we must trust our students as learners and enlist writers as our coteachers. Writers of children's books typically know their audience well and approach their craft with that audience in mind. We shouldn't feel compelled to interrupt the reading numerous times to explain and expound and share our interpretations and thoughts. We may actually handicap children by doing so.

Consider this: If we stop in the flow of an idea, turn from the text and toward the children to explain a word or offer our interpretation of a metaphor, then we are behaving like those birds who go out, find food, and fly home to regurgitate the nourishment into the eager open mouths of their young. If we share the goal of working toward developing strategic thinkers and readers, and we trust that the books we are presenting are actually within the conceptual grasp of students, then we must trust the children to learn and the writer to know the audience.

If this appeals to your logic, then we encourage you to try this out. Explain to the children that you will read some books twice. The first time is for listening for the big idea. There will be no stopping and talking, no added explanations from you. You simply read and they just listen. Explain that you will then read the book a second time, stopping at selected points to both offer and solicit ideas. Let them know that during that second reading they are also welcome to pose questions if something is not clear. Now, clearly you would not do this with *every book* you select to read aloud. However, if we approach *some* read-alouds in this way, we may actually nudge students to use the context of the language and the craft of the writer as building blocks to make meaning as they engage as listeners. We nudge them to sustain a line of thinking, to keep wonderings open as they move through the text on the current of our voices looking for connections further downstream.

When using a picture book or text with a substantial number of illustrations, another possibility is to take a picture walk through the pages. Slowly turn the pages and carefully examine the illustrations. Linger with the images and the language they can evoke in a viewer's imagination. Pause and wonder, talk and form theories as you slowly move through the images. Invite language and thought as you encourage students to wonder with you about people, relationships, objects, settings, and the like depicted in or evoked by the images or illustrations. As you and your students move through the images, it is likely that theories about the text will begin to emerge. Ask your students to point to specifics in the illustrations that could be used to support these emerging theories. Before moving into the text, take a moment to read any summary material or reviewers' comments on the flap or jacket. Use this language and the emerging theories from the picture walk to establish purposes for listening. Now, begin reading the story aloud, taking care to make the illustrations visible for your students.

The language and art in a picture book should be taken in simultaneously. Remember, when you read aloud for a child or a group of children, you are a living demonstration of the art of reading. Take your time; don't rush the language or the art. Keep in mind that students are trying to build meaning from the marriage of language and art and that your voice is the instrument playing the music of the language listeners hear. So, as the reader, you need to pay careful attention to pace, tone, inflection, and rhythm. The mood of the story should float on the sound of your voice and should be emanating from the art.

In this scenario, because you will have already taken the picture walk through the book slowly, talking through ideas and emerging theories, move through the reading at a comfortable but steady pace. Let the language carry the story. Let the art support the language. Trust the writer and the artist to know their audiences and trust your students to use the cues in the language to build meaning as you read. In other words, read through the story without pausing.

Obviously, reading aloud to students has tremendous potential in their lives as learners. But for us to realize that potential, reading aloud must be more than simply sitting in front of a group of children and saying the words on the pages. When a read-aloud is done well, it is a performance; in our view, it is an art very akin to storytelling. The telling is as crucial to the listeners as is the tale. If the tale is well crafted, intriguing, captivating even but the telling is monotone and dull, we will fail to create a current strong enough to sweep listeners away—to pull them into the flow of the story. There will be no magic.

As noted by Laminack (2000), it is our view that every book has a voice all its own. We have to read each book for ourselves and listen to find that voice before reading it aloud for students. There are quiet books such as *All the Places to Love* and *The Sunsets of Miss Olivia Wiggins, Saturdays and Teacakes, Twilight Comes Twice* and *Hello Harvest Moon* and *Barn Owls* and *Scarecrow* and *Whoever You Are.* There are boisterous books such as *Piggie Pie* and *Me First!* There are laughing-out-loud humorous books such as *Stephanie's Ponytail* and *Hooway for Wodney Wat* and *My Lucky Day* and *Diary of a Worm.* The writing in the book gives you signals not unlike notations in music guiding the musician's rhythm, pace, volume, and tone. Likewise, signals in the text tell you when to slow down, drift your voice to a trailing quiet pause, or stop dead still and wait.

Signals come in the writer's use of language, punctuation marks, capital letters, bold print, puffy letters, color print, line breaks, paragraphing, and other visual cues on the page. A long series of things connected by repeating "and" after every item, for example, could indicate the writer's desire for you to have a sense of the amount or quantity of things. We typically find this reads best in a long breathless string, which drives home the same point with sound that the writer is making with print. Such a series might also be used to have you feel the breathless rush of saying the items all at once or to show that the series taken together provide one image and that one image is really a composite of several individual things. In either situation we would need to read the piece aloud to find the right rhythm to best fit the meaning. A word or phrase written in bold, puffy, red letters twice the size of the surrounding text usually begs the voice for some form of exaggeration—increased volume; stretching out the words; showing audible and visible excitement, concern, fear, anxiety, or worry. Line breaks and paragraphing are more subtle signals that may suggest pauses or clustering phrases to create a rhythm.

There are rhythms in written language, as in music, that can make the oral rendition of a text sing to the ear and heighten the meaning. To find that rhythm we have to read the piece aloud for ourselves. At times, we can find it immediately and sometimes we have to try out a passage several ways to hit on the rhythm that sings for us. Usually, by reading a piece several times, like working through a piece of new music, we come to know the nuances in a text. We find those quiet spots where we need to slow the pace, soften the volume, and lean in a little toward the listeners, as if we are sharing something not meant for everyone. We find those places where the voice needs to slowly climb in volume to demonstrate emphasis. We find those spots where the voice needs to increase the speed as the action moves quickly and suspense is mounting.

The search for those signals can be made easier by coming to know the characters in the text. The characters, too, have a life of their own. Their personalities reveal to us how they might react. That will, of course, reveal how dialogue and descriptions of their actions might be read aloud. Shy, quiet Wodney Wat may speak softly and avoid making eye contact with the audience until he gains confidence toward the end of the story. The greedy and sneaky Gritch certainly does not whisper in her desperate search for eight plump piggies for piggie pie. In fact, she is loud and boisterous—bordering on being rude and obnoxious. Knowing the characters helps us know how to bring life to the language through our voices.

Settings also can be signals. A quiet pastoral setting may be a signal for a slow pace and a quieter tone. A busy, traffic-filled city block may indicate a louder volume or more rapid pace. Even so, setting alone may not be enough to make this decision. Refrains can signal rhythm, a rhythm that echoes, echoes and repeats, repeats and echoes through the text like this sentence. Or refrains may be ways to weave a thread throughout a story, a thread that our voices can highlight without exaggeration, a thread we can help the listener notice. We must come to know these signals so that we can make the read-aloud experience a magic one for students.

Reading aloud can be that current that sweeps students away from the banks of onlooking and into the flow of language itself. Our voices can be the magic. Our read-aloud times can be the introduction to new authors, new genres, new titles, new topics—new worlds. Through our voices, students may come to believe that there is something between the covers of a book that is worth the effort. And, as a result, they may well grow into writers themselves.

Once, when Lester was in an elementary school as a visiting author, a child asked him whether he had wanted to be a writer when he was a kid. Lester wanted to say yes, but knew he had to tell the truth and say no. As a child, Lester had not ever considered being a writer. He did explain that even though he enjoyed writing when he was younger, his school never had an author visit, he never saw writing samples from any of his teachers as demonstrations or examples, and none of his teachers presented writing as a career option. It was just a subject in school then. The same is true for Reba; writing was never seen as an option when thinking of a career. As children we studied writing but never lived it. Also, few of our teachers ever brought it to life. They never wrote in our presence and never mentioned the role that writing played in their own lives. It was as if writing was something done only by students and lonely, isolated people who created books. What an image!

Reading aloud can be our invitation for students to notice how writers craft their work. Reading aloud can lead us to discussions of authors' motivations and interests and knowledge bases. We and our students can live like writers if we take Mrs. Hand's lead and bring life to language with our voices. But it will take more than that.

We must pause to notice the signals writers carefully plan in the craft of their work. We must help students to not only notice them but also to begin trying them on for size. They must hear the rhythms in language, feel the current of the story, and know the magic of voice if they are ever to discover the power of written language for themselves. If they know it, we can show them how it is done and they can produce it on their own, making magic for others. They can envision themselves as the ones who write.

# 2

## Building Community by Reading Aloud the First Thing Every Day

I always read aloud, in my most dramatic voice, when I first meet students. It's the fastest way I know to bond with kids.

*Regie Routman*

**R**ALPH PETERSON (1992) contends that "[t]he primary goal at the beginning of a new year or term is to lead students to come together, form a group, and be there for one another. . . . In making learning communities with their students, teachers make use of ceremony, ritual, and rite in an effort to create a place where students feel they belong" (13, 15). Establishing ceremonies and rituals and routines with students gives them a sense of peace. There is a calming effect that comes from knowing what to expect, knowing the parameters, knowing how the day will pass, and sensing that you belong here—that you are cared for and needed. "Whether we're a preschooler or a young teen, a graduating college senior or a retired person, we human beings all want to know that we're acceptable, that our being alive somehow makes a difference in the lives of others" (Rogers 2003, 162).

The idea of setting the day in motion with a read-aloud is more than just a way to start the day. This particular ceremony is, as Regie Routman notes, the fastest way to bond with kids. Clearly, as we establish the pattern of opening the day with a read-aloud devoted to building community, we are bonding with our students; but they are also bonding with one another and with the authors, illustrators, and characters we feature. So opening the day with a carefully selected read-aloud has many layers of benefit.

Peterson (1992) goes on to say:

> Ceremonies aid students in making the transition between daily life and classroom living by turning thoughts toward schooling. . . . When ritual is incorporated into an opening ceremony, it gets everybody on the same page, so to speak. . . . Ritual has a centering effect. . . . Ritual makes it possible to dwell in an experience, to exist in feeling ways, to simply be one with the moment. (16, 20–22)

When we gather around a story first thing in the morning, we are leading students to lean in, to join with the characters and with each other as we examine the lives of those characters and the impact of their decisions. We lead them to examine life through the lens of another, to see the challenges faced; and, more important, to realize how our responses to life's challenges can make all the difference. The rituals involved in getting ready for the morning read-aloud will quickly become a shared routine in the community of learners; in many ways these will help define the community. "Ritual is a way of connecting to a larger community. It is more than talk. It is made up of symbolic acts that ground family and community life. Rituals such as taking up a position in a circle, taking oaths, making pledges, and lighting candles all symbolize that participants are entering into a different reality" (Peterson 1992, 20).

Every morning, as you begin the day with this first read-aloud, what rituals will you establish? Will there be a designated spot for all to gather? Will each student have a designated place? Will there be any talk before the book is shared? Will you always begin by telling how you selected the book? Will there be talk during the reading or after? Will there be clearly defined or understood ways of entering into the conversation? Obviously, these are issues to ponder as we make the first read-aloud of the day a significant part of the community's life. Whatever rituals you establish, we strongly recommend that you include the selection's title and introduce the author and illustrator (if appropriate) as if they are present and guests in your community that morning. When a familiar author or illustrator is featured, acknowledge what is known about the person.

Beginning the day with a read-aloud can yield benefits throughout the day and across the weeks and months of your time together. Consider the energy harnessed by having all the minds in your classroom community come together and focus on the language and events of the story you are putting in the air. Consider the power of beginning your day with all that energy traveling on a common current; every member of the community rubbing shoulders with the same characters—pondering their dilemmas, cheering their accomplishments, and sharing in the pain of their struggles and losses. Consider having the cumulative effect of all those readings as a common touchstone across the days and weeks and months of a school year.

Consider the rich discussions that could develop within your community and the opportunities that may arise for modeling how to explore a topic and form an opinion, how to dialogue with others, how to voice an opinion, or how to disagree in a civil and respectful manner. Consider the opportunities you could have for hosting frank conversations about choices, friendship, and treatment of others, respect for differences, and a myriad of other topics that could center on the characters in stories rather than on individuals in the classroom community. Consider the effectiveness of a well-chosen book at the most timely moment. And as we said in the introduction, consider the power of books that feature characters learning to recognize that our similarities as human beings are more powerful than the outward and the individual differences that distinguish us one from another. What if we had opportunities to get to know people as human beings with emotions and intellect and heart and soul before we knew the labels that separate and build walls and foster hatred? What if?

Mr. Rogers, our beloved television neighbor (and one of Lester's heroes), wrote that "[a]s human beings, our job in life is to help people realize how rare and valuable each one of us really is. . . . It's our job to encourage each other to discover that uniqueness and to provide ways of developing its expression" (Rogers 2003, 137). Clearly, this is one of the goals of this first read-aloud.

In this chapter we feature books to help you show children how rare and special they are while also coming to realize that each of their neighbors is equally valued. The books will help demonstrate that we can love and support the learning of one without diminishing the capacity to love and support others. We feature texts to help students understand that life brings challenges and joys and fears and worries. We can use the books to help students know that they, like the characters they meet, can face challenges and know the full range of human emotions in healthy ways. The conversations these texts can help us ignite are important. Through the first read-aloud of a carefully chosen book, we can help students recognize that it is a part of human nature to feel all the emotions. But, more important, we help them to internalize positive ways to react to those emotions.

## ■ *Books for Building Community*

This first collection of books is organized under one big umbrella: Building Community. Under that umbrella we have carefully clustered several sets of books around related themes. So now we invite you in to explore books from the following eleven shelves—books we believe will help you and your students establish a caring and thoughtful, open and accepting community.

- Celebrating Ourselves and Others
- Believing in Yourself
- Providing a Lens to View the World
- Learning to Value Special People with Special Ways
- Today I Feel . . .
- Overcoming Obstacles and Facing Life's Challenges
- Meeting Neighbors and Making Friends
- Coping with Taunting, Teasing, and Bullying
- It Happened at School
- A Family Is . . .
- Learning to Say Good-Bye

One final word before you begin perusing the shelves. We clearly recognize that these collections are only a beginning; this list is by no means intended to be exhaustive. At best we see the books here as the base from which we hope you will continue to build as you discover new titles with this first read-aloud in mind.

### *Building Community Bookshelf One: Celebrating Ourselves and Others*

Self-respect and a healthy sense of self-worth may be essential to our ability to appreciate others. Mr. Rogers (2003) said that "[w]e want to raise our children so that they can take a sense of pride in both their own heritage and the diversity of others" (146). For each of us to hold dear a personal identity does not prohibit any of us from recognizing and appreciating the value of the differences others may know as truth. "When you combine your own intuition with a sensitivity to other people's feelings and moods, you may be close to the origins of valuable human attributes such as generosity, altruism, compassion, sympathy, and empathy" (Rogers 2003, 147). Books selected for this shelf are intended to help you lead your students to discover or validate an identity as individuals who are important in their own right. In addition, these books can spark the conversations that can help them recognize the significant role each plays in creating community in the classroom, in the neighborhood, and in the world.

## All the Colors of the Earth

*Written and Illustrated by Shelia Hamanaka*
Mulberry Books/Morrow 1994, ISBN 0–688–17062–5

> Hamanaka's very short but glorious book tells the reader (and listeners) that regardless of the color of your skin it takes all the ethnic diversity found on earth to make us what we are. From phrases like *roaring brown, whispering gold, tingling pink* to others like *crackling russets,* the author's craft is a stunning work. The message of this seven-sentence book will surely become a favorite of yours to use for phrasing, beautiful language, adjectives, punctuation, leads, endings, but most of all message. . . . *Children come in all the colors of the earth and sky and sea.*

## Celebrations

*Written and Illustrated by Nancy Maria Grande Tabor*
Charlesbridge 2004, ISBN 1–57091–575–X

> Since Mexico and the United States share a border, they also share many citizens, customs, holidays, and celebrations. In this lovely bilingual text (the language appears on all pages in both English and Spanish), Tabor begins with: *All days are special. Every day an important event happens. We choose the days we want to make even more special, and we celebrate those days in many ways.* From the celebration of the New Year through all the major holidays, Tabor explains the customs of each country. What a wonderful resource this will become for the many U.S. classrooms that are home to bilingual children.

## Country Kid, City Kid

*Written by Julie Cummins*
*Illustrated by Ted Rand*
Henry Holt 2002, ISBN 0–8050–6467–2

> Ben lives in the country and Jody lives in the city, and this is where the book gets interesting. Ben's perspective about life in the country is told on the left

page while on the opposite page you find Jody's perspective about her life in the city. The text is interesting but the pictures make this one a must-have as you contrast their lives, their customs and culture. As readers move through the text, they will be there for all the daily occurrences including waking up to the different sounds, traveling to school, shopping for groceries, playing baseball, picking up the mail, shopping for Christmas trees, and finally getting ready for summer camp where the two kids finally meet each other. *Country kid, city kid—miles apart but two of a kind.*

## Feathers and Fools

*Written by Mem Fox*
*Illustrated by Nicholas Wilton*
Voyager Books 1989, 2000, ISBN 0–15–202365–8

What happens when we focus on differences in others and let those differences consume our thoughts? Read this enchanted allegory and guide your students to recognize how our fears can alter our perceptions and judgments and ultimately how the choices we make can affect our lives and the lives of others. In this story, the characters are the magnificent peacocks and the elegant swans that begin to distrust each other. Lots of layered meaning may be missed without a thoughtful and reflective teacher to guide and develop the deeper meaning of the story. This is truly a powerful and thought-provoking book.

## Giving Thanks: A Native American Good Morning Message

*Written by Chief Jake Swamp*
*Illustrated by Erwin Printup Jr.*
Lee & Low 1995, ISBN 1–880000–15–6

The author's note reads: *Native American children are taught to greet the world each morning by saying thank you to all living things. They learn that according to Native American tradition, people everywhere are embraced as family. Our diversity, like all the wonders of Nature, is truly a gift for which we are thankful.* This will be one of your favorite books to read aloud and get your children talking about what community means and how we should embrace diversity rather than let it divide us. Printup's art respects the customs and culture featured. This very simple message will become a standard for the beginning of your school year.

## Hooray for You!

*Written and Illustrated by Marianne Richmond*

Richmond Studios 2001, ISBN 0–93167444–1

What makes every one of us the special individuals we are? Explore these ideas with your students. Each of them will likely conclude that there is no one else in the entire world quite like him or her. This book will help us learn to appreciate and celebrate those differences. The art is so colorful and delightful that children will chant "read it again."

## I Am America

*Written and Photos by Charles R. Smith Jr.*

Cartwheel Books/Scholastic 2003, ISBN 0–439–43179–4

Charles R. Smith Jr. zooms in with his camera lens to feature boys and girls representing a variety of characteristics including color, ethnic background, size, religion, preferences, and more. This book contains bright, crisp photography and minimal text presented in enlarged font. Smith features his own beautiful children on the page with *I am a new branch sprouting in my majestic family tree.* This one makes a wonderful addition to the community-building focus with the embedded message: No matter how different we are, we are still more alike!

## I Call My Hand Gentle

*Written by Amanda Haan*
*Illustrated by Marina Sagona*

Viking 2003, ISBN 0–670–03621–8

This thoughtful book was written following Amanda Haan's observations of young children playing with each other on playgrounds across America and Europe. It features, in very simple language, many of the things little hands can choose to do: hug, throw, hold, protect, share, catch, hammer, write. It also contrasts the gentle with the not-so-gentle: grab, hurt, steal, break. This lovely, nicely written book can be used with children of all ages.

## I Like Myself

*Written by Karen Beaumont*
*Illustrated by David Catrow*

Harcourt Children's 2004, ISBN 0–15–202013–6

Karen Beaumont's dedication tells it all: *Wishing every child the magic of self-acceptance and love.* This very short, enlarged font text will be very appealing to young children. The story is written in first person with the tiny character drawn to be uniquely different. However, she likes everything about herself and will serve as a springboard for great knee-to-knee conversation.

### I'm in Charge of Celebrations

*Written by Byrd Baylor*
*Illustrated by Peter Parnall*
Aladdin 1986, ISBN 0–689–80620–5

This little book can become the opening to a new way of thinking for your classroom community. So many times, we either skip celebrations or think a celebration has to be an elaborate event for something truly magnificent. However, Byrd Baylor shows us that we can find reasons to celebrate the "everyday and ordinary" things in our lives. She demonstrates how we can have as many celebrations as we choose for any reason we find noteworthy. Read this one to open a tremendous opportunity to begin creating celebrations for the community developing within a new classroom.

### Ish

*Written and Illustrated by Peter H. Reynolds*
Candlewick 2004, ISBN 0–763–62344–X

Our years of work with young children and teachers have led us to value and celebrate approximations. That is why we have become so enchanted with this book: *Ish* is a celebration of approximations. In this tiny but awesome book, budding artist Raymon loses faith in himself when his brother's comments are less than positive. Raymon is on the verge of giving up when he notices that his sister Marisol has snatched one of his crumpled drawings. He dashes up the stairs and follows Marisol to her room only to find a gallery of his crumpled drawings that she has rescued. When Raymon learns to see his work through Marisol's adoring eyes, he begins to see potential in each of his efforts. Every reader will learn an important lesson along with Raymon, a lesson that invites him to savor his life and his efforts to express himself. *Ish* is a book that is simply too delicious for children to miss!

### Let's Talk About Race

*Written by Julius Lester*
*Illustrated by Karen Barbour*
HarperCollins 2005, ISBN 0–06–028596–6

Julius Lester writes on the front flap, *I write because our lives are stories. If enough of those stories are told, then perhaps we will begin to see that our lives are the same story. The differences are merely in the details.* His slant is refreshing yet so simple. As you delve deeply into the text, children will grow to realize that underneath their skin they are all exactly the same as every other human being. Lester is reminding us once again that we must lead children to know each other heart to heart, head to head, and soul to soul before we know the details of our differences.

## Peace Begins with You

*Written by Katherine Scholes*
*Illustrated by Robert Ingpen*
Sierra Club/Little, Brown 1989, ISBN 0–316–77440–5

This powerful picture book deals with difficult personal, national, and world issues relating to peace. You and your students will come back to this one again and again as a touchstone when peacemaking is called for. The story reveals the difficulties that occur as conflicts arise and how these can be resolved in ways that avoid having winners and losers—a difficult concept for young children. The text is rather long but valuable for knee-to-knee discussions.

## Shades of Black: A Celebration of Our Children

*Written by Sandra L. Pinkney*
*Photographs by Myles C. Pinkney*
Scholastic 2000, ISBN 0–439–14892–8

In this celebration of African American children the Pinkneys invite you to notice the many skin tones that cannot be described with the single word *black*. The beautiful children featured range in shades from creamy white to milky smooth brown, from radiant brassy yellow to gingery brown. In addition, the author and illustrator point out differences in hair—straight, twisted, short, and long. The final focus is eyes and the Pinkneys describe how each set of eyes is different from the other. As a transition from one section to the next, you find the words: *I am Black. I am Unique.* (Read this one along with *The Colors of Us, I Am America,* and *Brown Sugar Babies.*)

## Somewhere Today: A Book of Peace

*Written by Shelley Moore Thomas*
*Photographs by Eric Futran*
Albert Whitman 1998, ISBN 0–8075–7545–3

*Somewhere Today* is a strikingly simple text with one sentence per page followed by a full-page photograph illustrating the meaning of the sentence. Every page gives children an example of living peacefully together: *Somewhere today . . . . someone is being a friend instead of fighting.* The book provides an excellent lead-in to inviting your children to develop their own class book to extend the message of peace.

## A Tale of Two Goats

*Written by Tom Barber*
*Illustrated by Rosalind Beardshaw*
Barron's 2005, ISBN 0–7641–5847–3

When you first open this book, Beardshaw's lighthearted art might lead you to think this is just another cute book for children, but if you linger with it awhile and read the text, you will realize there is a much larger and deeper message. In the oversize book, two farmers live side by side with only two goats as companions. One farmer grows cabbage while the other grows turnips. A fence separates the farms because neither wants the goat of their neighbor to have any of their vegetables. However, the goats don't see things the same way as the farmers and begin exchanging food. The farmers don't like that so they build a larger, stronger fence. When that doesn't stop the goats, they build an even larger, stronger, taller fence. The normally healthy goats soon become sick when they stop eating. It doesn't take the farmers long to rethink their behavior and tear down the brick wall they finally created to keep the goats separated.

## The Way to Start a Day

*Written by Byrd Baylor*
*Illustrated by Peter Parnall*
Aladdin 1977, 1978, 1986, ISBN 0–689–71054–2

Baylor's text takes the reader on a journey that explores many different cultures (cavemen, Peru, Aztec, Congo, China, Egypt, and the Pueblo) and how they each celebrate the new dawn. What a perfect book to use to draw a parallel at the beginning of the year as you begin to develop ceremonies and rituals for your classroom community.

## We Share One World

*Written by Jane E. Hoffelt*
*Illustrated by Marty Husted*
Illumination Arts 2004, ISBN 0–9701907–8–6

*You and I, we share one world,*
*One golden sun,*
*One silver moon.*

So begins the musings of one young boy perched atop a rock formation staring toward the distant mountains and the pastel sky. As readers turn each page, our narrator speaks of the many things he shares with children everywhere—breathing the air, touching the wind, hearing the waves, and smelling the rain—he speaks of sharing one world. Our young narrator looks in from one corner of each spread into another part of the world where children are depicted in the context of their culture, sharing what our narrator speaks of. In the upper corner of each spread there is a small inset map showing the home continent and country of the children depicted. Hoffelt and Husted are sisters who merged their talents to celebrate life and help children recognize that as human beings we are more alike than different, to recognize that as citizens of the globe we are all neighbors. (Pair this one with the 1997 *Whoever You Are* by Mem Fox.)

### Whoever You Are

*Written by Mem Fox*
*Illustrated by Leslie Staub*
Voyager Books 1997, 2001, ISBN 0–15–216406–5

Mem Fox gently and quietly reminds us that no matter where we are or who we are there are others just like us all over the world. While our skin may be different, our homes and schools may be different. Our language may even be different but inside our hearts are the same. We all smile the same. We laugh the same. We hurt and cry the same. This wonderful book is an invitation to children to become aware of all the other ways we are the same, despite our differences. *Whoever You Are* is a great book to begin community-building on the first day of school. The book is gift enough, but our additional wish for you is that Mem Fox could read the book to your children.

## Building Community Bookshelf Two: Believing in Yourself

Some children seem to cross the threshold on the first day of school with confidence and poise. Yet some seem to doubt themselves and their worth to others. For this shelf we've pulled several books with characters that reveal a belief that being special is possible even in the face of factors that might defeat many. As you consider the titles here, think of how you could provide support for those who doubt themselves, even when they don't realize they need the support. Perhaps Mr. Rogers (2003) said it best when he wrote: "The world needs a sense of worth, and it will achieve it only by its people feeling that they are worthwhile" (175). During the opening read-aloud let these books help students explore the importance they each have as members of the classroom community you are developing day by day.

## Buzzy, the Bumblebee

*Written by Denise Brennan-Nelson*
*Illustrated by Michael Glenn Monroe*
Sleeping Bear Press 1999, ISBN 1–886947–82–1

> This book needs to be read and discussed near the beginning of the year as you are establishing the importance of believing in yourself. Buzzy reads the *scientific fact* that bees should not be able to fly due to their build. He begins to doubt himself and all of a sudden Buzzy really can't fly. The story takes the reader on Buzzy's journey of rediscovering how to get his head aligned with his heart! *Buzzy* . . . is a superb book for community-building at all levels during the elementary years.

## The Dot

*Written and Illustrated by Peter H. Reynolds*
Candlewick 2003, ISBN 0–7636–1961–2

> Vashti is a little girl who doesn't believe in herself or her ability to draw; however, she has a wonderful teacher who not only believes but makes Vashti believe as well. When asked to begin on her art project, Vashti resists and says she just can't draw. When all she gets out is a single dot, her teacher asks her to sign it. The next day that piece of art is framed and hung behind the teacher's desk. *The Dot* is a very short but oh so powerful book. This one would be a good read-aloud for your children *and* an excellent book to open a faculty meeting. It would also be a great gift for a special teacher who takes the time to value individual differences in children. (Pair this one with *Ish.*)

## Dumpy La Rue

*Written by Elizabeth Winthrop*
*Illustrated by Betsy Lewin*
Henry Holt 2001, ISBN 0–8050–6385–4

Everyone including his parents tells Dumpy La Rue that pigs can't dance but Dumpy knows that is not true. His sister teases him but still Dumpy believes. He is a pig who knows just what he wants to do. He slips, and he slides. He shimmies and he shuffles. He simply dances from the music in his head. Soon all the animals in the barnyard are following Dumpy's advice and listening to the music in their heads. Word spreads to all the other barnyards, and folks come from all around to see the amazing show led by Dumpy La Rue, a pig who knows just what he wants to do.

## Mr. Lincoln's Whiskers

*Written and Illustrated by Karen B. Winnick*
Boyds Mills 1996, ISBN 1–56397–805–9

Grace Bedell, an eleven-year-old girl, makes history in 1860 when she writes a letter to Mr. Abraham Lincoln to give him some advice about what is appealing to voters when he runs for President of the United States. At this time in history, women couldn't vote, but Grace strongly believes in the same things Lincoln believes in but she thinks his face too thin and sad for people to vote for him. So this young girl changes history by writing a letter (text is included) to Mr. Lincoln advising him to grow a beard. Not only does he grow a beard but he also writes her back. Shortly after winning the presidency, Mr. Lincoln, when traveling to be sworn in, has his train stop in the town where Grace lives so that he can meet his new friend.

## Odd Velvet

*Written by Mary E. Whitcomb*
*Illustrated by Tara Calahan King*
Chronicle Books 1998, ISBN 0–8118–2004–1

Velvet is an odd and strange little girl in the eyes of her classmates, but she follows her heart and mind regardless of the things they say about her. As the days unfold and the school year draws to a close, her classmates begin to understand and appreciate Velvet. They even begin saying that Velvet is not so strange after all. This is a wonderful book to spark conversations about friendship, valuing all people, and looking for the good in others.

## Pig Enough

*Written and Illustrated by Janie Bynum*
Harcourt Children's 2003, ISBN 0–15–216582–7

Willy is really a guinea pig but when he wants to join the Pig Scouts, all the other pigs make fun of him—*Willie, Willie, don't be silly! You'll never be a pig!* But the taunting and teasing doesn't deter him. He joins the Pig Scouts. On their very first outing, the only two pigs not chosen to be a partner for the hike are Willie and Peyton. Peyton is not happy to be paired with a guinea pig and he starts the chant, *Willie, Willie, don't be silly! You'll never be a pig!* By this time, you can guess that something is going to happen that will allow Willie to prove to the other pigs that he really is a pig—not just one that looks different but also one that has talents the other pigs don't have. This is an adorable read-aloud that you and your children will delight in spending time with.

### Stand Tall, Molly Lou Melon

*Written by Patty Lovell*
*Illustrated by David Catrow*
Putnam Juvenile 2001, ISBN 0–399–23416–0

Molly Lou is one spunky little girl who believes in herself regardless of the comments by the class bully. It doesn't matter that she is the shortest girl in first grade. It doesn't matter that her teeth stick out so far you could stack pennies on them. Her grandmother is a sage old woman who offers the best advice one can get. And Molly Lou is wise enough to listen. When her grandmother tells her to smile, that's what she does. Once read, this one will never leave your short list of books to read aloud!

### The Straight Line Wonder

*Written by Mem Fox*
*Illustrated by Marc Rosenthal*
Mondo 1997, ISBN 1–57255–206–9

Mem Fox uses her imagination in such a creative manner as she reveals the importance of believing in yourself and your worth while making three straight lines her characters. Line one doesn't like being a straight line and despite being criticized by his two friends, he delights in jumping and twirling and pointing his joints. His friends are embarrassed by his antics until he is discovered by a movie director who makes him famous. With a thoughtful, guided discussion, this book can become an important read-aloud for your students.

# Building Community Bookshelf Three: Providing a Lens to View the World

Books pulled for this shelf were selected because they enable us to look past ourselves. They help us recognize that our lives overlap the lives of others whether they live across the street or across the globe, whether they exist alongside us in this hour or have lived during other decades or centuries. As you share these books with students, everyone is exploring how much we have in common as members of one human family.

If there is one message that could capture the essence of the books on this shelf, it would be this: "As different as we are from one another, as unique as each one of us is, we are much more the same than we are different. That may be the most essential message of all, as we help our children grow toward being caring, compassionate, and charitable adults" (Rogers 2003, 184). Our one caution in sharing these books is to remind you that, as the adult, it is your responsibility to notice and name stereotypes and bias when it is evident and to provide other perspectives to make that bias visible. We hope you find this collection helpful in that endeavor.

## Alice Yazzie's Year

*Written by Ramona Maher*
*Illustrated by Shonto Begay*
Tricycle Press 2003, ISBN 1–58246–080–9

> Written as poems for each of the months of her year, this lovely book shows the contrasts between the childhoods of Alice Yazzie and her Grandfather Tsosie who remembers his days with his Navaho tribe. The book so nicely captures his feelings as he watches his precious granddaughter move into her world of school buses, Mickey Mouse, San Francisco, Levi jeans, and all the other things that are so far from his memories of growing up.

## Angel Child, Dragon Child

*Written by Michele Maria Surat*
*Illustrated by Vo-Dinh Mai*
Scholastic 1983, ISBN 0–590–42271–5

> This book takes you into the heart of a scared little Vietnamese girl named Ut. She becomes very sad and misses her mother when she must go to an

American school where the children make fun of her clothes and she doesn't understand their language. Ut's mother is not able to come with the large family when they immigrate because they do not have enough money for her mother's fare. One day when anger overpowers Ut's gentleness, she strikes back and gets into a fight with Raymond. When the principal breaks up the fight and makes Raymond write Ut's Vietnamese story, things change for everyone in the school. Suddenly, the words spoken between the two build a bridge of understanding, kindness, and generosity. This book helps children learn to live together as a community regardless of the many differences that may exist between members.

### The Caged Birds of Phnom Penh

*Written by Frederick Lipp*
*Illustrated by Ronald Himler*
Holiday House 2001, ISBN 0–8234–1534–1

Ary, a young girl, lives with her family outside the Cambodian city of Phnom Penh, a very crowded, dirty city full of merchants and air so polluted that it is difficult to breathe. Ary's family is very poor and they have little security in their lives. She longs to smell clean air, have good food to eat, and have steady work for her family. The sky is so polluted that the only birds she ever sees are in a cage at the market. The birds, like Ary, have forgotten what it's like to be free. According to tradition, if she can free a bird, it will carry her wishes into the open sky. The first bird Ary frees only returns very quickly back to its cage. It takes many days to save enough money to free another. This time she very carefully selects the bird to free. With wishes for the courage to find more knowledge, food for her family, and medicine for her grandfather's sores, she sends the bird to freedom.

### The Chief's Blanket

*Written by Michael Chanin*
*Illustrated by Kim Howard*
H J Kramer 1997, ISBN 0–915811–78–2

Long before the white man came to settle the land, the Navajo women of the Southwest were skilled weavers. In *The Chief's Blanket* Mockingbird Song is known throughout the land for her beautiful work and men from far and wide come to barter with her for the blankets she weaves. As she grows older, she teaches her granddaughter, Flower After the Rain, to weave as well. One day a chief and his braves arrive. When the chief sees Flower After the Rain's work, he longs to own one of her weavings. This heartwarming story goes on to reveal how the young girl decides to help her ailing grandmother by trading one of her lovely blankets for a horse.

## The Color of Home

*Written by Mary Hoffman*
*Illustrated by Karin Littlewood*
Phyllis Fogelman/Penguin Putnam 2000, 2002, ISBN 0–8037–2841–7

Hassan has just moved from his home in Somalia, a war-torn country in Africa. He begins school knowing little English and is very homesick. The school here is far different from his school back home. Read about the trials young children face when they enter a school where everything is strange and frightening . . . even lunch. The story also reveals children who are kind and a teacher who goes the extra mile to reach this young child and make him feel welcome, even using Hassan's artwork to build the bridge that connects strangers to friends. Littlewood's bright watercolor paintings fill the spreads and support the story well.

## Dancing with the Indians

*Written by Angela Shelf Medearis*
*Illustrated by Samuel Byrd*
Holiday House 1991, 1993, ISBN 0–823–41023–4

*Dancing with the Indians* is based on a story passed down through the generations from the author's great-grandfather who escaped from slavery in 1862. He traveled to the Southwest and a Seminole tribe took him in. He later married one of the Seminole women. Even though the marriage fails, he feels a strong bond with the Seminole tribe for the remainder of his life and travels back regularly to maintain those ties. Following the divorce, Papa John moves to Oklahoma and marries an African American woman. Their marriage produces several children, one of which is the author's father. Readers and listeners will find the lyrical prose of Medearis enchanting and pleasing. The author's note included at the end provides many interesting details about the historical information supporting this story.

## The Day of Ahmed's Secret

*Written by Florence Parry Heide and Judith Heide Gilliland*
*Illustrated by Ted Lewin*
HarperCollins 1990, ISBN 0–688–08894–5

As you turn page by page, you walk the dusty streets with this young boy as he delivers heavy bottles of fuel from his donkey-drawn cart in Cairo, Egypt. While traveling the long hot hours up and down the streets with Ahmed, you will learn all about the merchants and their goods. All day long, hour after hour, young Ahmed becomes more anxious to get home to tell his family his big secret. Finally at sundown, the time of day when you can't tell a black thread from a white one, he arrives home where his family is waiting for him. After a deep breath, Ahmed shares his secret . . . he has learned to write his name!

## The Day Gogo Went to Vote

*Written by Elinor Batezat Sisulu*
*Illustrated by Sharon Wilson*
Megan Tingley 1999, ISBN 0–316–70271–4

While this story, told through the eyes of Gogo's young great-granddaughter, is set in South Africa, the events parallel many of the events experienced in the United States as African Americans worked to gain equal rights under the law. Gogo, the great-grandmother, lives in South Africa and has never been allowed to vote. When she learns that she had been given that right under the law in her country, she is determined, despite her age, to participate in an election. This moving story of courage and determination and celebration is too important to miss.

## Dear Juno

*Written by Soyung Pak*
*Illustrated by Susan Kathleen Hartung*
Viking 1999, ISBN 0–670–88252–6

Juno lives in America but his grandmother lives in Korea. His grandmother's language is different from his, so his parents must read her letters to him. He is always excited to receive a letter from Korea. One day one arrives but his parents aren't available, but as he studies the contents of the envelope, he realizes he can make meaning from what's there while waiting for the words to be read to him. His grandmother has sent a picture of herself sitting under a tree and has also included a flower for Juno. This secret discovery helps Juno begin a long-distance relationship with his grandmother that isn't totally dependent on his parents. *Dear Juno* offers a comparison between two cultures and demonstrates how love often communicates without words.

## Faraway Home

*Written by Jane Kurtz*
*Illustrated by E. B. Lewis*
Gulliver 2000, ISBN 0–15–200036–4

Desta lives in America but her father grew up in Ethiopia and longs for his homeland. As he prepares for a trip home to see his sick mother, Desta begins to fear that he won't come back to her. Her father tries to make her understand his need to see his country one more time. In his attempt to soothe her, he describes his homeland so that she can make pictures in her mind and think of where he will be while he is visiting his mother. Before the night is over, his assurances have won out and little Desta wants him to continue telling his stories. The art of E. B. Lewis reflects little Desta's fears and her father's internal conflict between his love for his American family and his longing for his homeland of Ethiopia.

## Galimoto

*Written by Karen Lynn Williams*
*Illustrated by Catherine Stock*
Mulberrry Books/Morrow 1990, ISBN 0–688–10991–8

When Kondi, a young boy in an African village, wants to build a toy out of wire, his brother makes fun of him. But Kondi is determined to find enough wire to succeed because he wants the toy so badly. He collects wire from every source he can find in his village. Finally, after much searching, he has enough and through great effort he has a wonderful wire galimoto that all the village children admire. You will enjoy the softness of Stock's art as it captures the very essence of Kondi's character and the traits readers will admire.

## Good-bye, 382 Shin Dang Dong

*Written by Frances Park and Ginger Park*
*Illustrated by Yangsook Choi*
National Geographic 2002, ISBN 0–7922–7985–9

Jangmi is moving to America from Korea and is leaving behind her home and all the things she's grown to love—her clay roof, her best friend, the willow tree right outside her window, and the chummy they could buy at the open market. The authors contrast the differences found in homes in the United States to the home in Korea where young Jangmi lived. Rather than ondal floors they have wooden ones and rather than a willow tree, Jangmi has a maple tree outside her window. All things make her miss Korea until the girl next door comes for a visit and then Jangmi decides her dad might be right: Life can be good again even so far away from Korea.

## Hana in the Time of the Tulips

*Written by Deborah Noyes*
*Illustrated by Bagram Ibatoulline*
Candlewick 2004, ISBN 0–7636–1875–6

To build your background for this turbulent period of history in Holland, read the author's note before reading this rather long but very significant book to your children. Deborah Noyes hints about the importance of tulips in Holland on the first page: *Tulips in those days were as precious as gold.* . . . In the story, Hana's father grows tulips but he always has time for long walks and time for conversations full of imagination with young Hana. However, when the tulip fever hits Holland, her father becomes obsessed with greed and loses interest in spending time with her. Read to find out how Hana works to get her father to refocus on what is truly important in life. Ibatoulline's art is reminiscent of classical museum art. The book is lengthy, so will need to be read aloud in sections.

## I Hate English!

*Written by Ellen Levine*
*Illustrated by Steve Bjorkman*
Scholastic 1989, ISBN 0–590–42304–5

When little Mei Mei immigrates with her family to New York from China, she finds the new language confusing. In Chinatown, people look and sound like her but at her new school, it is far different. She loves everything about the Chinese language and especially the way it looks with all its fat and short strokes. She wants no part of learning to speak, read, or write in English. In fact, she resists it. Then one day when her teacher reads a book, she forgets all about not wanting to listen to the words spoken in English. Even though it is difficult, Mei Mei, with the help of her teacher, soon comes to realize that learning English only makes her world better because she can understand both languages.

## Jingle Dancer

*Written by Cynthia Leitich Smith*
*Illustrated by Cornelius Van Wright and Ying-Hwa Hu*
Morrow 2000, ISBN 0–688–16241–X

The jingle dance is a festive tradition in the Muscogee and Creek nations. The dancers wear dresses with lots of jingles sewed onto them. Young Jenna has grown up watching her Grandma Wolfe dance with a dress that tinks with each move she makes. Now it is her time because she is old enough to dance at the next powwow. Without enough time to order a dress that jingles, Jenna must borrow jingles to sew on her dress. From one cousin to the next neighbor, Jenna goes in hunt of the jingles. Before the big powwow her dress had four rows and with each bouncing step of the dance, Jenna knows she is dancing for each of the four people who shared their jingles with her. An author's note is provided at the back to give you the history of this tradition.

## Just Like Mama

*Written by Beverly Lewis*
*Illustrated by Cheri Bladholm*
Bethany House 2002, ISBN 0–7642–2507–3

*Just Like Mama* is a portrayal of life in an Amish community. Many feel that it is an excellent example of the family values, devotion, unity, and faith of the Amish people. In this story about Susie Mae's family, everyone says she looks just like Mama. She takes great pride in these compliments and then sets out to prove to her brother that she is just like Mama in all other ways. She works hard to be able to gather the eggs, milk the cows, and pick the berries without eating as many as she picks . . . just like her Mama. In the end, Mama gives her important advice about striving to use other people as your model. (Pair this one with Jane Yolen's *Raising Yoder's Barn*.) *Note:* Because this book contains direct references to Jesus, you may not be able to use it in public schools.

### The Last Dragon

*Written by Susan Miho Nunes*
*Illustrated by Chris K. Soentpiet*
Clarion Books 1995, ISBN 0–395–67020–9

> In the Chinese culture dragons are considered a force for good and therefore play an important role in celebrations. In this book a young boy is sent to Chinatown to spend the summer with his great-aunt. There in a shop window, he finds a very large and faded dragon he wants to restore. His aunt tries to talk him out of it but he pleads with her until she gives in. He spends the rest of the summer convincing several shopkeepers to assist him with the restoration. By the end of the summer, Peter's dragon is completely restored. All the neighbors who helped take great pride in the glorious dragon. The author's note in the back of the book describes the Chinese custom of dragons.

### Lily and the Wooden Bowl

*Written by Alan Schroeder*
*Illustrated by Yoriko Ito*
Doubleday 1994, ISBN 0–385–30792–6

> The author's note at the front tells us that this story actually began as a Japanese folktale but has been adapted for this book. We've chosen to include this in this read-aloud section because it is a wonderful tale that will enchant your children. The text is long, but it is an outstanding story of how kindness and honesty overcome dishonesty and cruelty. Lily lives with her grandmother. When her grandmother dies she asks Lily to wear a wooden bowl to shield her beauty from the world. When she goes to work in the rice fields with the bowl on her head, the other workers laugh at her. Soon Lily is asked by a wealthy farmer to come live in his house and nurse his sick wife. The wife is cruel to Lily, but the eldest son falls in love with this strange girl with the wooden bowl on her head. Despite the dishonesty and cruelty of his mother, he eventually marries Lily and receives the blessings of his father. During the wedding ceremony, the wooden bowl cracks, and Lily's beauty is revealed to the world.

### The Lotus Seed

*Written by Sherry Garland*
*Illustrated by Tatsuro Kiuchi*
Voyager Books/Harcourt 1993, 1997, ISBN 0–15–249465–0

*The Lotus Seed* is the story of a Vietnamese family who moves to America after a civil war begins. Before leaving Vietnam, the grandmother plucks a seed from a lotus pod in the Imperial garden to take with her on the journey. Throughout the years that follow she will take the seed out each time she becomes lonely and homesick. A young brother steals the cherished lotus seed and plants it, but forgets where. Later in the spring, the seed blooms into a beautiful lotus flower—the flower of Vietnam. An author's note provides you with more details about this period of history.

## Marianthe's Story: Painted Words and Spoken Memories

*Written and Illustrated by Aliki*
Greenwillow 1998, ISBN 0–688–15661–4

All of us can remember our fear of the unknown on that first day of school or in a new building or with a new teacher or new classmates. What most of us cannot relate to is facing that first day knowing we won't be able to understand a single word spoken to us. In this story, *Painted Words,* young Marianthe is facing a new school with all the normal fears of a young child, but she also faces a language barrier. What she can't predict that day is being placed in the classroom of an understanding teacher who reaches out to comfort her and to welcome her inside the new community. Marianthe soon learns her art can be used as words to communicate with her classmates. At the end of the story, readers turn the book over and the tale continues with the sequel in which Mari is learning to function in her new language. *Spoken Memories* tells the story of how Mari's family left their poor village to come to America to seek a better way of life.

## Mice and Beans

*Written by Pam Munoz Ryan*
*Illustrated by Joe Cepeda*
Scholastic 2001, ISBN 0–439–18303–0

Rosa Maria loves to cook and have her big family squeeze into her tiny house for one of her meals. The story progresses through the days of the week (with the name of each day enlarged and in a different color) as Rosa Maria plans for little Catalina's birthday. All week as she prepares for the dinner, things keep disappearing. She thinks she is in such a hurry she is simply forgetting. But Rosa is in for a surprise when the riddle is solved on the night after Catalina's party. Spanish vocabulary, which adds flavor to an already delightful book, is sprinkled throughout the story. But don't worry, Ryan has included a pronunciation guide in the back. The artwork is equally inviting and will appeal to students.

## My Name Is Yoon

*Written by Helen Recorvits*
*Illustrated by Gabi Swiatkowska*
Farrar, Straus and Giroux 2003, ISBN 0–374–35114–7

Little Yoon is from Korea and throughout the book she is trying to establish her membership in a new country, a new school, and a new classroom. It reminds us of the conflict children sometimes have when trying to merge into an established community. The book can also help you invite children to focus on what they have in common with others, not just see the differences. (Pair this with *Whoever You Are* by Mem Fox.)

## Mystic Horse

*Written and Illustrated by Paul Goble*
HarperCollins 2003, ISBN 0–06–029813–8

This legend is based on the oral traditions of the Pawnee tribe and tells of a young boy who lives with his grandmother. The tribe depends on horses to carry them to hunt for buffalo, but the boy and his grandmother are very poor and can't afford a horse. So they have to travel from one camp to another by walking and carrying everything they own on their backs. The young boy's adventure begins when he discovers an old horse. Although the rest of the tribe laughs at his plan, the young boy is determined to nurse the horse back to good health. As it turns out, the horse has magical powers and tells the boy exactly what to do to win the admiration of his tribe. However, the boy doesn't follow the horse's advice and the horse is killed. Because of the boy's true sorrow and regret, the horse is brought back to lead the boy to an entire herd of horses. The boy and his grandmother never have to worry about being poor again.

## Passage to Freedom: The Sugihara Story

*Written by Ken Mochizuki*
*Illustrated by Dom Lee*
Lee & Low 1997, ISBN 1–880000–49–0

This story is about a Japanese consul family living in Lithuania as World War II is beginning. Many of the Jewish citizens are gathered outside the consul seeking visas to Japan to escape the Nazi troops who are invading Poland. Each of Sugihara's three requests to his home country to accept these immigrants is denied, leaving him desperate to help all these people. He knows if he helps them, it will put his own family in danger. Read this one to students and ignite a conversation about what character is and how one human being can look beyond his own needs to serve others.

## Peacebound Trains

*Written by Haemi Balgassi*
*Illustrated by Chris K. Soentpiet*
Clarion 1996, ISBN 0–395–72093–1

*Peacebound Trains* is a complex story written in small chapters supported by stunning watercolor paintings. The first two chapters tell the story of a young Korean girl named Sumi who lives with her *Harmuny* (Grandmother) while her *Umma* (Mother) is away in the army. Sumi is very sad and misses her mother. Beginning with the third chapter, while comforting her granddaughter, Harmuny begins to remember how the sound of the train reminds her of life in Korea when she was a young wife and mother and war broke out in her homeland. Soon they had to leave everything behind to escape their country. However, when they arrived at the train, it was already full, so they had to ride to freedom on the roof leaving behind Harmuny's husband—a husband she never sees again. Korean words are sprinkled throughout the story. The author's note at the end will give you adequate background information to make the text even more powerful for students.

## Raising Yoder's Barn

*Written by Jane Yolen*
*Illustrated by Bernie Fuchs*
Little, Brown 1998, 2002, ISBN 0–316–07593–0

In this story the Amish are portrayed as a close-knit community where the belief is strong that neighbors support neighbors. The author's note in the back of the book gives supporting information about Amish culture that will enhance the wonderful *Raising Yoder's Barn*. You might want to consider reading the note to children before reading the story. In it eight-year-old Matthew's family loses a barn to fire. The loss of a barn is a major setback for any family within the Amish community. Therefore, all family members and most of the neighbors join together to raise a new barn . . . all in one day. Many practices of the Amish are embedded within the story told in Jane Yolen's poetic language.

## The Royal Bee

*Written by Frances Park and Ginger Park*
*Illustrated by Christopher Zhong-Yuan Zhang*
Boyds Mills Press 2000, ISBN 1–56397–867–9

Song-ho, a young boy dressed in rags, wants so badly to learn how to read and write. But in the days when Korea was ruled by emperors, the poor were not given the opportunity for education. Yet, because Song-ho is so determined, he goes to great lengths to gain knowledge. After many months of eavesdropping on the master giving instruction, Song-ho is ready for The Royal Bee—a yearly contest to determine which student has the most knowledge. Against the rules, the master teacher takes Song-ho. All the contestants are so bright that the questions and correct answers just keep going back and forth all day. Finally the Great Governor grows tired as darkness falls and asks one final question of each contestant: *What does winning The Royal Bee mean to you?* You must read this one to know Song-ho's answer and the wonderful ending of the story. The authors' note reveals that this true story is based on their grandfather's life.

## Sitti's Secrets

*Written by Naomi Shihab Nye*
*Illustrated by Nancy Carpenter*
Aladdin 1994, 1997, ISBN 0–689–81706–1

Sitti lives in a Palestinian village on the other side of the earth from her son and granddaughter. Nye does a beautiful job describing how a child would understand the distance between her home and her grandmother. Once during a visit, Sitti can't understand the little girl's language and her father has to translate. But love can overcome language and the grandmother and granddaughter learn to communicate. *Her voice giggled and whooshed like wind going around corners. She had a thousand rivers in her voice.* This little girl finally realizes that *people are far apart, but connected.*

### Songs of Shiprock Fair

*Written by Luci Tapahonso*
*Illustrated by Anthony Chee Emerson*
Kiva 1999, ISBN 1–885772–11–4

> Little Nezbah, a young Navajo girl, is excited about the coming of the Shiprock Fair. She looks forward to all the traditions her family shares at this event. Sprinkled throughout the text are Native American terms that add depth to the story of the parade and carnival that all children long for—scary rides, loud music, bright lights, cotton candy, and the Ferris wheel.

### The Trip Back Home

*Written by Janet S. Wong*
*Illustrated by Bo Jia*
Harcourt Children's 2000, ISBN 0–15–200784–9

> Many of the books we list show families leaving their homelands and traveling to America. However, this book features a family, who has lived in the United States for many years, planning a trip to show their child the family's homeland. They plan very carefully when choosing the gifts to take home to their parents. In Korea, as the family members are greeted, their Korean names are given. Wong does a lovely job allowing readers a glimpse of Korean family life as seen through the eyes of the small child.

### The Unbreakable Code

*Written by Sara Hoagland Hunter*
*Illustrated by Julia Miner*
Rising Moon 1996, ISBN 0–87358–638–7

> This outstanding book tells an astonishing story about how the Navajo code talkers used their native language to help win World War II by developing a code that the Nazis could not break. The story is embedded in a larger one that will be appealing to young children. John, a young Navajo boy, has never lived off the reservation until his mother remarries and is moving him to Minnesota. With fear in his heart, he feels he will never be happy again. But his understanding grandfather tells the boy that he carries with him a pride of his native language, faith, and ingenuity. The author provides a note to give you more background that will help extend the meaning for your students.

# Building Community Bookshelf Four: Learning to Value Special People with Special Ways

According to Rogers (2003):

> Part of the problem with the word *disabilities* is that it immediately suggests an inability to see or hear or walk or do other things that many of us take for granted. But what of people who can't feel? Or talk about their feelings? Or manage their feelings in constructive ways? What of people who aren't able to form close and strong relationships? And people who cannot find fulfillment in their lives, or those who have lost hope, who live in disappointment and bitterness and find in life no joy, no love? These, it seems to me are the real disabilities. (25)

It has been our experience that children come into the world with eyes that see the person from the inside out. Children seem to naturally see similarities between themselves and others. They learn from adults to focus on differences, and more important, they learn to let those differences make a difference in how they do or don't interact with people. We pulled books for this shelf that you can share with students as you help them see past a "label" or "inability," to see instead into the human being—to see the heart and mind and soul of another person. In short, to see our similarities.

## The Alphabet War

*Written by Diane Burton Robb*
*Illustrated by Gail Piazza*
Albert Whitman 2004, ISBN 0–8075–0302–9

> This book about Adam is a good one to have on your shelf in the event you have a child in your classroom with dyslexia. His story will help children understand how even a simple task can become very difficult for children with dyslexia. Adam began school like all children . . . eager to learn. He could run, play, and color like the other children. As he moved through the grades and his friends began to read and write, Adam struggled. He did learn to write his name, and he even knew his letters until they were put together to form words; then they were too confusing for him. Thus *The Alphabet War* begins. By third grade, he becomes a behavior problem and his classmates are no longer his friends. The ending of Adam's story is happy when he is placed with a special resource teacher who teaches him special tricks when

looking at letters. *Once he stopped noticing everything he couldn't do, he began to see everything he could. . . . He wasn't dumb. He was just a different kind of thinker.*

### Be Good to Eddie Lee

*Written by Virginia Fleming*
*Illustrated by Floyd Cooper*
Philomel 1993, ISBN 0–399–21993–5

This sensitive story is about Eddie Lee, a Down syndrome boy who lives across the street from Christy. The story takes place on a warm spring day when Eddie Lee shows Christy the wonders of nature that bring both pleasure and surprise to the healthy young girl. Within the pages of this text, Christy has to make choices between being kind to Eddie Lee and being with her friend JimBud. The book provides us with an excellent opportunity for children to think and talk about making choices, showing courage, and respecting differences.

### The Best Worst Brother

*Written by Stephanie Stuve-Bodeen*
*Illustrated by Charlotte Fremaux*
Woodbine 2005, ISBN 1–890627–68–2

All brothers and sisters alternate between feelings and actions that reflect adoration and love and frustration and anger. This book with its short text and soft pictures portrays this mix so perfectly. Into this blend Stuve-Bodeen adds the frustration young Emma must learn to work with when her baby brother is born with Down syndrome. Each spread takes the reader on the highs and lows of the journey as Emma learns important lessons of living with Isaac. For further reading there are two pages at the back of the book that list common questions and answers about children with Down syndrome.

### Can You Hear a Rainbow? The Story of a Deaf Boy Named Chris

*Written by Jamee Riggio Heelan*
*Illustrated by Nicola Simmonds*
Peachtree 2003, ISBN 1–56145–268–8

Third in the Learning Books Series is the story of Chris who was born deaf. The book explains how his parents detect Chris' inability to hear. We also learn some of what it is like to be unable to hear the sounds all around you.

One of the important lessons for children to understand is that deaf children sound different when they speak simply because they have never heard the sound of voices. We also learn about hearing aids, sign language, and lipreading, and what each can and cannot do for deaf people. In establishing a classroom community, the books in this series help children better understand others around them.

## Different Just Like Me

*Written and Illustrated by Lori Mitchell*
Talewinds Books/Charlesbridge 1999, ISBN 1–57091–490–7

All week long April is waiting to go see her Grammie. But during the week, she runs errands with her mother which allows her to see so many different people who are different but just like her. On the bus, she sees children using hand signals to talk to each other. Yet when they get off the bus, she waves at the girl and the girl waves back. Later she begins to notice people in the grocery store come in all shapes and sizes. On the elevator she meets a woman with a dog who must use her hands to read the Braille on the elevator buttons but she finds the right floor just like April.

## The Hickory Chair

*Written by Lisa Rowe Fraustino*
*Illustrated by Benny Andrews*
Arthur A. Levine Books/Scholastic 2001, ISBN 0–590–52248–5

This precious book belongs in so many categories (for example, A Family Is . . . , Today I Feel . . .), but we've chosen to place it on this shelf because of Louis and his gift of using his senses to accommodate his loss of sight. Louis has a wonderful relationship with his grandmother who has a *rich molasses voice and a good alive smell of lilacs with a whiff of bleach.* Gran always sat in her hickory chair to read aloud to Louis and this chair becomes very important to him after Gran dies. The surprise ending will keep children asking for it time after time.

## Howie Helps Himself

*Written by Joan Fasser*
*Illustrated by Joe Lasker*
Albert Whitman 1975, ISBN 0–8075–3422–6

This book begins with the recognition that it is sometimes difficult for the average child to not be curious or anxious about children who are physically handicapped. It was written in the hopes that it would encourage society as a whole to be more welcoming to these children. *Howie is a boy with brown eyes and brown hair and a soft, warm smile. Howie likes to watch the snow fall. He likes to eat chocolate ice cream. He likes to ride in the car with his daddy.* The book goes on to explain that while there are many things Howie can do, there are some he can't do and why. The tone is nonthreatening and very supportive, so children can understand similarities and differences. An additional element we hope children will notice following the reading of this book: pages alternate between color and black and white.

## Looking After Louis

*Written by Lesley Ely*
*Illustrated by Polly Dunbar*
Albert Whitman 2004, ISBN 0–8075–4746–8

Louis is autistic but he attends a school that values inclusion with classmates and a teacher who learns to support and value and encourage him. Everyone works to understand Louis and to invite him into their activities. This book is sure to help your students be more open to all children and to treat others with kindness and patience. A note is included that explains autism.

## Moses Goes to a Concert

*Written and Illustrated by Isaac Millman*
Farrar, Straus and Giroux 1998, 2002, ISBN 0–374–45366–7

Moses is a deaf child who goes to a school where all the children are deaf. Mr. Samuels, their insightful teacher, gives Moses and each of his classmates a balloon to hold at the concert. He shows them that by holding the balloons in their laps, they can pick up more vibrations. (Readers discover that you can feel sound through vibrations.) This book can heighten awareness of sign language because Millman provides phrases along with the appropriate hand motions at the bottom edge of the pages. Your students will delight in the opportunity to practice and use their hands to talk. Moses ends with good advice to all children: *When you set your mind to it, you can become anything you want when you grow up.* There are several more books about Moses.

### The Printer

*Written by Myron Uhlberg*
*Illustrated by Henri Sorensen*
Peachtree 2003, ISBN 1–56145–221–1

> Uhlberg's childhood plays an important role in this poignant story of the courage a deaf father shows in saving the lives of countless workers during a fire. When the newspaper printing presses are being consumed by fire, the deaf printer uses sign language to signal the other deaf employees to alert the hearing ones. Even though all the printing presses are destroyed, not a single life is lost that day due to the bravery shown by a deaf man. The end pages include a detailed description of how to fold newsprint into a printer's hat. In addition, the author's note is especially meaningful.

### Private and Confidential: A Story About Braille

*Written by Marion Ripley*
*Illustrated by Colin Backhouse*
Dial 2003, ISBN 0–8037–2900–6

> A powerful book about young pen pals in America and Australia. The excitement of getting letters is overwhelmed when one discovers the other is almost totally blind. However, soon a letter arrives written in Braille, and with it the realization that friends are friends regardless of differences. Backhouse's art is truly outstanding and supportive of this sweet and heartwarming story.

### Special People, Special Ways

*Written by Arlene Maguire*
*Illustrated by Sheila Bailey*
Future Horizons 2000, ISBN 1–885477–65–1

> The title is so appropriate for this wonderful poetic book about special children. The art is so childlike it serves to assist you in helping young children understand that despite our differences, we are still so very much the same. This book shows children of all exceptionalities right alongside children of all sizes and shapes. This can be an important book to use in your efforts to build a caring classroom community.

### Through Grandpa's Eyes

*Written by Patricia MacLachlan*
*Illustrated by Deborah Kogan Ray*
HarperCollins 1980, ISBN 0–06–024044–X

His grandpa is blind but he teaches John many things about how he "sees." Spend some time with this family as grandpa teaches John how to see using his senses of smell and hearing. Grandpa tells John that Nana's voice smiles at him. So when Nana reminds John its time to go to sleep, he closes his eyes to test his ability to hear a smile. Even though they are in different rooms, John finds out that his grandpa was right. He could hear her smile because he was looking through his grandpa's eyes.

 *Building Community Bookshelf Five: Today I Feel . . .*

Every morning children step from the bus or the carpool carrying the weight of those book-laden backpacks and the added weight of that invisible bundle of emotions they always have with them. Turning to Mr. Rogers again, he contends:

> Confronting our feelings and giving them appropriate expression always takes strength, not weakness. It takes strength to acknowledge our anger, and sometimes more strength yet to curb the aggressive urges anger may bring and to channel them into nonviolent outlets. It takes strength to talk about our feelings and to reach out for help and comfort. (2003, 15)

We have pulled the books for this shelf with these thoughts in mind.

As you share each of these titles with students, help them recognize that "[t]here is no 'should' or 'should not' when it comes to having feelings. They're part of who we are and their origins are beyond our control. When we can believe that, we may find it easier to make constructive choices about what to do with those feelings" (Rogers 2003, 20). So during this read-aloud explore the feelings featured in each title. Help your students recognize that these feelings are part of being human and that each of us will experience them. Help them notice how reactions to the feelings are what we must learn to control. Perhaps the most important insight that can arise from using this shelf is that we can't always control what happens to us, and we may not be able to curb our emotions, but we do have choices about how we channel those emotions.

## Beatrice Doesn't Want To

*Written by Laura Numeroff*
*Illustrated by Lynn Munsinger*
Candlewick 1981, 2004, ISBN 0–7636–1160–3

> Beatrice doesn't like to cooperate with others but most especially with Henry, her older brother. When Henry has an assignment that requires him to go to the library to do some research, he has to take Beatrice along. But since she doesn't like the library and she doesn't like reading and she doesn't like books, she fusses about having to go. Once there she gives him a hard time because she is bored. After her third trip, she changes her mind about reading when she gets to hear the librarian read aloud. Then she doesn't want to leave the library when it's time to go home. The font used is large and the illustrations will make you fall in love with Beatrice even when she is her most uncooperative self.

## I'm Not Invited?

*Written and Illustrated by Diana Cain Bluthenthal*
Atheneum 2003, ISBN 0–689–84141–8

> Have you ever felt left out of parties while your friends were excited about being invited? If so, this is a book you can relate to, and it is certainly a book that belongs in your classroom for reading aloud. When Minnie hears about Charlie's party at school, she rushes home to discover that she didn't get an invitation. Then everything in her young life reminds her of the party and that only reminds her that she's not invited. All week long she tries to get invited but doesn't succeed. Going to bed on Friday night is painful and then Saturday morning riding by Charlie's house is equally hurtful. Imagine the joy when Minnie learns that the party being held at Charlie's house isn't his party after all—it's his sister's.

## Noisy Nora

*Written and Illustrated by Rosemary Wells*
Puffin Books 1973, ISBN 0–14–056728–3

> This is a wonderful book for any child who is the middle child in a family. It's sometimes difficult to assert your individuality and get the attention all

children need when you're neither the oldest nor the youngest. Nora was no different. When she begins missing the attention of her parents, Nora decides that if she is truly noisy, they will pay attention to her. But when that doesn't work, Nora shouts, *I'm leaving, and I'm never coming back!* It doesn't take long for the family to miss their noisy Nora. She has finally got the attention she wanted so badly.

## The Way I Feel

*Written and Illustrated by Janan Cain*
Parenting Press 2000, ISBN 1–884734–71–5

This short, playful text helps kids explore various feelings while developing the language to talk about them. The story is printed in an enlarged font that is randomly placed on the page to entertain as it informs. This read-aloud can contribute to community-building because it stimulates discussion about the importance of trying to understand the needs of others and of working together to live in peace.

## What's That Noise?

*Written by Michelle Edwards and Phyllis Root*
*Illustrated by Paul Meisel*
Candlewick 2002, ISBN 0–7636–1350–9

When brothers Alex and Ben are put to bed and quietness settles around them, suddenly night noises become louder and louder. Young Ben begs big brother Alex to sing him a song to drown out the noise. But when Alex agrees to sing, Ben wants Alex to come to his bed to sing the song. The story has great dialogue for you to use in a writer's workshop as the young boys work together to overcome their fears. Also, when introducing this charmer, notice the endpapers; the front one matches Alex's blankets while the back one matches Ben's.

## When Sophie Gets Angry—Really, Really Angry . . .

*Written and Illustrated by Molly Bang*
Blue Sky Press 1999, ISBN 0–590–18979–4

Many children have trouble controlling their anger and Sophie is no different. However, an angry child in a class can cause the classroom community to suffer. Reading books that deal with anger helps children develop the language to describe their feelings and will help them learn to solve some of the problems. Bang uses lots of red as the background color for the pages on which Sophie is reacting in anger. The book is very short but quite powerful.

 ## Building Community Bookshelf Six: Overcoming Obstacles and Facing Life's Challenges

Life is filled with challenging moments. Knowing that we are not alone, that others have faced similar challenges, can bring us comfort when those overwhelming feelings begin to stir within. The books we pulled for this shelf feature characters facing big decisions or seemingly overwhelming hurdles. As you open each book and share it with students during the first read-aloud of the day, you will have the opportunity to open conversations about facing life's challenges and making wise choices. Explore how each challenge presents options and how the options we choose can make all the difference.

### An Angel for Solomon Singer

*Written by Cynthia Rylant*
*Illustrated by Peter Catalanotto*
Orchard Paperbacks 1992, 1996, ISBN 0–531–07082–4

> A lonely old man living in New York City is homesick for his old home in Indiana. He doesn't know anyone in the big city where he lives in a hotel for men. He dreams of the things he loved: a balcony, a fireplace, a picture window, a cat, and even walls of color. One night he wanders into the Westway Café—where all your dreams come true. There Solomon Singer meets a waiter with a voice that is quiet like Indiana pines. Over soup and a cup of coffee, Solomon finds a friend. Night after night, Solomon returns to Westway Café and to his friend whose smile brings the warmth of home to him. The details found in Catalanotto's art are worthy of several visits alone; together with the story, it makes this book a winner!

### Bob

*Written and Illustrated by Tracey Campbell Pearson*
Farrar, Straus Giroux 2002, ISBN 0–374–39957–3

> Bob may be the best-looking rooster in a children's book. Once you get beyond Pearson's gorgeous art, you will fall in love with this adorable story

about Bob, a rooster who doesn't understand his role as he clucks his day away—just like all the other hens. All is fine until Henrietta, the cat, tells him roosters aren't supposed to cluck. She tells him a rooster is supposed to crow, to wake the girls every day. So Bob sets out in search of someone who can teach him to crow. Children will delight as Bob travels across the barnyard and into the woods on his search. The story becomes a cumulative tale as each of the animal sounds is repeated throughout his journey. Bob does learn the correct way to wake the girls with his cock-a-doodle-do but he doesn't forget all the other greetings he has learned.

### Chicken Chickens

*Written and Illustrated by Valeri Gorbachev*
North-South Books 2001, ISBN 0–7358–1541–0

When Mother Hen takes her little Chickens to the park for the first time, they are overwhelmed by all that is going on around them. All the animals call to them to join their fun. Yet they refuse each invitation to play because, after all, they're just little Chickens. However, once they make it to Beaver, who is going down the slide, he figures out a way they can slide without doing it alone. He places them on his tail and down they go. Once they've overcome their initial fear, up and down they go together without the safety net of Beaver's tail. This one will speak to young children who feel fear at many new situations.

### Felix and the Worrier

*Written and Illustrated by Rosemary Wells*
Candlewick 2003, ISBN 0–7636–1405–X

Every night after Mom tucks Felix safely in bed, the Worrier sneaks into his room for a visit. During the visit, the Worrier fills Felix's mind with fears about all the things that *could* happen to him the next day. Mom tries to assure Felix that he has nothing to worry about, but Felix worries anyway. The Worrier even visits Felix the night before his birthday. But Felix worries for nothing because he is given a puppy as a birthday gift and puppies worry the Worrier more than anything.

### Good-Bye, Hello

*Written by Barbara Shook Hazen*
*Illustrated by Michael Bryant*
Atheneum 1995, ISBN 0–689–31665–8

*We're moving, so I have to say good-bye. Good-bye for good, old neighborhood. Good-bye, swings. Good-bye, park.* Walk through the pages with this little girl as she says good-bye to all the familiar things she is sad to be leaving. *Soon though, it's time to say hello. Hello, brand-new neighborhood with a Pizza Pit and a Toys Are Good. Hello, new park with a pond and a great big hill for sledding on . . .* This is an exceptional book to use with young children who must move to new things and leave familiar things behind. It could also be useful as a read-aloud on the first day of school as you say hello to a brand-new room and new friends and new routines.

## My Best Friend Moved Away

*Written and Illustrated by Nancy Carlson*
Viking 2001, ISBN 0–670–89498–2

A story for young children that shows the feelings children have when things change suddenly. The book features two young girls who have been best friends forever and begin school together. Then one of them moves away. Of course, the one left behind is sad and wonders who she will have to share things with. One day a new family moves into her old friend's house and that family has a dog and toys and a girl who is the same age. The last page shows two happy new friends!

## Quiet, Wyatt!

*Written by Bill Maynard*
*Illustrated by Frank Remkiewicz*
Putnam 1999, ISBN 0–399–23217–6

Most everyone grows up thinking "if only" I were older . . . Wyatt is no different. No one in his family thinks he's big enough for anything he wants so badly to do. It seems that they are forever telling him to be quiet! Finally, even others begin telling him to be quiet, so Wyatt decides he'll just quit talking altogether. Read to find out what happens when Wyatt isn't talking anymore. Your children will make connections with young Wyatt.

## Saving Strawberry Farm

*Written by Deborah Hopkinson*
*Illustrated by Rachel Isadora*
Greenwillow 2005, ISBN 0–688–17400–0

During the Great Depression, there was little money in anyone's pocket. But when young Davy learns that Miss Elsie, his neighbor, is about to lose Strawberry Farm, he talks his family and the other people in town into helping save the farm. All the townspeople go to the auction where the farm is to be sold off with only pennies in their pockets. When the bidding begins, each bidder raises the previous bid by only a penny. When finally a bid of $9.75 is made by Miss Elsie herself, the town has to pass the hat to collect enough pennies to pay off the bid. The story is heartwarming and will be a welcome gift to the class as you work to build a supportive community among your children.

## Someplace to Go

*Written by Maria Testa*
*Illustrated by Karen Ritz*
Albert Whitman 1996, ISBN 0–8075–7524–0

In this story Davy, his brother Anthony, and their mom live in a homeless shelter. For two years, Davy has had to walk the streets until his mom gets off work because the family can not check into the shelter until 8:00 PM. Through Testa's carefully chosen words readers feel the pain of not having a mom pick you up after school, of having to eat in the soup kitchen without your mom, and of not having warm clothes to ward off the cold while walking the streets after school every afternoon. Sad, sensitive, yet hopeful, this story will serve as a powerful springboard into discussions about overcoming great obstacles in life.

## Something Beautiful

*Written by Sharon Dennis Wyeth*
*Illustrated by Chris K. Soentpiet*
Doubleday 1998, ISBN 0–385–32239–9

The young girl in this story personifies *something beautiful* from the inside out. She reveals her character throughout the book as she strives to see beyond the graffiti walls of scarred buildings to find something beautiful in her neighborhood. Walk with her throughout her neighborhood as she sees everyday sights: a homeless person, a dark alley full of trash, a lunch counter, a launderette. The comments of her neighbors help her realize we each have a role in making our surroundings more beautiful. We can all learn an important lesson from her *can do* attitude. Soentpiet's art is so thoughtful, with the careful attention to every detail we have come to expect of him. (*Note:* If you or your students are wondering what Chris Soentpiet looks like, check out Mr. Lee, the owner of the fruit store.)

### You've Got Dragons

*Written by Kathryn Cave*
*Illustrated by Nick Maland*
Peachtree 2003, ISBN 1–56145–284–X

Children (and even adults) experience dragons—worries and anxieties and fears. And dragons, once dreamed up, just get bigger and bigger unless we resolve them. Cave gives us this precious little book to help get children into discussions that will help them understand their worries and put them into perspective. The last line of the book is one you will want to let linger in the air for a moment before asking children to get knee-to-knee for conversation: *No dragon is more powerful than YOU.*

 ## *Building Community Bookshelf Seven: Meeting Neighbors and Making Friends*

All of us, at some time or other, need help. Whether we're giving or receiving help, each one of us has something valuable to bring to this world. That's one of the things that connects us as neighbors—in our own way, each one of us is a giver and a receiver. (Rogers 2003, 136)

Meeting the new neighbors in our classroom and school communities can be an opportunity for making new friends.

Building friendships and learning to both give and receive help is one of the ways we gain a sense of pride and accomplishment as we grow and develop. This shelf features books that demonstrate how important friendship is in our lives. Share these titles with your students and help them discover how valuable each of them is to the community. And as you read each book, you will have yet another opportunity to explore how friendships help shape our community.

### Best Friends

*Written and Illustrated by Steven Kellogg*
Dial 1986, ISBN 0–8037–0099–7

Louise and Kathy are best friends. They do everything together and like all the same things. Everything is absolutely perfect until summer when Louise has to leave to visit her aunt and uncle. Kathy is miserable and lonesome for her best friend. Then a postcard arrives and Louise tells Kathy what a wonderful time she is having. But Kathy feels Louise is a traitor for not missing her. This book will take you back to those days of childish feelings that were so powerful when you harbored them. It will also appeal to students because they share some of those miserable, sad feelings Kathy feels. This is one of Kellogg's best as he offers a resolution for the conflict young children often feel when they get jealous of their best friends!

### Big Al and Shrimpy

*Written by Andrew Clements*
*Illustrated by Yoshi*
Simon & Schuster Children's 2002, ISBN 0–689–84247–3

The dust jacket wrapping this book on friendship says it best: *Poor Shrimpy! He wants to be like Big Al, loved and adored by all the other fish. But who would want to be friends with such a teeny, tiny fish? Big Al, that's who! He's big and scary looking, and he remembers what it was like to be friendless. Still, all the other fish think Shrimpy's just a nuisance. Then one day, when Big Al's life is in danger, Shrimpy is the only one brave enough and smart enough to save the day.* Children will cheer for Shrimpy and adore the art.

### A Box of Friends

*Written by Pam Munoz Ryan*
*Illustrated by Mary Whyte*
Gingham Dog Press/McGraw-Hill 2003, ISBN 1–57768–420–6

Annie has to move away from her home and all her friends. She is very sad until her grandmother gives her some advice: *Everyone has a box of friends that they can take with them wherever they go.* So Annie begins to make a box of friends to take with her. To fill the box Annie gathers familiar items that will remind her of each of her friends. The watercolor illustrations are very supportive of this tender story that may help ease the pain of moving away.

### Enemy Pie

*Written by Derek Munson*
*Illustrated by Tara Calahan King*
Chronicle Books 2000, ISBN 0–8118–2778–X

This book won't stay on your shelf after you read it aloud to the children; it is sure to become a favorite of children of all ages. Derek Munson writes the Dad into the story as the problem solver and baker who understands his young son's summer disaster when a new boy moves into a house down the street—one he is sure will be his worst enemy. Dad explains how to rid yourself of an enemy by feeding them *enemy Pie,* but first you must spend a whole day with the enemy—and you have to be nice to him. After the day of play, the enemy pie is served and a friendship is developed.

## Fox Makes Friends

*Written and Illustrated by Adam Relf*
Sterling 2005, ISBN 1–4027–2756–9

Little Fox is bored and wants friends to play with so he gathers his butterfly net to go out and catch some. His wise mother tells him that you don't *catch* friends, you *make* friends. He takes his mother's words very literally and tries to *make a friend* by putting sticks, an apple, and some nuts together. When that doesn't work, a rabbit comes by and tries to help him. They make and even bigger friend, but that doesn't work either. Then a squirrel comes along and the three of them make an even bigger friend and, of course, that doesn't help either. The three little folks have tried their hardest to make a friend, but to no avail. Nothing they do works and soon all three become very sad. When Little Fox's mother comes along and asks him about his friends, the three little animals suddenly realize they'd been making friends all along . . . just not the one they thought they were making! Relf's art is just delightful on the oversized pages and the large font is a perfect fit for this very simple text. This one would be an excellent choice for the first days of making friends.

## Horace and Morris but mostly Dolores

*Written by James Howe*
*Illustrated by Amy Walrod*
Atheneum 1999, ISBN 0–689–31874–X

Horace, Morris, and Dolores had been friends forever. The three of them enjoy doing everything together until one day the two boys join a club that girls can't join. Dolores is hurt and lonely so she forms her own club that doesn't allow boys. But the problem is that girls don't enjoy doing the things she had done with Horace and Morris. So she decides to quit the girl's club. Chloris, another club member, decides to join Dolores on her walkout. They are soon joined by not only Horace and Morris but also a few other boys who want to join them in one thing they all enjoy—exploring. The story helps children realize that we will be happier when we make our own decisions rather than doing what others think we should do. And there is a powerful message that friends are those who enjoy doing things together—regardless of gender.

## Miz Berlin Walks

*Written by Jane Yolen*
*Illustrated by Floyd Cooper*
Philomel 1997, ISBN 0–399–22938–8

Friendships are meant to be shared regardless of age. This one is a delightful story about the friendship that grows between an old woman, Miz Berlin, and her young neighbor. Most people think Miz Berlin rather strange as she walks the block and talks to herself. But as the young girl soon discovers, Miz Berlin makes a wonderful storytelling friend who tells *block-long* tales.

## Mr. George Baker

*Written by Amy Hest*
*Illustrated by Jon J. Muth*
Candlewick 2004, ISBN 0–7636–1233–2

The text is short but is so cleverly written with Harry, our young narrator, turning to talk directly to the reader: *See this man? This one here, sitting on the porch? That's Mr. George Baker, and he's a hundred years old, no kidding.* Harry is friends with his neighbor, Mr. George Baker, the hundred-year-old musician. Every morning they wait for the bus together on the front porch. Mr. Baker still loves to dance and play his drums but he can't read and he wants that to be corrected. So each day while Harry is learning to read just down the hall, George is learning with the other grown-ups in room 7. Jon J. Muth's soft watercolor illustrations are truly outstanding and help set the tone for this tender story of friendship and working toward a dream.

## Not Norman: A Goldfish Story

*Written by Kelly Bennett*
*Illustrated by Noah Z. Jones*
Candlewick 2005, ISBN 0–7636–2384–9

Norman, the goldfish, is not the pet our young narrator wanted for his birthday. He is determined to take the goldfish back to the pet store and trade him for a pet he really wants. However, time after time, Norman somehow pleases the little boy and slowly, slowly with each episode, he begins to notice how Norman smiles at him and seems to gulp at just the right time. Slowly our narrator decides that Norman might be a pretty good pet. So when Saturday comes with the opportunity for exchanging, he decides Norman really is the pet he wanted after all. The large font paired with minimal text on each page makes the book very appealing to young children.

## One Stormy Night . . .

*Written by Yuichi Kimura*
*Translated by Lucy North*
*Illustrated by Hiroshi Abe*
Kodansha International 1994, 2003, ISBN 4–7700–2970–5

This is a tale you will need to read and think about several times before reading it to children. It is a powerful story that will linger in your mind as you think about friendship and differences. In it a young hungry goat is caught out in a thunderstorm after dark but struggles against the wind and rain to find a tumbledown hut for shelter. Before long, with the storm raging, a wolf slips into the same hut for shelter. Throughout the stormy night, the two frightened animals cling to each other and become friends. Neither of them knew during the long night that they were supposed to be enemies. The ending will invite lots of predictions.

## A Splendid Friend, Indeed

*Written and Illustrated by Suzanne Bloom*
Boyds Mills Press 2005, ISBN 1–59078–286–0

This very simple text is one that young children will adore. The illustrations are so lovable and when combined with the powerful message in the large font, you will want this one on your community-building shelf. Goose is just full of questions when he comes upon Bear. He wants to know all about what Bear is doing. But Goose answers his own questions before Bear can. Goose likes to do everything that Bear is doing—reading, writing, and thinking. The expression on Bear's face makes you think that Goose is truly bothering him. But when Goose goes off to make a snack, Bear writes him a note. When Goose comes back to share, he reads Bear the note he's written: *I like you. Indeed I do. You are my splendid friend.* Bear finally admits he likes Goose, too!

## The Other Side

*Written by Jacqueline Woodson*
*Illustrated by Earl B. Lewis*
Putnam 2001, ISBN 0–399–23216–1

Here's another outstanding book to show children the power of friendship. *The Other Side,* written by the sensational Jacqueline Woodson and illustrated by the equally significant talent of E. B. Lewis, uses a fence as a metaphor to show the division between races. Woodson gives us Clover who lives in a yellow house on one side of the fence and Annie who lives in a white house on the other side. The two girls' mothers tell them they must never play on the other side, it isn't safe. Clover watches Annie play and wants to talk with her. Finally, the girls decide that sitting on the fence will allow them to be together without defying their mothers. The story is so lyrical you will adore reading it to children and sharing the magic of the friendship that develops between these two young girls. We once heard E. B. quote the entire text from memory and to this day his voice still resonates with us when we use this precious book.

## That's What Friends Are For

*Florence Parry Heide and Sylvia Van Clief*
*Illustrated by Holly Meade*
Candlewick 2003, ISBN 0–7636–1397–5

From the gorgeous endpapers to the lush collages revealing the animals in the forest, this is a charming tale of Theodore the elephant who is suffering from a hurt leg and can't travel to see his cousin on the other side of the forest. All his friends begin giving Theodore advice about how he can get across the forest to visit his cousin. But when Opossum comes along, he doesn't give advice. Instead, Opossum devises a plan to bring the cousin to Theodore. The book ends with this advice: *To give advice is very nice, but friends can do much more. Friends should always help a friend. That's what friends are for!* This is a good one to share on those occasions when actions are needed.

## And to Think That We Thought That We'd Never Be Friends

*Written by Mary Ann Hoberman*
*Illustrated by Kevin Hawkes*
Crown Publishers 1999, ISBN 0–517–80068–3

This cumulative tale introduces a brother and a sister who fuss, who thwack each other and whack each other; a brother and sister who just don't get along. If their older sister hadn't interfered, the fight might have gone on and on. Argument after argument occurs throughout the text and each episode is connected to making up with the words, *and to think that we thought that we'd never be friends.* We believe this book is important because it invites children to take a look at the choices they make. It also allows them to examine their own behavior, not only with their siblings but also with their classmates.

## What Lies on the Other Side?

*Written by Udo Weigelt*
*Translated by S. Allison James*
*Illustrated by Maja Dusíková*
North-South Books 2002, ISBN 0–7358–1677–8

When we first found this book, we decided to buy it simply for the lead: *It was a clear, crisp morning after a stormy night. Little fox was exploring a new part of the woods when he came upon a stream. It wasn't terribly wide, it wasn't too deep, but it was just wide enough and deep enough to stop him from going across. "I wonder," he said, "I just wonder what it's like on the other side."* But before the last page was read, we were stunned to discover the powerful portrayal of friendship used to overcome suspicion and fear of the unknown. Building a bridge to allow the animals to cross from one side of the river to the other becomes a metaphor for learning to live together. The ending is equally charming: *Everybody pitched in, and the bridge was finished that afternoon. As the sun sank into the forest on Fox's side, and lit the trees on Raccoon's side until they glowed like fire, the animals sat on the bridge and told stories of witches and dragons and giants and trolls, and no one was afraid at all.* One reading will begin teaching us to accept differences in others, to trust the good and face the rumors.

## You're Not My Best Friend Anymore

*Written by Charlotte Pomerantz*
*Illustrated by David Soman*
Dial 1998, ISBN 0–8037–1559–5

All friends sometimes disagree on things. Like all relationships, there are also highs and lows to go through. The friendship of Ben and Molly, who do everything together, is no different. As they are getting ready for their birthday party, the friends can't agree on what kind of tent to buy with the money they've saved. Not until they finally exchange presents, do they realize how much their friendship means to them. They realize that their disagreement is not nearly as important as having a true friend.

## Building Community Bookshelf Eight: Coping with Taunting, Teasing, and Bullying

Children learn all too soon that some neighbors can be cruel. "There's the good guy and the bad guy in all of us, but knowing that doesn't ever need to over whelm us. Whatever we adults can do to help ourselves—and anybody else—discover that that's true can really make a difference in this life" (Rogers 2003, 176). On this shelf of books you will find titles that feature characters where the "bad guy" inside is coming out; however, "good guy" characters are there as well. In some books children will see the bad guy and the good guy in the same character. Every read-aloud from this shelf will be an invitation for open and frank conversations about being a good neighbor.

### Alley Oops

*Written by Janice Levy*
*Illustrated by CB Decker*
Flashlight Press 2005, ISBN 0–972–92254–7

A very clever book that will reveal to children the pain suffered by others who become the target of a bully. Taunting and teasing and bullying will at one time or another become a problem for every teacher in every school and classroom. Jonathan Jax begins to make fun of Patrick, a boy in his school who is very overweight. Patrick's dad visits Jonathan and his dad. After that visit Jonathan's dad gives him some advice that is worth the price of this book: *Your grandpa used to say we have two dogs inside of us. One dog is bad. The other dog is good. The two of them fight all the time. (Then Jonathan asked his dad) Which dog wins? (His dad answers) The one you feed the most. You get to decide.* The story ends with Jonathan agreeing to go over and apologize. During the visit, Jonathan finds out that Patrick is a master at hand wrestling, which is very impressive to the young boy.

### Chrysanthemum

*Written and Illustrated by Kevin Henkes*
Greenwillow Books 1991, ISBN 0–688–09699–9

At one time or another we all wish our parents had named us something other than the name we have. Chrysanthemum shares this feeling about her unusual name until she has a wonderful teacher named Delphinium Twinkle. Of course, after meeting Mrs. Twinkle everyone wants flower names . . . even the children who had made fun of Chrysanthemum's name. All along, as Chrysanthemum is made sad by her classmates, her parents support and give good advice. Read this one and explore how our comments can hurt others and how looking for good often brings it.

### Dog Eared

*Written and Illustrated by Amanda Harvey*
Doubleday 2002, ISBN 0–385–72911–1

Want to meet a bully whose taunts are overcome? What classroom doesn't face this problem at sometime during the year? Well, just pull this one off the shelf and invite your kids in to meet Otis with his rather big ears. This one is delightful and very short, but packed with meaning that will reassure children who sometimes question their self-worth when others say hurtful things.

### Don't Laugh at Me

*Written by Steve Seskin and Allen Shamblin*
*Illustrated by Glin Dibley*
Tricycle Press 2002, ISBN 1–58246–058–2

The flap of this book uses these words to introduce it: *For anyone who's ever been bullied—or been a bully themselves—it's time to change your tune. This is not a book for whiners, but a new language that will give you the words you need to take charge and stop the cycle of teasing.* It will indeed give children the opportunity to talk about words that hurt others. The art presents caricatures of children and supports the short explicit text. The afterword was written by Peter Yarrow of Peter, Paul and Mary.

### Hooway for Wodney Wat

*Written by Helen Lester*
*Illustrated by Lynn Munsinger*
Walter Lorraine Books/Houghton Mifflin 1999, ISBN 0–395–92392–1

Rodney Rat couldn't pronounce his *r*'s so all his rodent friends called him Wodney Wat. They teased him so badly that Rodney became very shy and withdrawn. He ate his lunch alone and didn't play with his classmates at recess. One day a new rodent—a big, mean, bossy rodent—moves into their classroom. Camilla Capybara, the new rodent, becomes the bully who rules the classroom and the playground. No one will stand up to her. Read this scrumptious tale to find out how Wodney becomes the hero when he rids the class of the bully Camilla. This one is a great book to begin a discussion on bullies.

## The Littlest Wolf

*Written by Larry Dane Brimner*
*Illustrated by Jose Aruego and Ariane Dewey*
HarperCollins 2002, ISBN 0–06–029039–0

What does a little wolf do when his brothers and sisters make fun of him and tease him, saying that he cannot do any of the things they can do? As you might guess, he hides! However, a very wise daddy searches him out only to reassure him that all things will come in time. When it's time for him to roll in a straight line, he will be able to. When it's time for him to run very fast, he will be able to. For each worry, little wolf is assured by his dad that when the time comes, he will be able to do what is needed. As the story ends, all little wolves are called for nap time under the big oak tree. There nestled under the tree, Big Gray reminds little wolf that once that very big oak tree was just a tiny acorn.

## Me First

*Written by Helen Lester*
*Illustrated by Lynn Munsinger*
Houghton Mifflin 1992, ISBN 0–395–58706–9

Pinkerton, a pink, plump, and pushy pig, would do anything to be first even if it meant stepping on his classmates! Lester (that's Helen Lester) takes the reader through several days of school with Pinkerton rushing and pushing to be first in line, first to eat, and first to board the bus for the field trip to the beach. When the group of Pig Scouts arrives at the beach, Pinkerton pushes to be the first in the water. And then, when he hears a faint voice calling *who wants a sandwich*, Pinkerton dashes toward the voice to be first for a sandwich. Instead he meets the *sandwitch* who takes him to visit her castle.

During his time at the castle, Pinkerton learns that being first is not always the best thing. There is no doubt that children will get the message of this charming but influential story.

## My Secret Bully

*Written by Trudy Ludwig*
*Illustrated by Abigail Marble*
Tricycle Press 2005, ISBN 1–582461–59–7

Most children have a difficult time identifying bullying of this type because it is so easily denied. Even for adults who observe and work with children, emotional bullying is extremely difficult to work with. Therefore it is crucial that we be observant of social interactions and help children acquire the language to express their feelings. Emotional bullying can be as damaging as physical aggression; however, in an open and nurturing community, we can provide supports and opportunities for children to care for one another. Katie is the secret bully who fools people into thinking she is Monica's friend. As you read this story, students will likely realize Katie's behavior, all too often something they can recognize. Read this book several times before your read-aloud because it will certainly be an impetus for lots of knee-to-knee and whole-class discussions.

## The Recess Queen

*Written by Alexis O'Neill*
*Illustrated by Laura Huliska-Beith*
Scholastic 2002, ISBN 0–439–20637–5

This read-aloud will get children howling with laughter as they recognize the Mean Jean of the story can be found in many of them at one time or another. Mean Jean, the Recess Queen, wants to be first in everything and will do anything to get her way. None of the other children will stand up to her but this changes when a Katie Sue moves to their school. Katie Sue shocks everyone as she talks right back to Mean Jean and even dares her to jump rope with her. While everyone holds their breath, Mean Jean joins Katie Sue and a friendship is born. This is a truly delightful book and your students will love the quick-paced, rhyming, chanting language.

## The Sissy Duckling

*Written by Harvey Fierstein*
*Illustrated by Henry Cole*
Simon & Schuster 2002, ISBN 0–689–83566–3

Elmer, a young duckling, is different. He doesn't like all the things other boy ducks enjoy. He is a duck that likes to bake, paint, and put on performances while the other boy ducklings build forts and play football. Elmer's dad isn't happy with his son and expresses his displeasure to his wife. When Elmer overhears his father talking, he is devastated and moves out on his own. However, when Elmer's dad is shot by the duck hunters, Elmer saves his life. Throughout the winter he teaches his dad some important lessons about respecting differences and looking at the talents that each of us has and that who we are helps make the world a better place.

## *Building Community Bookshelf Nine: It Happened at School*

School stories have a special appeal to us (go figure), and we found that our collections were filled with titles for this shelf. Because you are reading this book right now we suspect that you, like us, find delight in the sounds of children moving through the hallways and in the smells of new school supplies and in the feel of a new notebook in your hands. Books from this shelf feature school as the setting or as a significant part of the plot. As you share these books with students, you'll find opportunities for many discussions ranging from myths about school to fears and worries faced by students and teachers alike. There will be opportunities to explore our feelings about learning and meeting the challenges when learning. This shelf offers laughter and lighthearted chatter along with serious conversations. So just pull a title and read it aloud.

### Amber Waiting

*Written by Nan Gregory*
*Illustrated by Kady MacDonald Denton*
Red Deer Press 2003, ISBN 0–88995–258–2

Amber, a new kindergartener, can tell you lots of good things about being old enough to go to school. Although there is far more good than bad, there is one thing that is really, really bad—being picked up late. The majority of the book describes Amber's fears and despair as everyone leaves with their parents while she is left waiting and waiting and waiting. When her dad finally arrives, Amber tries in her kindergarten language to make her dad understand how afraid she was that he had been late. At last dad understands as he swings her up on his shoulders for a ride home. Use this one to lead your children toward inferring. The language doesn't tell you what dad says to make it all right but the illustrations help your children understand that Amber's world is secure again.

## A Fine, Fine School

*Written by Sharon Creech*
*Illustrated by Harry Bliss*
Joanna Cotler Books/HarperCollins 2001, ISBN 0–06–027736–X

A delightful book that will thrill children as they hear about a principal who loves his fine, fine school so much that he decides the children need to attend school every day—even in the summer. As the story peaks, the principal realizes that while he does indeed have a fine, fine school, children will be missing a lot of the pleasure of growing up if they attend school every day. The book is sure to get children talking about the things they know best: school, swinging, skipping, and climbing trees—being kids.

## First Day Jitters

*Written by Julie Danneberg*
*Illustrated by Judy Love*
Whispering Coyote/Charlesbridge 2000, ISBN 1–58089–061–X

Read this book aloud on the first day of school. It will give children a new perspective on the role of a teacher. It will also invite them to see that teachers have worries and anxieties that are often similar to their own. You see, this book is all about the jitters teachers feel on the first day of school, but they won't know its talking about the teacher until the end of this delightful book.

## Jake's 100th Day of School

*Written by Lester L. Laminack*
*Illustrated by Judy Love*
Peachtree 2006, ISBN 1–56145–355–2

What's a principal to do when a student forgets his 100th day collection of things? Well, of course, she must help him collect them right there at school and what better 100 items could you imagine in a collection than an inviting set of 100 books! Read along as the problem is solved much to the delight of Jake. Lester couldn't resist turning this event into his fourth picture book after he visited Reba's school and heard the story. It really happened and Chase (aka Jake) was one happy boy as he pushed those 100 books back to his classroom.

## Jeremiah Learns to Read

*Written by Jo Ellen Bogart*
*Illustrated by Laura Fernandez and Rick Jacobson*
Orchard 1997, ISBN 0–531–30190–7

Jeremiah is a wonderful grandfather who knows how to do many things. He can build a split rail fence. He can make a table out of a tree. He knows how to make syrup from sap but he doesn't know how to read. His wife, Juliana, tries to convince him he is wonderful just the way he is, but Jeremiah thinks if he learns to read he will be even better. So one morning he gets up very early and joins the children as they make their way to school. He becomes the new student. They even help him as he practices learning his letters and their sounds. Soon he is reading—even to his Juliana who admits that now she wants to learn to read as well. The art is spectacular. Don't be surprised if children think Jeremiah looks just like Santa!

## Mr. Lincoln's Way

*Written and Illustrated by Patricia Polacco*
Philomel 2001, ISBN 0–399–23754–2

Mr. Lincoln is an outstanding principal who enjoys children and appreciates their difference—differences that make them the special individuals they are. What will Mr. Lincoln do with his positive outlook when Mean Gene, the school bully, continues to pick on little kids and call them names? He does what good teachers throughout the world do every day: He finds the one thing that will interest Gene and gets him involved. *Mr. Lincoln's Way* is a heartwarming story that will make you proud you are an educator.

## Next Year I'll Be Special

*Written by Patricia Reilly Giff*
*Illustrated by Marylin Hafner*
Doubleday 1980, 1993, ISBN 0–385–30903–1

Marilyn thinks her teacher is mean and dreams about next year when she will have a nice teacher who loves her. Everything about next year's teacher is appealing to Marilyn. She just knows that Miss Lark won't say mean things and will let her be a board washer, a line leader, or a door monitor. She will even be a better reader—even the best in the class! The children will be her friends and will share things with her. Even though her dad assures her she is special now, Marilyn just knows next year it will be better.

## School Picture Day

*Written by Lynn Plourde*
*Illustrated by Thor Wickstrom*
Dutton Children's Books 2002, ISBN 0–525–46886–2

School picture day is like no other as children show up for school with their faces clean and shining, hair slicked down, and clothes pressed ready for pictures. However, there is usually one in line who is more interested in how that camera works than in getting a picture taken. Well in the starring role of *School Picture Day* that kid is Josephina Caroleena Wattasheena the First. Josephina is too curious and busy trying to understand how everything works to be concerned with looking her best for school pictures. However, when her class is all set for the picture and the camera breaks, Josephina saves the day! Read with laughter as you walk with this group of kids to have the class picture taken.

## Sit Still!

*Written and Illustrated by Nancy Carlson*
Puffin 1996, 1998, ISBN 0–14–056202–8

Most every classroom has a Patrick who simply cannot sit still and no matter where he is, he can find any number of ways to sit in a chair. Finally, the teacher gets frustrated and Patrick's mom takes him to his doctor to see whether something is wrong with him. Following the visit, everyone knows what they need to do to keep Patrick busy and the problem is resolved by everyone working to develop the plan. Not only should this book be read to children, but it could also be used in a faculty meeting to remind teachers of the need to be flexible when planning for all children.

## Sumi's First Day of School Ever

*Written by Soyung Pak*
*Illustrated by Joung Un Kim*
Viking 2003, ISBN 0–670–03522–X

The first day of school can be so overwhelming for all of us but imagine what it is like when you can't speak the language spoken at school. Sumi, frightened and unsure, must learn how to live in this new country and in this new environment called school. Her mother teaches her a few phrases but little Sumi still sees the school as a lonely and scary place. Thankfully, Sumi is placed in a classroom with a sensitive teacher who tenderly develops a special place for her before the first day is over. Friendship wins out over fear and Sumi goes home thinking that school is not such a scary place after all. This special book cleverly exposes fears and insecurities for new classmates making it just right for extending the boundaries of our community when any new child enters a classroom.

## Testing Miss Malarkey

*Written by Judy Finchler*
*Illustrated by Kevin O'Malley*
Walker Books 2000, ISBN 0–8027–8737–1

You know those annual standardized tests that the "outside world" puts so much emphasis on? Well if you are one of the many teachers who has to give those annual standardized tests and has to watch your students fret for days and weeks, then you need this book. It shares universal truths about our behavior but will even be enjoyed by children as they prepare for the "testing season." Only educators can appreciate this story as the entire school staff gets into the groove of preparation for the I.P.T.U. exam. Read as the principal ensures that all the children have #2 pencils, the custodians are guarding the halls, the teachers are all biting their nails and some are even throwing up. The moms are packing just the right kind of brain food and giving comprehension exams before bedtime. The art is totally playful and sets just the right mood for this hilarious story. This one gives us a bit of levity around the serious business of testing. We think it will bring chuckles during a time of stress.

## Too Loud Lily

*Written by Sofie Laguna*
*Illustrated by Kerry Argent*
Scholastic 2004, ISBN 0–439–57913–9

Lily Hippo is just too loud. She doesn't mean to be, she just is. Even when she is trying to be quiet, she is still too loud. Learn how Miss Loopiola, the new drama teacher at Lily's school, solves the problem. The story is charming and children will adore the art as well as the problems Lily has as she tries to do what is right . . . even when it is hard because your voice is just too loud.

## Trevor's Wiggly-Wobbly Tooth

*Written by Lester L. Laminack*
*Illustrated by Kathi Garry McCord*
Peachtree 1998, ISBN 1–56145–175–4

> Every classroom needs this book on the day a tooth finally comes out. Trevor has a loose tooth but he is not sure he is ready for someone to pull it out. Of course, all his friends have solutions . . . none of which is very appealing to young Trevor. Finally, Grandma Sally provides the best solution and everyone is happy with the results. The art is very appealing and children will want this one read over and over again. As a principal, teacher, or counselor, it will be read often to lots of children as this special time arrives in their lives.

## What Did You Do Today?

*Written by Toby Forward*
*Illustrated by Carol Thompson*
Clarion 2004, ISBN 0–618–49586–X

> A good read-aloud for the beginning of school because every child (and mom) plans for that first day and all the things he or she will get to do. The story is reassuring for young children because it shows what mom is doing on her first day and how her thoughts keep coming back to her child. Before long the kids begin preparing to go home where they will find out how mom has spent her day. Thompson's illustrations will be most appealing to your children because she playfully supports the story with her art.

## When It's the Last Day of School

*Written by Maribeth Boelts*
*Illustrated by Hanako Wakiyama*
Grosset & Dunlap 2004, ISBN 0–399–23498–5

> *When It's the Last Day of School* so perfectly goes into the head of this little boy as he tries his best not to get in trouble and to keep his excitement in check until that final bell rings. He relives many of the routine things he's done all year and with each task he tries so hard to stay focused. However, when that final bell rings, he is finally free and ready to *explode*!

## Building Community Bookshelf Ten: A Family Is . . .

"I believe it's a fact of life that what we have is less important than what we make out of what we have. The same holds true for families: It's not how many people there are in a family that counts, but rather the feelings among the people who are there" (Rogers 2003, 38). Books for this shelf were selected to help children recognize that family is less about who lives with them and more about how they are loved and cared for by those they live with. We recognize that all children will not see their families in these stories. We know that children come to us from many different family groupings. This shelf includes books with various definitions of family, but it cannot reflect every child who will fall under the spell of your voice. We struggled with that concern as we selected the books.

We were guided by our memories of how it felt to think the families of our friends were somehow more "in step" and went to neater places and never said or did things that embarrassed their children. Neither of us grew up with books that helped us understand that the love within a family had nothing to do with clothes or vacations or its makeup. In the libraries of our childhood, books showed families with a dad who went to work in pressed slacks and a starched white shirt. The mom wore a dress to clean house and do the dishes and prepare delicious meals and freshly baked cookies. The children were polite and siblings looked out for each other. And every family had a delightful dog or a perky kitten who stayed by the children's sides.

Today, there are so many books for children to help them understand that family is about the love shared, about developing a sense of independence and belonging, and about one's worth as an individual who is needed and treasured. Children's books can help them understand that family can be defined in numerous ways. Whatever the definition, "[t]here's something unique about being a member of a family that really needs you in order to function well. One of the deepest longings a person can have is to feel needed and essential" (Rogers 2003, 70).

Perhaps the best lens for viewing the titles on this shelf was given to us by Lucy Calkins (1991) when she wrote: "We cannot give children rich lives with long family suppers full of shared stories but we can give them the lens to appreciate the richness that is already theirs in their lives" (35). So think of the children in your classroom. Think about the lives they live and the families they go home to at the end of a day in school. Think of them as you look across this shelf and pull a few titles that have special appeal. Take time to read several of these and select those that will validate the lives of the children you teach. Then select a few more to grow the definition of family beyond what is already familiar and known. Help each child come to value the family structures that others may know.

### The Bat Boy & His Violin

*Written by Gavin Curtis*
*Illustrated by E. B. Lewis*
Simon & Schuster 1998, ISBN 0–689–80099–1

> Papa is manager of the Dukes, the worse baseball team in the Negro National League. And he doesn't like it because his young son, Reginald, would rather play his violin than baseball. To get Reginald's attention away from the violin, Papa makes him a batboy for the team. Rather than disappoint Papa, the young violinist uses every free minute he has to continue to practice his beloved violin. Reginald's music begins to influence the luck and attitude of the team, but most of all it changes his Papa. In a gentle and thoughtful way the story tells of the unkindness and hardships faced by African Americans during this time in history. And it also pushes the issue of gender roles just a bit.

### Before I Was Your Mother

*Written by Kathryn Lasky*
*Illustrated by LeUyen Pham*
Harcourt 2003, ISBN 0–15–201464–0

> When you read this one, you will want to pull your children in close. It is a perfect selection to share during an All About You unit. Since most children cannot imagine their parents as young children, this story is one to be cherished. The book is told in a first-person narrative and the mom always begins a new episode of her story by saying to her child, *I wasn't always your mother. . . .* Then she goes on to tell what she did as a little girl when she loved to play with friends, make lots of noise, roller-skate, and wear cowboy boots to weddings. Not only does Lasky use a repeating line *(I wasn't always your mother)* but she also enlarges the word *once* as another signal that a new episode is about to begin.

### Black Is Brown Is Tan

*Written by Arnold Adoff*
*Illustrated by Emily Arnold McCully*
Amistad/HarperCollins 1973, 2002, ISBN 0–06–028776–4

From the inside flap you learn that this book about an interracial family was first printed in 1973. We are introduced with these words: *a brown-skinned mama, the color of chocolate milk and pumpkin pie and a white-skinned daddy, not the color of milk or snow, but light with pinks and tiny tans. And two children, the beautiful colors of both.* Now several decades later, the family is recaptured in watercolors assuring that a family is a family regardless of the shades of their skin.

## Daddy, Will You Miss Me?

*Written by Wendy McCormick*
*Illustrated by Jennifer Eachus*
Aladdin 1999, ISBN 0–689–85063–8

When Daddy has to leave his little son behind while he goes to do a job in Africa, the little boy is desperately sad. This story shows a sensitive Dad who shares his own sadness with his boy and takes the time to describe things he will do every day to help get through the four weeks before he can come back home. McCormick does an amazing job of crafting the story to show the depth of Dad's understanding of what the boy needs to feel safe. The beautiful art created by Eachus makes this book truly memorable.

## Daniel and His Walking Stick

*Written by Wendy McCormick*
*Illustrated by Constance R. Bergum*
Peachtree 2005, ISBN 1–56145–330–7

Here's a wonderful book to use in your classroom on the day grandparents are to visit. It will also spark an interest in having an older person visit your classroom to tell stories. Young Jesse doesn't remember either of her grandfathers, even though both parents are forever telling her family stories to help her know them. But Jesse isn't satisfied, even with the stories and pictures. On a family vacation, Jesse's parents take her to meet Daniel, a friend of one of her grandfathers. The longing for a relationship with a "grandfather" is satisfied as Daniel takes her on long walks and helps her see the world through his old and wise eyes. On their walks, Daniel, who always uses a walking stick, finds another smaller walking stick that had washed up beside a lake. The stick is just right for Jesse. When she returns home, Jesse takes far more from her time with Daniel than the walking stick. Jesse learns from the wisdom only the older generation can give our young.

## Goin' Someplace Special

*Written by Patricia C. McKissack*
*Illustrated by Jerry Pinkney*
Atheneum 2001, ISBN 0–689–81885–8

> *Goin' Someplace Special* is a memoir of growing up in the 1950s when the pains of racial segregation were experienced by African Americans. The story tells of our narrator's first trip alone out into the segregated world. To get to the library in town, she rides a bus and has to sit in the back. The library, where all were welcome, is her "someplace special." The author's note gives a brief history of segregation and ends with an acknowledgment of Andrew Carnegie whose great wealth built the library—the *Someplace Special*—that served as her doorway to freedom.

## Grandpa's Corner Store

*Written and Illustrated by DyAnne DiSalvo-Ryan*
HarperCollins 2000, ISBN 0–688–16716–0

> *Mr. Butler sold his hardware store when a bigger one opened nearby. Then the building was torn down to make way for a new supermarket.* And soon after more businesses on the block were sold and torn down. *Old stores are out. New stores are in. But my grandpa's store stays the same. . . . Grandpa lives in a room in the back. . . . Saturday mornings I'm at the grocery to give Grandpa a hand. . . . Firefighters from across the street line up at the deli counter. Mrs. Kalfo takes their orders and bags them up to go.* Most children today won't have these memories, but many adults can remember those small stores before large supermarkets moved in to take their place. Let this book be a walk down memory lane and open a discussion contrasting old ways with newer ones and as a lead-in to a conversation about the timeless ties between grandchildren and grandparents.

## Grandpa's Face

*Written by Eloise Greenfield*
*Illustrated by Floyd Cooper*
Philomel 1988, ISBN 0–399–21525–5

> Tamika loves her grandpa. She loves everything about him. She even loves all his many faces that tell her how he is feeling. One day she walks in while he is rehearsing for a play and sees a face she doesn't recognize—a face that

scares her, a face she knows wouldn't love her. By suppertime, she is so upset that she spills her glass of water and it splashes on her grandpa's shirt which worries her even more. With love and understanding of the special relationship shared by this granddad and granddaughter, all the misunderstanding is resolved and the bond between the two becomes stronger than ever.

## The Hello, Goodbye Window

*Written by Norton Juster*
*Illustrated by Chris Raschka*
Hyperion 2005, ISBN 0–7868–0914–0

> *Nanna and Poppy live in a big house in the middle of town. There's a brick path that goes to the back porch, but before you get there you pass right by the kitchen window. That's the* Hello, Goodbye Window. *It looks like a regular window but it's not.* These are the words that begin the charming story of our narrator's visits to her grandparents' house where she is greeted by a wave from the kitchen window. And after the visit it is through this window that our narrator sees her grandparents blowing kisses to her as she leaves. The book gives you such a warm and safe feeling—it is simply delicious. The back flap of this lovely text tells us this is Juster's first picture book. We think after only one reading you'll be hoping it won't be his last.

## Just One More Story

*Written by Jennifer Brutschy*
*Illustrated by Cat Bowman Smith*
Orchard 2002, ISBN 0–439–31767–3

> This story will warm your heart as you follow an unusual vagabond family of three traveling night after night to entertain people with their music while living in a very small camper trailer. The family bonding and rituals clearly describe for children the essential elements of what it means to have a "home." This is a book you will come back to over and over again.

## Little Rabbit Runaway

*Written and Illustrated by Harry Horse*
Peachtree 2005, ISBN 1–56145343–9

In this one Little Rabbit struggles with learning how to navigate life. When his parents scold him, he gets so angry he decides to run away. His family tells him they love him and will miss him but he is determined to make his own decisions. So he packs the things he will need, ties them in a knapsack, and begins his journey. He meets Molly Mouse and they decide to set up a home together. Little Rabbit soon learns what it means to live with someone else as Molly becomes more bossy by the day. It doesn't take him long before he is ready to go home and be his Mama's Little Rabbit again.

## The Memory String

*Written by Eve Bunting*
*Illustrated by Ted Rand*
Clarion Books 2000, ISBN 0–395–86146–2

Are all stepmothers like the one in Cinderella? Of course not! But so often they are painted in a negative light. This Eve Bunting book was long overdue because she provides us with the rare portrayal of a stepmother who is kind and generous and thoughtful. Young Laura has a treasured memory string, left to her when her mother died. The string holds buttons that were precious to her mom and now to her. When Laura's memory string breaks, the buttons are scattered. However, Laura's stepmother and her father are there ready to comfort her and to help her search for the lost buttons. Yet, one button, the one most treasured by her mother can't be found. When Laura sees her new stepmother on her knees searching through the grass with a flashlight for the button, she is touched. And when Laura overhears a conversation between her father and his new wife, she has a change of heart.

## Me Too!

*Written and Illustrated by Jamie Harper*
Little, Brown 2005, ISBN 0–316–60552–2

Growing up with brothers and sisters can sometimes make children wish they were the only child in the family. This kid-friendly book will help students develop the language needed to express some of the frustrations that come along with those feelings. Grace's little sister, Lucy, simply drives her crazy because not matter what Grace says or does, Lucy always says *Me, too!* Grace is not comforted even when she is reminded by her parents that it is a compliment to have Lucy want to do everything just like her. Life with Lucy proves to be a hardship until one day at her swimming lesson, Grace finds herself trying to be just like her coach. All of a sudden Grace realizes her situation with Lucy has now been repeated by her. This one will generate far more than just a knee-to-knee conversation about family situations; it can also include relationships that occur at school.

## Morning on the Lake

*Written by Jan Bourdeau Waboose*
*Illustrated by Karen Reczuch*
Kids Can Press 1998, ISBN 1–55074–588–3

*Grandfather stops the canoe in the center of the lake. He does not speak. This is his special place. Morning is his favorite time, and so it is mine.* This is a lovely story about the special relationship between a Native American grandfather and his grandson who love spending the day together—from early morning to night. It reveals the grandfather clinging to many of his early customs: wearing moccasins, building a canoe, and teaching his grandson the wise ways of understanding nature. Waboose's writing shines as she describes how the quiet of morning transcends into the birds chirping, animals stirring, the mist leaving the top of the lake, and the leaves swaying gently in the breeze. By noon the description changes again as they begin to climb the mountain feeling hot and thirsty. Once at the very top, *Grandfather sits down and motions for me to sit beside him. I do. He does not speak. Neither will I. This is his special place. Noon is his favorite time, and so it is mine.* Eventually night comes and together they study the stars. At the door of the forest, they pause: *I have been in the bush with Grandfather many times, but not at night. I know this is his special place. Night is his favorite time, and so it is mine.* The art so softly reflects the tender relationship of the grandfather and his grandson making this one more of a treasure for us.

## My Daddy Is a Giant

*Written by Carl Norac*
*Illustrated by Ingrid Godon*
Clarion Books 2004, ISBN 0–618–44399–1

In our adult world we often forget what the world looks like through the eyes of a child. This book brings that viewpoint to the forefront. The large font and short text make this book even more delightful for young eyes. *My daddy is a giant. When I want to cuddle him, I have to climb a ladder.* From this point on the young boy tells you all the things that happen because his daddy is so-o-o big. His sneezes are like a hurricane that blow the seas away, his laughs are so strong they blow the leaves off trees, and his kicks are so strong they send balls as high as the moon. Then, as this tender story ends: *My daddy is a giant, and when I grow up, I'm going to be a giant too!*

## My Friend Grandpa

*Written by Harriet Ziefert*
*Illustrated by Robert Wurzburg*
Blue Apple Books 2004, ISBN 1–59354–063–9

When Emma goes to her Grandpa's farm every summer, she leaves the city and her best friends behind. But in the country her best friends are her Grandpa and the big tree that lives on his farm. That tree provides her many hours of enjoyment as she watches squirrels play and bugs crawl and she swings very high on a swing hanging from a limb. One morning when she wakes up, her tree has been damaged badly by a summer storm. As Grandpa is hauling her tree off, Emma notices a large hole in the trunk. She asks him to leave it for her to explore. Grandpa is too big to climb inside, but with his help Emma crawls in. She loved her tree and now it provides her with a wonderful playhouse.

## My Two Grandmothers

*Written by Effin Older*
*Illustrated by Nancy Hayashi*
Harcourt 2000, ISBN 0–15–200785–7

Often children are torn between differences that can exist between two sets of grandparents. Differences in life styles, religious beliefs, or culture may raise confusion for some children. *My Two Grandmothers* was written for just such a family situation. In the story, a young girl has one grandmother who lives on a farm and celebrates Christmas. The other grandmother lives in a city apartment and celebrates Hanukkah. After the story goes back and forth between visits, the granddaughter decides on a very different celebration that both grandmothers can attend. She names her new celebration the First Traditional Grandmothers' Party.

## A New Room for William

*Written by Sally Grindley*
*Illustrated by Carol Thompson*
Candlewick 2000, ISBN 0–7636–1196–4

This is a sweet story about a young boy and his mom during a move from their old house and his dad to a new house (probably following a divorce but it doesn't say). William is not happy in his new house and he misses everything about his old one. To help him overcome his sadness, his wise mom lets him select new wallpaper for his room. While she is putting it up, he meets the little boy next door who offers to let him play on his swing set since William had to leave his at his old house. This precious little book will provide a ray of hope for any child who is new to your classroom or is about to make a move away. This is one you don't want to miss.

## No Place Like Home

*Written by Jonathan Emmett*
*Illustrated by Vanessa Cabban*
Candlewick 2005, ISBN 0–7636–2554–X

Take your children on a journey with Little Mole after he begins to believe that his home is dull and he wants to live somewhere that is bright and beautiful. Readers will love the full-color art that surrounds the large font and they will without doubt grow to adore this little character. When Little Mole finds that there is *No Place Like Home,* you and your children will cheer. This delightful book will fill your classroom with joy and goodwill. Save it for a day when you need to put joyful language in the air.

## Old Bob's Brown Bear

*Written and Illustrated by Niki Daly*
Farrar, Straus and Giroux 2001, ISBN 0–374–35612–2

Old Bob never had a teddy bear until he was given one by Gran for his birthday. Granddaughter Emma can't understand why an old man would want a teddy bear and she wants Old Bob's bear for her own. When she cries, the bear goes home with her. On each subsequent visit the teddy bear travels with Emma and ends up going back home with her. He is her constant companion for many years. One day Emma no longer needs Teddy so he ends up in her toy box. It is there, during a visit, that Old Bob finds him. While cuddling Teddy, Old Bob can smell all of Emma's love and adventures on the old bear which makes him love it even more.

### One Magical Morning

*Written by Claire Freedman*
*Illustrated by Louise Ho*
Good Books 2005, ISBN 1–56148–472–5

> If you teach very young children, the words in this tender rhyming story need to float in the air of your classroom: *In the shadowy woods, one clear summer's morning, Mommy took Little Bear to see the day dawning.* Walk through the forest with Mother and Little Bear as they watch the moon fade and the stars slip away one-by-one to reveal fox cubs playing and pigeons soaring above. The beautiful art embraces the language helping readers feel the strength of the relationship between parent and child as they move through this lovely story.

### One of Three

*Written by Angela Johnson*
*Illustrated by David Soman*
Orchard 1991, ISBN 0–531–07061–1

> This short little text invites you into the troubled heart of the youngest of three sisters who have always done everything together. But, by the middle of the book, the two older girls outgrow the youngest of the three and move in a different direction, leaving her out of their activities. She is lonely and sad until her mom and dad save the day by making her a part of a threesome again with them. *One of Three* is priceless for opening a discussion about family issues with older or even younger brothers and sisters. It is simply irresistible.

### Our Gracie Aunt

*Written by Jacqueline Woodson*
*Illustrated by Jon J. Muth*
Jump at the Sun 2002, ISBN 0–786–80620–6

> If you want to define what a family really is, you need to read this book as two young children enter into foster care and experience the worry of wondering what happened to their mother. Young Johnson and his big sister Beebee have experienced their mama leaving for days at a time, but this time she doesn't come back. A neighbor reports this to the agency, and Miss Roy comes to the apartment to take them to live with their mama's sister Gracie.

Because of an argument, the sisters had not spoken to each other for years; therefore, the children did not know their Aunt Gracie. As the story unfolds, you learn their mama has gone away to a hospital where she will have to stay for a long time. So the children must stay with their aunt. By the end, they realize that this is where they want to be because though they still love their mother, they love the security they have found in their Aunt Gracie's care.

## Our Tree Named Steve

*Written by Alan Zweibel*
*Illustrated by David Catrow*
G. P. Putnam's Sons 2005, ISBN 0–399–23722–4

This moving tribute to strong family ties and the memories of traditions is written as a letter from Dad to his children to tell them what has happened to their beloved tree. When the children were still very small, they found some land where they were going to build a house. The three children fell in love with one tree on the property and begged and begged that it not be cut down. When baby Sari tried to say tree, it sounded like "Steve." And so the tree became Steve and the family made many memories with him as the children grew. Over the years, he had been a swing holder, a third base, a hiding place, a jump-rope turner, and even held a line to dry clothes. Through those years, many things happened to Steve as he grew older. But one day while the children were away visiting grandma, a storm moved through and knocked Steve over. This time nothing could save him.

## Papa, Do You Love Me?

*Written by Barbara M. Joosse*
*Illustrated by Barbara Lavalle*
Chronicle Books 2005, ISBN 0–8118–4265–7

When a young African boy asks his Papa if he loves him, his Papa answers: *You came from your mama, whom I love, your grandpapas and grandmamas, whom I honor, and from me. You are my Tender Heart, and I love you.* Each page poses another question from the boy to his Papa and each time his Papa tells him of all the ways he is loved—*How much? How long? What would you do if I was hot? What if I was thirsty?* With each answer, Papa assures his young son of his deep and abiding love. The metaphors and language are as abundant and rich as the story is touching and tender.

### Remember, Grandma?

*Written by Laura Langston*
*Illustrated by Lindsey Gardiner*
Viking 2004, ISBN 0–670–05898–X

> From the lush front endpapers, where the title page begins, to the back ones with Grandma's apple pie recipe, this book is sure to become a favorite for a read-aloud for children of all ages. The story unfolds as Margaret introduces the reader to her wonderful Grandma who is in the early stages of forgetfulness. The font size is large and its placement varies from page to page which makes the book artfully appealing.

### Something Special

*Written by Nicola Moon*
*Illustrated by Alex Ayliffe*
Peachtree 1997, ISBN 1–56145–137–1

> Charming endpapers give the reader a peek at the days of the week and sets up the pace of the story throughout an entire week with a new baby sister as Charlie tries to find that *something special* for show-and-tell at school. The days are stressful for young Charlie as he learns to live with this new baby in his house. The story is sure to charm young children who have had or will have the same experience at home.

### Stars in the Darkness

*Written by Barbara Joosse*
*Illustrated by R. Gregory Christie*
Chronicle Books 2002, ISBN 0–8118–2168–4

> *Stars in the Darkness* is a powerful heart-wrenching story of a young boy and his brother who live with their mother in an inner city. The brothers use their imaginations to pretend they live somewhere else. In their pretend world the city lights are stars and the sirens are wild wolves howling at the moon and the shots fired are the stars cracking the darkness. What happens when suddenly the older brother, Richard, doesn't come home and becomes one of "them"? What happens when a new basketball appears and he knows Richard doesn't have the money to buy one? How does his Mama battle her own son? This book deals very frankly with a social issue many children have to live with every day. And it does so with great care and insight.

### Sunshine Home

*Written by Eve Bunting*
*Illustrated by Diane de Groat*
Clarion Books 1994, ISBN 0–395–63309–5

This is a story like no other to describe the love family members feel for each other even in tough times. Gram lives with Timmy and his family until she falls and breaks her hip. When it doesn't heal properly, the doctors feel she needs full-time care that can be given only in a nursing home. For their first visit to see her, each member of the family puts on a brave front and pretends to be so cheerful. However, as soon as they leave, Timmy's mom bursts into tears, then realizes she forgot to give Gram Timmy's new picture. So Timmy volunteers to go back in to give it to her. When he finds Gram, he discovers her in tears just like his mom. Now Timmy realizes that everyone was pretending to be happy to protect the people they love. de Groat's art is gorgeous and beautifully reflects the strong emotions in this story.

### Tell Me One Thing, Dad

*Written by Tom Pow*
*Illustrated by Ian Andrew*
Candlewick 2004, ISBN 0–7636–2474–8

Oh, you will love this one! Not only is Andrew's art so sensational but the story with its enlarged font is delicious too. Molly and her Dad have a bedtime ritual every night. Following the reading of a bedtime story, Molly asks Dad a question and he must tell her everything he knows about the subject. Embedded in this entertaining book are facts about each of the questions asked by Molly. What a clever way to build concepts and ideas in the heads of children! Then just as you settle in to that structure, Pow changes and reverses the role and lets Dad ask Molly questions. The last one of the day is: *What's the most important thing you know about me? (Molly starts to think but daddy fills in the answer. . . . You know that I love my baby!)* This one is not only a keeper for your classroom but it also would make a treasured Father's Day gift for someone who is a very special Dad.

### Today I'm Going Fishing with My Dad

*Written by N. L. Sharp*
*Illustrated by Chris L. Demarest*
Boyds Mills Press 1993, 1997, ISBN 1–56397–613–7

Our narrator is going fishing with his dad and the story is filled with all the preparations the little boy and his dad make to be ready. The little boy is overjoyed at the prospect of the day of fishing . . . at least that is what you think for the first half of the book. Then in a twist in the narrative, the story shifts and readers find out the little boy doesn't like fishing at all. What he loves is spending the day with his dad. What a lovely demonstration of the selfless things we do for those we love. And what an affirmation for little boys who are not avid sportsmen.

## Two Mrs. Gibsons

*Written by Toyomi Igus*
*Illustrated by Daryl Wells*
Children's Book Press 1996, 2001, ISBN 0–89239–170–7

Written as a memoir by Igus, *Two Mrs. Gibsons* is just begging to be read and discussed in your classroom community. The words are short and simple but the story is long and deep in meaning. Igus' Japanese mother and her African American grandmother are the two Mrs. Gibsons in her life: *one with skin the color of chocolate; the other with skin the color of vanilla.* While both these women have many differences, their sameness—their love for the little girl and her daddy—are more important.

## Uncle Willie and the Soup Kitchen

*Written and Illustrated by DyAnne DiSalvo-Ryan*
Mulberry Books/Murrow 1991, ISBN 0–688–09165–2

This one opens with a brief introduction explaining what a soup kitchen is and the important role it plays in the lives of many families in America. Uncle Willie works in the soup kitchen and after school he sits with his nephew until the boy's parents get home from work. Because of his many outstanding traits, Uncle Willie would be a great character study for students. Uncle Willie explains why he devotes time to help the needy and he introduces his nephew to his friends at the soup kitchen. In simple ways Uncle Willie demonstrates great respect for each of those who eats with him every day. Eventually, his nephew goes to work with him and learns another important lesson—even a child can make a difference.

## Visiting Day

*Written by Jacqueline Woodson*
*Illustrated by James E. Ransome*
Scholastic 2002, ISBN 0–590–40005–3

> A timely book that deals with the very sensitive subject of a father who is in prison while his young daughter lives with her mother and travels on a bus to visit him every month. Woodson shows great sensitivity toward a difficult subject that others have not addressed in a picture book. The dust jacket bears the following words: *Love knows no boundaries. Here is a strong family that understands the meaning of unconditional love.*

## We Wanted You

*Written by Liz Rosenberg*
*Illustrated by Peter Catalanotto*
Roaring Brook 2002, ISBN 0–7613–1597–7

> This is an adoption story like no other. On the back flap you read that Liz Rosenberg is a poet and once you read this stunning book, you will know she is truly a talented wordsmith. We promise that after you read it while preparing to use it in your classroom, you will read and reread it several times. Every page is just stunning. The text is short with a slightly enlarged font that makes it a great book to share with children. If you need another reason to buy the book, Catalanotto's art is simply divine.

## When Jo Louis Won the Title

*Written by Belinda Rochelle*
*Illustrated by Larry Johnson*
Sandpiper/Houghton Mifflin 1994, 1996, ISBN 0–395–66614–7

> This story will enchant you and your children as it unfolds. As the grandfather tells his young granddaughter the history of her name, a name she doesn't like, we learn about his life and the times he lived through. This family story of pride will take you from the fields of Mississippi with a young man and one tattered suitcase to the city where he seeks his fortune in Harlem. He arrives on the night Joe Louis wins the title fight and as the city erupts into a celebration, he meets his future wife. They name their first born, Joe Louis and he names his first born (a girl) Jo Louis.

## While You Are Away

*Written by Eileen Spinelli*
*Illustrated by Renee Graef*
Hyperion Books 2004, ISBN 0–7868–0972–8

> A powerful book told from the point of view of three small children whose parents are away serving in the armed forces (one in the navy, one in the air force, and one in the army). The words are reassuring and will inspire children to think of ways to find comfort during difficult times. Renee Graef's soft and tender art is outlined with ribbons on every page.

## You're Not My Real Mother!

*Written by Molly Friedrich*
*Illustrated by Christy Hale*
Little, Brown 2004, ISBN 0–316–60553–0

> In this touching story an adopted child realizes she doesn't look like her mother and says, *You know, Mom, you're not my real mother.* The rest of this reassuring book gives her daughter all the reasons she is her real mother. A real mother lets you put on twenty bandages when only one is needed. A real mother drives you back to pick up a beloved polar bear you've left at a friend's house. A real mother lets you help her cook. A real mother teaches you to say please and thank you. A real mother teaches you your ABC's. And the reasons go on. . . . Hale's watercolor art is the perfect match for this heartwarming story for adoptive mothers and children the world over.

 *Building Community Bookshelf Eleven: Learning to Say Good-Bye*

It is our hope that you will never need to pull books from this shelf. But we realize that sadness and death are part of life's journey, so we've selected some helpful books that have served us well in difficult times. We hope they will be a valuable resource should you ever need them. During sad times, children need the school community to be sensitive and understanding. Such a time may be difficult for children because they often suffer in silence and confusion. Saying good-bye is difficult for adults, which only makes it more uncomfortable for children.

We believe the books featured here need to be in every school library and available to teachers and families who may need them as bridges to conversation, to offer scaffolds for children to encourage their questions and the pouring out of their grief. And clearly, we believe every school counselor, who may be one of the most valuable resources in your school in times of loss, should know about these books.

## Always and Forever

*Written by Alan Durant*
*Illustrated by Debi Gliori*
Harcourt 2003, ISBN 0–15–216636–X

Durant did us all a huge favor by writing this sensitive book about losing a loved one. Because he used animal (personification) friends to explain how devastating it is to lose someone you love, the story will bring comfort to children as well as help them understand loss. In the beautifully illustrated book, Mole, Hare, and Otter are heartbroken when their friend Fox dies. They can't imagine what they will do without him and his memory only brings sadness. However, their friend Squirrel comes to visit and helps them understand that memories can also comfort. Squirrel reminds them that through those memories their beloved Fox will always be with them. The endpapers are worth the price of the book! The front one shows the entire group of friends with their arms around each other while the back one pictures the group of friends without Fox.

## Grandad's Prayers of the Earth

*Written by Douglas Wood*
*Illustrated by P. J. Lynch*
Candlewick 1999, ISBN 0–7636–0660–X

*When I was little, my Grandad was my best friend. Being with him always made the world seem just right.* This selection is soothing, significant, and indispensable for this bookshelf on learning to say good-bye to people we love. While the story never uses words of a religious nature, it does talk in an unforgettable way about how all things in nature pray—the tall trees, old mossy rocks, the splashed and sparkling water as it flows across the face of the earth. Only you, by knowing your community, will know whether you can use this book in the classroom. It is written so thoughtfully and with such passion it deserves to be placed in the hands of children who are confused and desperately need comfort when they lose people or pets they love. What Wood docs with his language is memorable, but when joined by Lynch's truly mesmerizing art, the package is sheer elegance.

## Little White Cabin

*Written and Illustrated by Ferguson Plain*
Pemmican 1992, ISBN 0–921827–26–1

This is one you'd better practice because it contains many Native American (Ojibwa tribe) phrases that may prove difficult, but the story is worth the effort of learning how to pronounce the words. Plain includes a glossary in the back and readers will find it very helpful. While walking through the woods a little boy comes upon a little white cabin. And then every time he passes ol' Danny is sitting on the porch. At first he doesn't speak, even though he is spoken to. Days and days later, the little boy begins speaking. Slowly the boy and ol' Danny become friends, dear friends: *As I grew up, ol' Danny grew older, until one day as I was walking though the bush like I always did, I came upon the little white cabin. Danny wasn't sitting on his porch, staring into the distance.* Not to worry, ol' Danny had prepared his young friend for the day he wouldn't be waiting for his visit: *Little one there will be a time when I will no longer take walks in the bush and enjoy the pleasures of Mother Earth—like the sound of a raindrop, the scent of burning sweetgrass—for I will be the wind, the moon, and the stars in the sky. So when I'm gone, it's up to you to carry on.* This tender tale is yet another story to help children understand this difficult part of living.

## Mending Peter's Heart

*Written by Maureen Wittbold*
*Illustrated by Larry Salk*
Portunus 1995, ISBN 0–9641330–4–0

These words from the book jacket capture the very essence of this story: *Sometimes life is hard. It's especially hard when someone you love is gone— And you know you'll never see him again. This is Peter's challenge—his beloved dog Mishka is gone, and Peter feels so bad he won't even eat ice cream! He sees no way out of feeling bad until he meets Mr. MacIntyre.* Every classroom needs this book when talking to children about loss. Wittbold does an exceptional job of evoking the sadness of Peter who so loved his dog. Salk's art will leave a lump in your throat as he extends this lovely and incredibly sensitive story. Walk in the shoes of young Peter as he seeks to ease his aching heart, and sit on the porch with kind Mr. MacIntyre as he tells Peter about his loss. Help children learn of the healing power of sharing the burdens of your heart.

## A Name on the Quilt

*Written by Jeannine Atkins*
*Illustrated by Tad Hills*
Athenum 1999, ISBN 0–689–81592–1

> This sensitive story allows us into the grief and loss Lauren feels after losing her uncle. There are many things she misses about him while her little brother fills the air with his questions. The uncle lived with Michael in his apartment where Lauren's artwork covered the refrigerator and where she was allowed to eat brownies off china. The family decides to honor their memories by using some of Uncle Ron's clothes to make a quilt. For more mature children there are sentences that tell of the separation within the family over Ron's life with Michael. This very sensitive subject (AIDS) is presented with kindness, understanding, and respect.

## The Next Place

*Written and Illustrated by Warren Hanson*
Waldman House 1997, ISBN 0–931674–32–8

> This is one of the most sensitive books you will ever read, but not one we would recommend to read to children. It is, however, a glorious message of assurance for someone suffering from loss. It has become one of the books both of us have put in the hands of loved ones left behind. The words are not only comforting to read but the art is also breathtaking and extends those words in such a powerful way. Before giving it as a gift, read it carefully because it reflects a very personal choice and belief.

## Poppy's Chair

*Written by Karen Hesse*
*Illustrated by Kay Life*
Scholastic 1993, 2000, ISBN 0–439–16130–4

> While most of us think of Karen Hesse as the author of many fine novels, she has crafted this deeply moving story about a young girl who goes to visit her grandmother for the first time following the death of Poppy. Within the story, Hesse deals with the sad moments the little girl encounters as she sees his chair for the first time and how she is afraid to go near it. She also fears getting into bed with her grandmother because it is the same bed her Poppy slept in and his picture is still on the nightstand. This book is so sensitively

written it reveals the fears young children face after losing someone who was very important to them. Because of this, it is a must-have for your shelves. We all know the time will come when it will be needed.

## Old Coyote

*Written by Nancy Wood*
*Illustrated by Max Grafe*
Candlewick 2004, ISBN 0–7636–1544–7

> *Old Coyote* has lived a full life and remembers many trips across the land and up the mountains, but now his muzzle is turning white and he knows his days are growing short. In the story you will travel with him as he begins to say all his good-byes. Within the lines, you will hear many of the habits and ways of coyotes. However, the beauty of this book is that Wood explains death in a tender and sensitive tone and ends with *finally, he dreamed his way into a whole new world.*

## Rudi's Pond

*Written by Eve Bunting*
*Illustrated by Ronald Himler*
Clarion Books 1999, ISBN 0–395–89067–5

> This is a sensitive story about coping with the loss of a good friend when Rudi dies. Bunting provides background at the beginning of the book to show you a tender relationship between the two friends, who despite being different genders, enjoy many of the same things. Rudi is born with a problem with his heart, so he is sick a lot but even on those days, the two are friends who understand. When Rudi begins *sinking* and is taken to the hospital, his classmates make a large sign for his room. Bunting does a remarkable job of exploring the many feelings and fears young children experience when facing a loss. She provides words of comfort after Rudi dies by showing his classmates doing something concrete that helps to commemorate their lost classmate. Himler's watercolor illustrations reflect the tone of this important story.

## Saying Goodbye to Lulu

*Written by Corinne Demas*
*Illustrated by Ard Hoyt*
Little, Brown 2004, ISBN 0–316–70278–1

Many classrooms will experience having to say good-bye to someone special—many during the school year, others in the past, but everyone at some time. *Saying Goodbye to Lulu* is a sensitively told story that will help you with a difficult subject for young children. This lovely remembrance is told from the viewpoint of a young girl who has had Lulu all her life to run with, talk to, play with, and *just love*. When the time comes that Lulu cannot do any of those things, the little girl hurts very badly and longs for those fun, playful days. When the time comes to say good-bye, Demas handles the text so tenderly you won't hesitate to use this story with your children.

## Thank You, Grandpa

*Written by Lynn Plourde*
*Illustrated by Jason Cockcroft*
Dutton Children's 2003, ISBN 0–525–46992–3

Grandpa helps his granddaughter discover the world around her. When she is barely old enough to toddle beside him together they wobble *side by side, hand in hand, smile to smile*. Throughout their walks together the grandpa teaches his granddaughter how to marvel at nature's gift and also how to say, *thank you and good-bye*. As Cockcroft's gentle art caresses Plourde's memorable story, your children will be reassured about the difficult process of saying good-bye.

## When Someone Dies

*Written by Sharon Greenlee*
*Illustrated by Bill Drath*
Peachtree 1992, ISBN 1–56145–044–8

The first time we read this deeply compassionate book for children about death, it took our breaths away with its gentle tone and caring words. Not until we read the author's biography did we know how this book could show such tenderness and understanding of the grieving process of children. Greenlee, an elementary teacher, has also taught courses in counseling at the university level. Thus she has gifted us with a book that, if ever needed, will help you reassure children that all feelings following the death of a loved one are okay. Notice the dedication page and the notes about the illustrator. Once again it took reading that note to see that the book was completed shortly before the death of Bill Drath.

# 3

## Putting Language in the Air—Sharing the Music—by Reading Aloud

. . . Anthony Browne and Bill Martin and Jane Yolen may have written the words, but we've written the music to make those words sing.

—*Lucy Calkins (1991, 137)*

**W**E BELIEVE THAT writers are like composers. Writers put words on paper just like composers put notes on the page. Each of them hears the sound of what they are committing to paper. In a similar vein a teacher who reads aloud is like a musician. Just as musicians read the notes as they make music in the air with an instrument, we make music in the air with our voices every time we read aloud. In that sense a teacher's voice is an instrument and language is the music we play. Writers give readers cues as to how a piece might sound just like composers provide signs for a musician with rests, crescendos, and legato and staccato notations.

As writers put words down in print, they hear the music in language. Writers work toward a rhythm and flow that will feel natural to the reader's voice and the listener's ear. There is an intended music in their crafting of the language. The musician takes the composer's work, reads the notes and various signals, and then interprets the sound of it while playing the instrument to create a rendition of a piece. In a similar way a reader takes the writer's work, reads the words and various signals, and then interprets the sound of it while using his or her voice to create a rendition of the music the writer heard while writing. Will every reading sound the same? That is very unlikely because each of us will interpret the tone, mood, rhythm, and pacing for ourselves; so, there could be as many variations as there are readers.

Every time we hear a favorite book read aloud we will notice places where we feel the reader rushed the words or talked too loud or became too animated. We will notice other places where there was too little enthusiasm or not enough variation in the voices of characters or perhaps the personality of a character doesn't shine through the voice of the reader. We notice the variations played out by different readers. We connect with some and not with others. We are also influenced by some. Lester has had numerous teachers tell him that every time they read one of his books aloud to students, they can hear him reading in the back of their minds.

When we read to students, our voices are the instruments on which the music of language is played. The same instrument can take on many moods in the hands of a single musician. So, too, can our voices as we read to children. Return to Chapter 1 and review our comments on finding the voice of a book and attending to the signals. Try reading a favorite picture book aloud paying attention to these ideas. Read it the way you always do and then slow down, return to the book and spend time with the written language. Notice what the writer has done to signal to you how the music might sound. Try reading it aloud again and again playing with the sound of it. Search for places where your voice can show the feeling of the book and the tone of the story and the mood of the scene with subtle changes in pacing and volume and pitch. Play with it, have fun with it, find joy in it and your students will hear that magic.

We believe this is essential to making the read-aloud experience the most meaningful, the most engaging, and the most influential in the learning lives of students. Lester has been saying for years now that we must put the music of written language in the air if our students' ears are to arrest its rhythm. And their ears must arrest the rhythm of language if their voices are ever to echo it. And their voices must echo that rhythm and music if their pencils are ever to capture it. He jokingly calls it a *Lesterism*. So it would follow something like this:

- *Mouth:* We put the sound of the music of language in the air through reading aloud on a consistent and predictable basis.

- *Ears:* The sound, the music and rhythm of language, becomes natural to their ears and children begin to recognize it when they hear it.
- *Mouth:* The rhythms and sounds of written language begin to filter into children's talk as they begin to use words and phrases from writers they admire.
- *Hand:* As children write, those words and phrases, rhythms and sounds begin to be layered in among their own.

## ■ *Books for Putting Language in the Air— Sharing the Music*

This second opportunity for reading aloud every day is about immersing students in the sounds and the rhythms, the tones and the beauty, and the delight and humor written language can convey. On these shelves we feature books that have the potential music to be "played" by a reader. We include quiet books and boisterous books, books that will make you laugh out loud, and books that will bring you to the edge of tears. We feature those books you can read aloud and close as the language begins to settle in like silent fog wrapping the community in a shroud of awe.

For this read-aloud opportunity, we have divided the books into the following three shelves:

- Beautiful Language
- Just for the Fun of It . . .
- Just Because It Needs to Be Read

So now we invite you to peruse our shelves and search for titles that can sing for you. Take the time to search out a few, open the covers, and let your voice become the instrument that will find the music waiting on every page. Your students deserve nothing less.

### *Putting Language in the Air Bookshelf One: Beautiful Language*

"Everything we know as writers, we knew as readers first." We first heard this from our friend Katie Ray and we so firmly believe in the notion that we are devoting the second opportunity for read-alouds to filling the ears of students with the sounds and rhythms of language. Over and over again we have witnessed the influence that reading aloud to children can have on their writing. We have seen them become fascinated with the way a favorite author uses a repeated phrase or line. We have been with a group of children when one leans in with widening eyes and announces that the same word is used to start each new segment. We have been there when an entire class begins to take notice of the way writers use sound and other sensory details in evocative ways. And we have been there when these writing moves (and so many more) begin to work their way through the ears and mouths of students and finally appear on a page of a child's writing.

Because we have been privileged to witness the influence of reading aloud in the writing lives of children, we feel compelled to share the wealth. When you read books from this shelf, read them as Cynthia Rylant (1990) says:

> [Read] with the same feeling in your throat as when you first see the ocean after driving for hours and hours to get to it. Close the final page of the book with the same reverence you feel as you kiss your sleeping child goodnight. Be quiet. Don't talk the experience to death. Shut up and let these kids feel and think. . . . Do this a lot. Teach them to be moved and you will be preparing them to move others. (19)

Just read as if you are giving your children a gift. Don't talk it to death. Don't test it. Trust it. Let it stand on its own and just give the gift. The gesture will be powerful and the language will be potent. The influence will be long lasting. Trust it.

## All the Places to Love

*Written by Patricia MacLachlan*
*Illustrated by Mike Wimmer*
HarperCollins 1994, ISBN 0–06–0210098–2

This beautifully written and illustrated book will warm your heart and flood you with memories of your favorite places. The story, told through the eyes of a young boy, reveals all the favorite places on the farm where he and his family live. Join the young boy as he and his grandfather await the birth of his sister. Listen closely and enjoy the music of MacLachlan's language that begins on the very first page: *On the day I was born my grandmother wrapped me in a blanket made from the wool of her sheep. She held me up in the open window so what I heard first was the wind. What I saw first were all the places to love: The valley, The river falling down over rocks, The hilltop where the blueberries grew. . . .*

## Anna the Bookbinder

*Written by Andrea Cheng*
*Illustrated by Ted Rand*
Walker Books 2003, ISBN 0–8027–8831–9

Long before books were printed and bound by machine, each book had to be stitched by hand. The job took long hours and great patience. Anna's father was a bookbinder who took great pride in his work and felt his careful stitches were far superior to the glue used by machines. On the night of the birth of his son, the father was behind on completing three books that had to be finished. They knew the future depended on getting the job done on time so when the father is called to be by the mother's bedside, little Anna set out to complete the job with the same skill and dedication she had witnessed with her father. The job takes all night but Anna succeeds only minutes before her father comes to tell her about the birth of her new baby brother. The book is a lovely addition to beautiful language but could also be used with a section about family to show the tender relationship between father and daughter. Ted Rand's art is glorious and perfectly complements Cheng's story.

## Billywise

*Written by Judith Nicholls*
*Illustrated by Jason Cockcroft*
Bloomsbury 2002, ISBN 1–58234–778–6

Cockcroft's soft, calming art will take your breath away. So take your time with this one—saunter through the book with your children and introduce them to Billywise before you read it aloud. The lead captured us on first read: *From a mole-black hole in the oldest oak, deep in the heart of the fern-brushed wood . . . a scritch, a scratch, a tap, a crack!* Remember that pacing is critical for this one; take your time and relish the music in the language. Billywise is an owlet that isn't quite sure he's brave enough to be an owl and despite the repeated and poetic reassurances from his mother, he is scared of all the things in his world. You just can't afford to have children miss having the rhythm and music of this one resonating in their ears.

## Canoe Days

*Written by Gary Paulsen*
*Illustrated by Ruth Wright Paulsen*
Doubleday 1999, ISBN 0–385–32524–X

> If you are a fan of *Hatchet*, you already know Paulsen as a talented writer, but none of the novels you've read will prepare you for this lovely picture book. In *Canoe Days* he has broken away from his usual adventure focus to invite you to float along in the canoe and listen to the *shish of a butterfly's wings . . . and become part of the sky as you slide in green magic without a ripple.* While the words are truly powerful, his wife's stunning art embraces the language in a visual landscape that makes this one irresistible. Pull children close, open this book slowly, and fill the air with language that shows them the fawn peeking, the butterfly pausing in its flight, the ducklings fanning out.

## The Harmonica

*Written by Tony Johnston*
*Illustrated by Ron Mazellan*
Charlesbridge 2004, ISBN 1–57091–547–4

> This hauntingly beautiful book belongs with your curriculum books in a collection designed to build background for a study of the Holocaust. However, the language is so striking, we could not resist putting it on this shelf. The story itself was inspired by a true story and is crafted for us by Tony Johnston. In it a young family is split because they are Jewish. The parents are sent to one concentration camp while their child (who is our narrator) is sent to another. The young boy carries with him the one thing that keeps his parents close to him and keeps hope alive—a harmonica given to him by his father. One night the Nazi commandant hears him play and demands the young boy play for him every night during his dinner. The boy feels such guilt as he plays for the commandant, but miraculously this one ability ensures his survival. From the first page onward your heart will race and you will hang on each word as each page is turned—long after the book is closed.

## Hello, Harvest Moon

*Written by Ralph Fletcher*
*Illustrated by Kate Kiesler*
Clarion Books 2003, ISBN 0–618–16451–0

On a day when you want to let beautiful language quietly float in the air, this is the book for you. Fletcher's language is poetic and lyrical while informing the reader/listener about the time when the light of the moon is so bright that *you can read your favorite book without even turning on the lamp.* The tone he sets is one of a soothing, quiet conversation. Hover with it, relish the language. Read this book with a pace that matches the flow of honey on a cold morning. Slow down the day and treasure the soft glow of language and art. Kiesler's art is in harmony with the tone of Fletcher's language. If these two didn't collaborate closely to give us this treasure, their hearts must surely beat the same rhythm. This is their second time to work together; their first production, which is equally as delightful, was *Twilight Comes Twice* (Clarion Books, 1997).

## The Last Dance

*Written by Carmen Agra Deedy*
*Illustrated by Debrah Santini*
Peachtree 1995, ISBN 1–56145–109–6

Love is something special when it begins first as a deep friendship. This is proven by the relationship between two young friends. Bessie and Ninny have a friendship that binds them through the years of their marriage, the war that separates them, and ultimately to Ninny's death. As a young child Ninny's grandfather, Oppa, made him promise to dance forever on his grave, to sing and to tell stories. This promise was passed on to the new relationship between Bessie and Ninny. Deedy (also the author of *The Library Dragon* and *The Yellow Star*) shows the range of her craft with this lovely story. Santini's soft pastel watercolor paintings make this a memorable read-aloud.

## My Wishes for You

*Written by Adele Geras*
*Illustrated by Cliff Wright*
Simon & Schuster 2002, ISBN 0–689–85333–5

This book is an important reminder of what is important in the lives of children. It helps us to refocus on what we hope and wish for all children—happiness, security, dreams, smiles, and love. We want light to shine on them to warm their faces and we want kisses to awaken them. We want their laughter to ring out and fill their world. Geras' poetic language provides words to express all those cherished wishes and Wright's art adds depth and texture to the words. In addition to the beautiful language, *My Wishes for You* is an outstanding book for community-building and offers an opportunity to get knee-to-knee in deep conversation about the important things in life. (This one is also a touching gift for someone you cherish.)

## Night in the Country

*Written by Cynthia Rylant*
*Illustrated by Mary Szilagyi*
Aladdin 1986, 1991, ISBN 0–689–71473–4

We believe that your children will be captured by the rhythm of Rylant's language right from the opening lines: *There is no night so dark, so black as night in the country. In little houses people lie sleeping and dreaming about daytime things, while outside—in the fields, and by the rivers, and deep in the trees— there is only night and nighttime things.* The language, though sparse, is luscious and rich as it describes night in the country. For those of you who have spent time in the country, this book will only stir up memories of night sounds and starlight and the flicker of fireflies. But for children who have lived their entire lives in the city, it provides a delicious picture of night life in another setting.

## Nocturne

*Written by Jane Yolen*
*Illustrated by Anne Hunter*
Harcourt 1997, ISBN 0–15–201458–6

This out-of-print picture book will take your breath away with its luscious language. Yolen cleverly puts two common words together for that just-right rhythm and tone—*In the night, in the velvet night, in the brushstroked bluecoast velvet night. . . .* And so begins the journey through the night. Hunter's art is equally charming, and if you can find this lovely book, you will want to let children spend time pouring over the pages as they explore the well-matched balance of art and language.

## In November

*Written by Cynthia Rylant*
*Illustrated by Jill Kastner*
Harcourt Children's 2000, ISBN 0–15–201076–9

*In November, the earth is growing quiet. It is making its bed, a winter bed for flowers and small creatures. The bed is white and silent, and much life can hide beneath its blankets.* If you want children to fall in love with language, this is surely one of the books for your collection. The quiet rhythm, the careful choice of words, the thoughtful use of metaphors will draw your children in like moths to a flame. Let your voice be an instrument that will alert their ears to each beautiful word as Rylant's language spills into the air. The art is equally pleasing as Kastner enfolds the lovely words in a gentle caress.

## Owl Moon

*Written by Jane Yolen*
*Illustrated by John Schoenherr*
Philomel Books 1987, ISBN 0–399–21457–7

*It was late one winter night, long past my bedtime, when Pa and I went owling. There was no wind. The trees stood still as giant statues. And the moon was so bright the sky seemed to shine. Somewhere behind us a train whistle blew, long and low, like a sad, sad song.* Yolen's poetic story is one of gentle words describing a tender relationship as a father takes his daughter for her first owling. You will feel the icy wind blow in your face. You will hear the crunching of your feet in the snow. And finally, you will feel your heart race as the owl calls back. Despite the cold and despite the joy of seeing the owl, the little girl realizes that *when you go owling you don't need words or warm or anything but hope. That's what Pa says. The kind of hope that flies on silent wings under a shining Owl Moon.*

## A Quiet Place

*Written by Douglas Wood*
*Illustrated by Dan Andreasen*
Simon & Schuster 2002, ISBN 0–689–81511–5

There are days in each of our lives when we seek a quiet place far away from the chatter of children, the rushing of shopping and running errands, the hectic pace of the day. Each of us has felt that desperate need to escape to a place that can envelop us with a calming sense of peace and solitude. That place is different for every person. For some it is the mountains, for others it is the beach; still others find it in the breezes in their own backyard or in the gentle motion of a porch rocker. *A Quiet Place,* written in poetic and gentle prose, reminds us that no matter where we seek it, sometimes the very best place to search for that peace is to look within ourselves and create our own quiet place.

## Scarecrow

*Written by Cynthia Rylant*
*Illustrated by Lauren Stringer*
Harcourt Brace 1998, ISBN 0–15–201084–X

*Scarecrow* is such a memorable book because of the well-chosen words, the careful attention to rhythm, and the clear and uncluttered language Rylant uses to tell this story. It begins: *His hat is borrowed, his suit is borrowed, his hands are borrowed, even his head is borrowed. And his eyes probably came out of someone's drawer.* But in those borrowed clothes, he finds his life to be lovely because his pleasure is found in having the *time for long, slow thoughts.* He enjoys being present for the other events of the field—the weaving of a spiderweb, the chatting of the birds, and the planting of crops. Even the birds appreciate him for his gentleness as he stands watch over the seasons. Once you've read and reread this treasure, you will find it one that children begin to read along with you on.

## The Seashore Book

*Written by Charlotte Zolotow*
*Illustrated by Wendell Minor*
HarperCollins 1992, ISBN 0–06–020213–0

A young boy wonders what the seashore must be like. In a game of pretend, his mother describes the essence of the sea and the glories of the sights surrounding it. The jacket flap provides you with an additional reason to add this book to your shelf: *Charlotte Zolotow's affectionate text and Wendell Minor's stunning paintings immerse the reader in a tender world of sensory pleasures and evoke the rhythm of a perfect day at the seashore.* In versatile and very descriptive prose, Zolotow provides you with a text that can put beautiful language in the air and launch wonderings and reminiscing about the seashore.

## The Sunsets of Miss Olivia Wiggins

*Written by Lester L. Laminack*
*Illustrated by Constance R. Bergum*
Peachtree 1998, ISBN 1–56145–139–8

This is a touching generational story whose words will play in your mind long after the book is closed. Miss Olivia lives in a nursing home and her daughter Angel takes her own grandchild Troy to visit. Miss Olivia doesn't speak anymore even when her family visits. Rather they sit and talk to her but their voices and actions cause Miss Olivia to retreat into her memory of times when she was young. The words are poetic and will move you to make connections with your own life. A reading will also invite children to acknowledge the aging process with more kindness and understanding. Bergum's soft paintings are so evocative that this book will become a favorite part of your collection on family relationships.

## Welcome, Brown Bird

*Written by Mary Lyn Ray*
*Illustrated by Peter Sylvada*
Harcourt 2004, ISBN 0–15–292863–4

The language in *Welcome, Brown Bird* is beautiful. As you fill the air with the sound of the well-crafted lines, there will be a hush in your classroom because the words just sound good lingering there. And along the way you learn a few things as well because this lovely book could easily be included in Chapter 6, Building Bridges Across the Curriculum by Reading Aloud, when studying about migration. Once the concept is introduced, the children will become fascinated with the concept of how birds know when to leave and where to go. And as a little bonus, the author's note in the back of the book will make you appear really smart.

## The Whales

*Written and Illustrated by Cynthia Rylant*
Scholastic 1996, 2000, ISBN 0–590–61560–2

*The Whales* is a lovely book to read over and over again, but the last we heard it had gone out of print. So if you own one, protect and cherish it. Better yet, write Scholastic and request that they reprint it for all those who don't own it. We love this one. The words just feel good flowing across your tongue, so the language should be put into the air often. These are the opening lines: *In the blackness of the Black Sea, the whales are thinking today. Thinking of those things that matter most to them: friends, family, supper.* The lyrical language throughout the short text visually lets you glide through the sea with the whales. Don't let Rylant's beautiful words lull you into thinking this book is just about the lovely language; she has also carefully layered in many facts about whales.

## *Putting Language in the Air Bookshelf Two: Just for the Fun of It . . .*

If you know either of us, one thing you are bound to understand is that we love to laugh. Laughter is so good for the mind and the soul. It takes talent to write the beautiful, lush, and lyrical language we featured in Bookshelf One. But, it also takes talent to write humor. So when we find books that bring grins to the faces of children and fill the air with the sounds of giggles or books that have a spot or two where laughter erupts like an ancient volcano, then we know we have something special. When you scan the titles on this bookshelf, you'll find those kinds of books. When you and your students need a good chuckle to make the day, just pull one of them and get ready to giggle and wiggle and laugh out loud. You could also use this shelf to launch a study of writing humor. Read these and examine how writers make us laugh.

### Alice the Fairy

*Written and Illustrated by David Shannon*
Blue Sky Press 2004, ISBN 0–439–49025–1

Alice is a delightful child but with tremendous imagination. You see, Alice is a temporary fairy who can do magic tricks like turn her daddy into a horse so she can ride on his back around the room. And better still is her ability to turn her daddy's cookies into hers with a wave of her wand! Your children will squeal with delight as they watch the art further define the animated words. Shannon's art is unmistakable and will be easily recognized by read- ers/listeners who are familiar with his David stories.

### Bad Boys

*Written by Margie Palatini*
*Illustrated by Henry Cole*
Katherine Tegen Books 2003, ISBN 0–06–000102–X

Oh those *Bad Boys* were really bad! On the opening spread you'll find not only Little Red Riding Hood but also the Three Pigs chasing them off in their obvious attempt to fool everyone into thinking they were good little boys. With these words—*Oh yeah! We're bad. We're bad. We're really, really bad*—they take us on an adventure on the wild side of bad. Read with delight as they will once again meet their match when they try to make a meal out of some ewes. Palatini is at her best with this humorous story and Cole does an outstanding job of breathing life into the two *Bad Boys*.

## Bubba and Beau Meet the Relatives

*Written by Kathi Appelt*
*Illustrated by Arthur Howard*
Harcourt 2004, ISBN 0–15–216630–0

You've never met a baby like Bubba or a dog quite like Beau. And together, well sister that is just about the most special team you are likely to ever meet in all your born days. So pull this book off the shelf, open to the first page, lean back, and get ready to have yourself a bodacious good time while you and your students laugh out loud. Appelt writes the tale in five very short chapters as Bubba moves through the plot of the story. (See also: *Bubba and Beau: Best Friends* and *Bubba and Beau Go Night-Night.*)

## Diary of a Worm

*Written by Doreen Cronin*
*Illustrated by Harry Bliss*
Joanna Cotler Books 2003, ISBN 0–06–000150–X

Have you ever considered how the world looks from a worm's point of view or even thought about how a worm spends the day? Well, get into a worm mode—that's it, wiggle a bit and get flexible—and enjoy a few minutes taking a new look at the world. This hilarious book is tucked within endpapers that simulate a worm's scrapbook—family photos are labeled just like those in your own family album. Beginning on March 20 and moving through the events of one worm's life, this diary carries us through August. Practice this one several times before reading to your class so that *you* can find the perfect *worm mode*. It takes a reading or two to find all the perfect rhythm and master all the dramatic pauses needed to set up the "punch lines." When the giggling is over and they catch their breaths, children will beg to hear it again. Bliss' art is every bit as blissful (chuckle, chuckle) as Cronin's crack-up choice of words. This one won't stay on your shelf once you've blessed it with a reading. Say, maybe you should get more than one copy. (See also Cronin's *Diary of a Spider*, 2005.)

## Epossumondas

*Written by Coleen Salley*
*Illustrated by Janet Stevens*
Harcourt 2002, ISBN 0–15–216748–X

*Epossumondas,* once a part of storytelling lore, becomes a mischievous little possum in Miss Coleen's retelling. That little possum pushes his mama to her wits' end. Epossumondas takes his mama's every word literally and, like *Amelia Bedilia,* that takes him into situations that will have you chuckling and shaking your head in disbelief at his mischief and downright silliness. Coleen (pronounced Co–leen) Salley, a master storyteller from New Orleans, turns her little possum into a *sweet patootie.* Practice reading this one several times before sharing it with children—better yet find Miss Coleen's CD and have a go at her southern-cajun dialect. Then just cut loose as you put the language in the air and let the music flow, like the slow waters of the Mississippi, from the pages of this adorable book.

## Hungry Hen

*Written by Richard Waring*
*Illustrated by Caroline Jayne Church*
HarperCollins 2001, ISBN 0–06–623880–3

*There once was a very hungry little hen, and she ate and ate, and grew and grew, and the more she ate, the more she grew.* With this clever lead, Waring sets the theme for his entire story, which will become a favorite of young children. The very short text paired with the large font makes this one a great read-aloud for the very young, but older children will find the story equally delicious. As with many stories in which there is a hen, we also find a crafty fox who keeps watching over the little hen down below in the farmyard. The greedy fox waits and waits as the hen grows bigger and bigger and you can just see him thinking about how much better the meal will be. The problem is (of course there has to be a problem) that as the hen is growing bigger and bigger, the fox grows hungrier and hungrier (and we assume weaker and weaker). Finally, the day comes when, with great speed, the fox runs down the hill and right into the hen's house. *And just as the fox was about to pounce . . . the hen bent down—and gobbled him all up!* Your children will squeal with glee (we know because even adults cannot contain their laughter when we read it aloud).

## My Lucky Day

*Written and Illustrated by Keiko Kasza*

G. P. Putnam's Sons 2003, ISBN 0–399–23874–3

This one is so delicious and we warn you . . . don't use it unless you are willing to give kids time to snicker, hoot, and chatter. Kasza's story of the little piglet, a hungry fox, and a lucky day is told so cleverly that you will wish you'd written it! Mr. Wolf, hungry as all wolves are, tries his best to get piglet into the oven. Every time he is near to succeeding, piglet thinks of something Mr. Wolf might want to do to make his piglet meal better. But each time the piglet is sure to remind the wolf that his suggestion is "just a thought." By the end of the day, Mr. Wolf is exhausted and piglet is clean from a delightful scrubbing, full after a lovely dinner, and tender from a terrific massage. When Mr. Wolf passes out from sheer exhaustion, piglet returns merrily home to sit in front of a roaring fire to plan for his visit to Mr. Bear's house. The art is delightful and the perfect match for the charming story.

## Piggie Pie!

*Written by Margie Palatini*

*Illustrated by Howard Fine*

Clarion Books 1995, ISBN 0–395–71691–8

Gritch is a very hungry witch and all she can think of is *Piggie Pie*. But as Gritch pours over the recipe, she has everything she needs except eight plump pigs. Her problem is solved when she finds an ad for Old MacDonald's Farm advertising ducks, chickens, and piggies. She jumps on her broomstick and heads out to the farm. She made a huge mistake when the pigs are forewarned of her arrival. Then the fun begins. The pigs, who are much smarter than Gritch, anticipate her every move and outwit her at every turn. Practice this one several times if you want your children to be pulled into the story because with a playful voice and a little drama this one will have them rolling with laughter as they cheer the piggies to victory.

## The Three Armadillies Tuff

*Written by Jackie Mims Hopkins*

*Illustrated by S. G. Brooks*

Peachtree 2002, ISBN 1–56145–258–0

You will adore this armadillo retelling of the *Three Billy Goats Gruff*. This is one you'll have to practice before reading to children to get the true flavor of the language, which will only make the story more memorable. The more animated you are, the more the children will enjoy this unique retelling of the classic. Just a little hint—work on the Armadilly Shuffle in your dance studio. Children are sure to ask whether you know how to do it.

## Wiggle

*Written by Doreen Cronin*
*Illustrated by Scott Menchin*
Atheneum 2005, ISBN 0–689–86375–6

Have you ever been teaching a concept when your young children became so consumed with the wiggles that you knew it was hopeless to expect them to concentrate one more moment? If that has ever happened to you, this new book of Cronin's won't be a surprise for you as you see her take the wiggles into new territory. So the next time those wiggles take over the bodies of your children, pull this one off the shelf and get their little bodies engaged for a few minutes so that they can (hopefully) settle back down for a more serious moment.

## *Putting Language in the Air Bookshelf Three: Just Because It Needs to Be Read*

Some books don't fit neatly in a single category. In fact many books could fit easily on several of the shelves we have included in our read-aloud library. The books for this shelf are the sort that plainly refused to be tucked into one specific place. But we love them so and have had such a good response when we have shared them in classrooms. We had no choice but to put them on a shelf of their own. (Books can be bossy little creatures.) So here is a set of books that you simply must read. The language in them is worthy of sharing and each title has features children will surely be "stealing" for their own writing. So go ahead and take a look. We are certain you'll find them delightful and a few are likely to become favorites.

## Author: A True Story

*Written and Illustrated by Helen Lester*
Houghton Mifflin 1997, ISBN 0–618–26010–2

The *New York Times* said this little book "should be an anthem for young writers" and we agree. After you read all the notes surrounding it, you find out it is a biography of Helen Lester's life as a writer. Knowing this makes the book a treasure for reading aloud to young writers. The process of growing as a writer is described so clearly you will find it to be a very helpful resource when children grow discouraged with their own process. Don't miss this one.

## Bear Wants More

*Written by Karma Wilson*
*Illustrated by Jane Chapman*
Margaret K. McElderry 2003, ISBN 0–689–84509–X

*Bear Wants More* is a lyrical tale of a bear who wakes up very thin from not eating during his long winter nap. This bear is very, very hungry. However, the more he eats, the less he is satisfied. So he enlists all his friends to help him find more and more food. Finally, when his stomach is so full that he can eat no more, all his friends realize that they are now so very hungry. The full-page illustrations will be so appealing to your young children. Read along with Wilson's other bear tale, *Bear Snores On* (2002), also beautifully illustrated by Chapman.

## The Butterfly Kiss

*Written by Marcial Boo*
*Illustrated by Tim Vyner*
Harcourt 1995, ISBN 0–15–200841–1

*The Butterfly Kiss* will take your breath away. The gorgeous butterfly has no family and is so lonesome. He wants only to give a kiss away, but all the animals of the forest reject it. The butterfly flies first to the tiger for a kiss, but the tiger is ready for a nap and doesn't want to be bothered. The butterfly darts next to the elephant who says he doesn't need anymore kisses since he has lots of them stored in his trunk. The butterfly visits others but no one wants a kiss until he floats into a window where an old man is tucking his grandson into bed. And finally the butterfly flutters down to give his *Butterfly Kiss*. This one is a keeper.

## Daddy Played Music for the Cows

*Written by Maryann Weidt*
*Illustrated by Henri Sorensen*
Windward 2004, ISBN 0–89317–060–7

After reading this book to children, you will wish you could gift every child with a daddy like this one. Regardless of the task at hand (and with a dairy farm there are many), the dad always takes time to play with his daughter. The story begins at the birth of the little girl (in the barn). Throughout the pages of this treasure you watch the girl grow up and discover the many wonders around the barn. You will marvel at Sorensen's art while you witness the many stages of this young girl's life among the cows (each has a name) and her discoveries of chickens laying eggs, learning to read in first grade, learning to yodel, and eventually being old enough to drive a tractor. For those of you who are lucky enough to make connections to this story, it will bring sweet memories. And for others, children and adults who've never experienced life around a barn and cows, it will open new doors. This one is just too good to miss.

## Go to Sleep, Groundhog!

*Written by Judy Cox*
*Illustrated by Paul Meisel*
Holiday House 2004, ISBN 0–8234–1645–3

We all know that the groundhog sleeps all winter and wakes in time to step outside in early February. And we know what happens if he can see his shadow. But what happens when the groundhog can't sleep and stumbles out only to see pumpkins in October and then again to see a turkey in November and once again in December? Well, if you don't know the answer, you'll just have to pick up this amazingly clever book to inform yourself and your children. Meisel's playful art is just the perfect companion for the text in this adorable book. You don't want to miss this one.

## Hot City

*Written by Barbara Joosse*
*Illustrated by R. Gregory Christie*
Philomel 2004, ISBN 0–399–23640–6

Where is the coolest place to escape to in a hot city, a city so hot the cement steps are like a frying pan? Where can children go to get away from the *blah, blah* ladies and their grown-up talk? To the library, of course! The library, they learn, is not only the coolest place to visit but it is also a place where a child can escape to be a princess or a king. Once they fall into the story,

Christie provides several full-spread illustrations inviting children to use their imaginations to provide the words.

### How Groundhog's Garden Grew

*Written and Illustrated by Lynne Cherry*
Blue Sky Press/Scholastic 2003, ISBN 0–439–32371–1

This book could easily be used in Chapter 6, Building Bridges Across the Curriculum by Reading Aloud, to provide you with step-by-step instructions on how to prepare and plant and then harvest a garden. Cherry explains the cycle of nature, when birds and a praying mantis eat harmful insects and the bees and butterflies eat the nectar and carry pollen from flower to flower. When Groundhog's garden begins to produce food, everyone joins him in celebrating. You won't be disappointed by Cherry's art especially if you have followed her work over the years and come to expect a focus on detail and conservation. It is colorful, full of information, and, in a word, outstanding.

### Imagine a Day

*Written by Sarah L. Thomson*
*Illustrated by Rob Gonsalves*
Atheneum 2005, ISBN 0–689–85219–3

Let imagination float with your voice as you put the words of this charmer into the air. There is only one sentence on each page of the oversized book and that sentence always begins with the phrase, *Imagine a day—Imagine a day . . . when you don't need wings to soar. Imagine a day . . . when autumn is a yellow canopy above you, a burnt orange carpet underneath, a road you have never ridden on before.* Paired with each sentence Gonsalves' evocative images illustrate the imagining language. This book is so unusual, so evocative, and too striking to miss.

### John Philip Duck

*Written and Illustrated by Patricia Polacco*
Philomel 2004, ISBN 0–399–24262–7

Polacco dedicated this book to the wonderful memory of Robert McCloskey whose *Make Way for Ducklings* has been shared with children since 1941. If you are not familiar with the story of the ducks at the Peabody Hotel in

Memphis, Tennessee, you will need to read the last page as well as the back flap before reading the story to children. Although Polacco wove this fictional story around the actual event she witnessed at the Peabody, it will be difficult for you to tell fact from fiction as you become captivated by the plot. However, children need to know that the parade of ducks has been an event at the Peabody for more than sixty years. In this astonishing tale, young Edward works with his dad at the Peabody during the week but goes home on the weekend to a little farm outside Memphis. While home one weekend, Edward sees wild ducks flying south in a perfect V. From that moment on, he is fascinated with the ducks. Read with wonder and amazement as you find Edward adopting a wild duck and training it to march to the John Philip Sousa March. This duck later becomes the leader of the daily marching of the ducks at the Peabody (or so the story goes). Is it fact or fiction? Mmmmm, let's just say it will certainly make for an interesting discussion.

## Kitten's First Full Moon

*Written and Illustrated by Kevin Henkes*
Greenwillow 2004, ISBN 0–06–058828–4

> *Kitten's First Full Moon* is sure to bring giggles from young children as they begin to understand why the kitten can never quite reach his saucer of milk. Once he sees that little bowl of milk in the sky, Kitten is on a mission to reach it. Just as he closes his eyes and stretches for that giant bowl, all he gets is a mouthful of bugs . . . then a tumble . . . then stuck up high in a tree. Poor Kitten! Will he ever get to his bowl of milk? Henkes is at his best as he so cleverly solves the problem for the hungry kitten. In a departure from the art we have come to expect from Kevin Henkes, this winner of the 2004 Caldecott Medal is illustrated in black, gray, and white drawings. We think this one belongs on the shelf in every primary-grade classroom.

## Knuffle Bunny

*Written and Illustrated by Mo Willems*
Hyperion 2004, ISBN 0–7868–1870–0

> Before you begin the visual treat of a picture walk through this text, don't forget to include the cover page. Willems shows a family album beginning with the wedding of her parents up to the birth of the main character, Trixie. Before reading the story of how little Trixie loses her treasured *Knuffle*

*Bunny,* show the children how Willems blends his cartoon-style art with photographs. Now the tale begins: *Not so long ago, before she could even speak words, Trixie went on an errand with her daddy.* Many of your young children will fondly remember their *Knuffle Bunny* from preschool days and will quickly relate to the panic when it is misplaced. If they can make this association, then you know this book will be a winner in your classroom.

## Little Pea

*Written by Amy Krouse Rosenthal*
*Illustrated by Jen Corace*
Chronicle Books 2005, ISBN 0–8118–4658–X

Children will love the twist in this little gem. It is filled with humor that will have students wide-eyed and erupting with laughter once they get the little twist in this one. Here's a little taste to whet the appetite: *Little Pea was a happy little guy. He liked to do a lot of things. He liked rolling down hills, for example, super fast. But there was one thing that Little Pea did not like . . . CANDY. That's what you have to eat for dinner every night when you're a pea.* This is an argument children hear all the time about eating their vegetables. Read this short one to determine how Papa and Mama Pea convince Little Pea to eat his candy. We guarantee chuckles.

## Little Raccoon's Big Question

*Written by Miriam Schlein*
*Illustrated by Ian Schoenherr*
Greenwillow 2004, ISBN 0–06–052116–3

This one will be a great read-aloud for younger children since they are always the ones with the big question: *When do you love me the most?* Throughout this little book an adorable raccoon appears in every situation of the day. And in every one he just has to ask his mom whether this is the time she loves him the most. His mother, his very wise and insightful mother, keeps saying, *Oh, no, that's not when I love you the most!* After a full day of seeking her answer, as he is being tucked into bed with sleepy eyes, his mom finally tells him, *It is always right now when she loves him the most!* This is such a "feel-good" book and the art is so scrumptious, you will want to read it over and over.

## The Magic Hat

*Written by Mem Fox*
*Illustrated by Tricia Tusa*
Harcourt Children's 2002, ISBN 0–15–201025–4

This infectious book comes with a warning: Read this book at the risk of becoming a chanter of the text. You'll be swaying and chanting, *Oh, the magic hat, the magic hat! It moved like this, it moved like that! It spun through the air and over a road and sat on the head of a . . . warty old toad!* You and every child within the sound of your voice will adore this one. Tusa's kid-friendly art makes the book as much a treat for the eyes as Fox's rhythmic language is for the ears. Oh, we almost forgot. There is a second warning: After you read this book, you will be found purchasing several extras to give as gifts.

## Mole and Baby Bird

*Written by Marjorie Newman*
*Illustrated by Patrick Benson*
Bloomsbury 2002, ISBN 1–58234–784–0

Mole finds a baby bird that has fallen from its nest and when no one comes to rescue it, he takes the baby home to care for it. Despite the warnings and misgivings of his mother and father, Mole is determined that the baby bird will live. As the baby grows, Mole begins to think of it as his pet, but his mother reminds him that birds don't belong in cages, they are meant to be free and fly. Though the bird does grow, it becomes sad in the cage. Mole loves his baby bird and finally after a stroll with a wise granddad, Mole realizes that love is greater than ownership. *Mole and Baby Bird* is an extraordinary metaphor showing us that letting the things we love be shared or the people we love be allowed to grow and spread their wings requires more courage and deeper love than keeping them all to ourselves.

## Mr. Wolf and the Three Bears

*Written and Illustrated by Jan Fearnley*
Harcourt Children's 2001, ISBN 0–15–216423–5

Would you believe that Mr. Wolf is actually having a birthday party for Baby Bear? Well, Fearnley just turns the original tale upside down, to the delight of children, with her *Mr. Wolf and the Three Bears*. Even Grandma Wolf comes over to help with the cooking and cleaning to get ready for the party. Just as the party begins, guess who crashes? Goldilocks! In this version of the story, Goldilocks is very rude and does everything in her power to ruin Baby Bear's party. During a game of hide-and-seek, Goldilocks is never found. And Grandma Wolf is the only one who knows for sure what happened. What fun you and your children can have searching for clues as you try to figure out what happened to that little party-crashing Goldilocks.

## Mrs. Watson Wants Your Teeth

*Written by Alison McGhee*
*Illustrated by Harry Bliss*
Harcourt 2004, ISBN 0–15–204931–2

Many kids have a bit of anxiety on the first day of first grade. But our narrator has an added worry when a second grader fills her head with all kinds of scary things about Mrs. Watson, the first-grade teacher. With charming wit, McGhee gets into the head of a typical first grader who believes her new teacher is out to get her first loose tooth. And so she makes her first day miserable by attempting to keep her mouth shut all day and refusing to talk to anyone. Bliss adds speech bubbles to the art to help readers know who is talking. (Read along with *Trevor's Wiggly Wobbly Tooth* for more fun exploring the anxiety associated with losing that first tooth.)

## My Favorite Bear

*Written and Illustrated by Andrea Gabriel*
Charlesbridge 2003, ISBN 1–58089–038–5

*My Favorite Bear* will be loved by young children with its luscious illustrations that present a variety of bears. The enlarged font makes the book even more appealing for a read-aloud. The story is told by Mother Bear as she tucks her favorite bear in for a nap. Although bear facts are included, the book is quite soothing because it both entertains and informs.

## Oliver Finds His Way

*Written by Phyllis Root*
*Illustrated by Christopher Denise*
Candlewick 2002, ISBN 0–7636–1383–5

*Oliver Finds His Way* is a good choice for a fall read-aloud—just as leaves are beginning to turn into sensational oranges and yellows and reds. Teachers who carefully schedule this read-aloud to coincide with the season will help their children identify more readily with Oliver. In this story Oliver's attention is so captivated by a floating leaf that he wanders off trying to catch it. But when he looses sight of the leaf, Oliver realizes he is no longer in the yard with his Mama and Papa. He runs from place to place but finds nothing familiar. He cries. He rubs his nose. He tries to think. Finally, he just roars and roars and roars! That's when he finally hears his Mama and Papa calling back to him. He runs toward their roaring . . . *all the way to Mama and Papa with tumble-down hugs . . . and a big yellow leaf just for Oliver.* Many interesting discussions could follow this one.

## Paul Needs Specs

*Written by Bernard Cohen*
*Illustrated by Geoff Kelly*
Kane/Miller 2004, ISBN 1–929132–61–1

This punchy, well-paced story is told from the perspective of a sister named Sal whose brother Paul gradually becomes aware of his need for glasses. When things begin to get a "bit fuzzy," the font is enlarged and printed in red and is fuzzy around the edges. As some things appear a "bit blurry" the font, again printed in red, is slightly out of focus. Similar techniques are used with the words *misty* and *foggy.* As Sal begins describing Paul's increasing number of accidents, the final letters on the words *bumped* and *tripped* and *dropped* and *spilled* are toppling and turning to match the meaning. As Paul visits the eye doctor, the reader gets a simulated view of the world through all the lenses used as Kelly's art playfully distorts images until there is finally no focus. Then there is a visit to the optician to select frames and get the new glasses followed by those awkward moments of adjustment to the newly focused view. True to form for many new to spectacles, Paul hides out in fear of being teased about the glasses. So readers join Sal as she sneaks up on him to give us a peek. Young readers will love the splash of an ending. Cohen's humorous tale paired with Kelly's vibrant art provide a wonderful opportunity for open discussions about the issues that often surround the experience of getting new glasses.

## Pie in the Sky

*Written and Illustrated by Lois Ehlert*
Harcourt Children's 2004, ISBN 0–15–216584–3

With a two-layered text, Ehlert has gifted young children with a delightful story about trees, leaves, grass, and other beautiful things. One layer of the text is a little girl talking about the pie tree that her Dad told her about but she can't find. The second layer, presented in a different font, gives a listing of everything you can see on the page. Both layers lead to the same conclusion—there is not a pie tree in the picture. Many of the pages are just half a page, which adds interest to the book. When the tree finally produces cherries, there are directions for getting them ready to make a pie. Now you have a pie tree.

### Plaidypus Lost

*Written by Janet Stevens and Susan Stevens Crummel*
*Illustrated by Janet Stevens*
Holiday House 2004, ISBN 0–8234–1561–9

Once you read this book aloud and the language gets in your head, watch out! You will find yourself thinking (and sometimes saying out loud), *Plaidypus lost, Plaidypus found. This story goes around and around.* Plaidypus, a beloved stuffed animal, was made from grandpa's old plaid shirt (the endpapers are plaid like the shirt) with button eyes and it becomes the little girl's constant buddy. Like all small children that means trips to the park and down the slide, swinging with lots of spills, and even trips to the supermarket. On each adventure, Plaidypus has a tendency to get lost, but you (and your young listeners) know what that means—the search is on. And each time we chant the words: *Plaidypus lost, Plaidypus found. This story goes around and around.* The large font and Stevens' art are so inviting children will be unable to resist falling in love with this read-aloud. Memories will be sparked with this one. Take advantage of those connections.

### "Slowly, Slowly, Slowly," Said the Sloth

*Written and Illustrated by Eric Carle*
Philomel 2002, ISBN 0–399–23954–5

This is a must-read for your classroom. The words roll off you tongue and sound so good lingering in the air. In addition to the lovely language, Eric Carle informs readers and listeners about many of the animals living in the Amazon rain forest. For more detailed background information about the sloth, read Jane Goodall's foreword. Carle's choice of rich language will add depth to the community vocabulary when talking about the rain forest and the animals that live there. So you want a few examples? Consider these taken from only one page: *lackadaisical, dawdle, dillydally, unflappable, languid, stoic, impassive, sluggish, lethargic, placid, calm, mellow, tranquil, relaxed, yawned.* What is it research says about a read-aloud exposing children to a broad vocabulary? Oh yes, this one is a treasure.

## Someday Is Not a Day of the Week

*Written by Denise Brennan-Nelson*
*Illustrated by Kevin O'Malley*
Sleeping Bear 2005, ISBN 1–58536–243–3

Every adult should read this outstanding book to remind them how grown-up language can often be misunderstood by young children. Once you read this adorable little book, you will understand just how clever Brennan-Nelson was to feature this situation in a picture book. *Max and Momma sat at the kitchen table together. Max ate blueberry waffles while Momma made a list of the things she had to do that day. It looked very long and boring to Max.* Like most children, Max begins thinking and suggesting things he wants to do instead. For every suggestion, Momma replies, *Someday, Max, but not today!* Later when Max begins singing the song he learned at preschool about the days of the week, he discovers that *someday* is not a day of the week. He runs to say, *Momma, Momma, we can't go to the fair someday! Because someday is not a day of the week. We have to pick one of these, he exclaimed, waving the calendar.* Just think of the number of times we say, "in a minute" or "maybe later" or "next time" or "someday." This one will have your students buzzing about the things adults are always saying to them. And it was cause you to pause and reflect.

## The Teddy Bear

*Written and Illustrated by David McPhail*
Henry Holt 2002, ISBN 0–8050–6414–1

This book will warm your heart and if you don't already appreciate David McPhail, you will after one read. In this tender story a little boy takes his teddy bear everywhere he goes. Then one day when he goes out to eat with his parents, quite by accident, he leaves it behind in the restaurant. The beloved bear ends up in a trash bin behind the diner where a homeless man finds it and tucks it safely away under his coat. The boy, of course, misses his teddy but soon thinks of him less and less. Many days later he sees the bear sitting alone on a bench in the park. As the boy walks away reunited with his bear, he hears the old man crying. When he and his parents move closer, he discovers the old man truly loves the bear. With kindness and courage, the little boy hands over his beloved bear to the old man. This one will be a keeper for you to read time after time and year after year. Think of the discussions that could follow this act of kindness.

## Treasures of the Heart

*Written by Alice Ann Miller*
*Illustrated by K. L. Darnell*
Sleeping Bear Press 2003, ISBN 1–58536–115–1

In the story a little boy wants to share all the things he treasures most in his world with his mom. *Come along with me to see, the greatest treasure that will ever be! It's not in chests on pirate ships or in your favorite birthday wish. It's buried deep and very safe. I have it in my special place. Come along, it's through this door.* He leads her by the hand to crawl along the floor to peer under his bed at all his treasures, which he wants to be sure she won't throw away. His treasures are special only to him—a paper clip, a potato chip, a broken pen, and three toy men are among the many treasures. The art is soft and tender like the message, extending the tone and mood of this read-aloud experience.

## What's the Magic Word?

*Written by Kelly DiPucchio*
*Illustrated by Marsha Winborn*
HarperCollins 2005, ISBN 0–06–000578–5

Just read this lead and you'll be hooked: *In a tree, in a nest, on a gusty spring morn, a speckled egg cracked, and a small bird was born. A wind spun round, making blossoms fly, and WHOOSHED Little Bird up into the sky!* Little Bird is blown from the homes of one animal to another. At the door of each, the animal living there asks, *What's the magic word, Little Bird?* Of course, Little Bird finds out that the magic word sounds different from each animal. The cow says the magic word is *Moo-Moo* and the bee thinks it is *Buzz-buzz* and the dog says it is *Bow-wow*, while the owl says it is *Hoo-hoo* and the pig thinks it is *Oink-oink*. But Mama Bird tells Little Bird the real magic word is *Please!* The delicious art and predictable lines offer a combination that is not to be missed.

## Yesterday I Had the Blues

*Written by Jeron Ashford Frame*
*Illustrated by R. Gregory Christie*
Tricycle Press 2003, ISBN 1–58246–084–1

> Have you ever thought about how colors become associated with certain feelings and most often how each of us experiences them differently? In this short read-aloud told in first person, our narrator explores his own blue and green days, his mom's red days, and dad's gray days along with his grandmother's yellow ones. This book is sure to serve as a springboard for lots of discussion about feelings and the colors each of us associate with a feeling.

## You Read to Me, I'll Read to You: Very Short Fairy Tales to Read Together

*Written by Mary Ann Hoberman*
*Illustrated by Michael Emberley*
Little, Brown 2004, ISBN 0–316–14611–0

> If you are familiar with Hoberman's earlier book *You Read to Me, I'll Read to You,* then you will have to add this one to your shelves. The children we've read to loved the first one, but they absolutely adored this one! Hoberman takes several of the fairy tales and turns them into verse for two voices. As with the earlier book, the language in this one is printed in three colors (one for you, one for me, one for us). Emberley's art is delightful and frames each of the tales perfectly! Read it aloud, show them how it works, and invite them to try it out for reader's theater. Then stand out of the way for their creative juices to flow. We only wish it were longer with more fairy tales. . . . Well if you like this one, you'll absolutely have to get *You Read to Me, I'll Read to You: Very Short Mother Goose Tales to Read Together* (2005).

## Wild About Books

*Written by Judy Sierra*
*Illustrated by Marc Brown*
Alfred A. Knopf 2004, ISBN 0–375–82538–X

> Dedicated to the wonderful Theodore Seuss Geisel (Dr. Seuss), this rollicking rhymed story will pull children right into the story as each of the animals in the zoo tries to find the perfect book. After Molly, the bookmobile librarian, reads aloud to the animals, they go absolutely *Wild About Books.* Molly fills every request with delight: tall books for the giraffes, small books for the

crickets, stick-to-the-wall books for the geckos, and even waterproof books for the otter. The animals become such lovers of books and reading that they convince Molly they need a zoobrary! Now on a visit to the zoo, you'll find the *animals just a bit hard to find—They are snug in their niches, their nests, and their nooks, going wild, simply wild, about wonderful books.* What great fun.

### Zoom!

*Written by Diane Adams*
*Illustrated by Kevin Luthardt*
Peachtree 2005, ISBN 1–56145–332–3

With an enlarged font this father–son roller-coaster adventure is filled with onomatopoeia as the coaster *click-click-clacks up the track . . . edging closer to the drop and suddenly AAAAAAHHHHH!* The story is very short but jam-packed with the thrill of the ride. The language clearly follows the show-don't-tell adage in describing the action in the story. And just as the once-reluctant little boy exits the ride, he immediately gets back in line for the next trip. Your children will be just as eager for another reading of this adventure.

# 4

## *Continuing the Music with Poetry Throughout the Year by Reading Aloud*

**P**OETRY IS SO frequently neglected in the lineup of material for read-alouds. Somehow we tend to think of picture books and short stories and novels shared in chapter installments when we think of reading aloud. Here in this chapter we encourage you to pause a moment every day to put the rhythms and cadences of poetry into the air and into the ear. Day after day, as you layer poem upon poem, those sounds begin to gather in the silent spaces and hover there like bees gathering one by one, gathering into a swarm. As poems accumulate, language begins to hum and the sound that language creates soon resonates throughout the day and takes on a life of its own.

It is that resonating hum that will linger in the ears of students, the hum that will become the familiar sound they will recognize when you read yet another poem and another. It is that familiar sound, that cadence and rhythm, that choice of words that will resonate in their ears and inform their mouths and pens when, for the first time, they begin to write poems of their own. And of course, the cadence and rhythm, the careful selection of just-right words will also find a way into their prose. Poetry will breathe life into all writing if we honor it with our voices and time.

We must read poetry aloud every day. It must become so much a part of the routine that children feel they have missed lunch if they fail to hear a poem read to them. Poetry is the rich, artful language that may be in the simple, direct, and forthright statement of an observation or truth perceived by the poet. The art may be in the layered-language concentrate potent with metaphor or symbolism for each reader to interpret as he or she is ready and able. The art may be in the ability of the poet to evoke image or emotion, to connect to the reader's life, to point out simple and often missed beauty in the world, or the art may be in a thousand other things. Poetry is a powerful form of writing that can say big things in small spaces and give students more control over their choices as writers.

## ■ *Making It Work*

Poetry isn't just for memorizing and analyzing—even if that is what we remember doing in school. We are suggesting that by making poetry an integral part of the daily routine, both you and your students will begin to see all the new possibilities poetry can bring to all aspects of the curriculum. Consider featuring it in this third read-aloud opportunity as a "poetry pause." Here's one way to make that work for you.

Find a spot in the room that will be easily visible to students. Attach a coat hook to the wall and designate this spot as the "poetry place." You might even paint a background in some contrasting color to "frame" the poem. Select thirty-six to forty poems and print each one on a chart. Make a collection of coat hangers with clips—the kind intended for holding a skirt or slacks. Feature one each week by clipping it to a hanger that will be placed on the coat hook. We recommend either laminating the charts or covering them in a clear contact paper so that they can be "loved" by children in the weeks to follow and used with other classes in the future. Post a new poem each Monday and revisit it throughout the week.

On the Monday for the third read-aloud, signal the children it is time for a poetry pause and then read the poem once so students can hear the pacing, cadence, and meaning of the language. Think of this as a brief shared reading and invite them to read along the second time through. Leave the poem posted so students can reread it at any spare moment during the day. On Tuesday during the poetry pause read the poem together once, and then on the second reading divide the group (those with buttons/without buttons on their shirts, those with strings/without strings in their shoes, etc.) to read alternate lines, or stanzas. Play with the sound of it, experiment with the rhythm, find a sound that fits the poem. On Wednesday have a copy of the poem for each student to add to a cumulative personal anthology binder. During the poetry pause read through the posted poem once as a group, then have them read the personal copies in pairs or small groups.

On Thursday and Friday devote the poetry pause to performances or readings of the poem by individuals, pairs, or small groups.

Throughout the week you will be constantly demonstrating the sound of poetry read aloud. More important, you are slowly transferring the voice of poetry to the readers and writers in your learning community. Once again, we know time is a critical factor, so let the reading of a poem be another hinge in the day. The poetry pause could take place as a second transition, perhaps just before lunch so that the language of poetry will resonate among the usual buzz in the hallway.

Featuring one poem each week requires that you select thirty-six poems. If you are working with kindergarten or first-grade learners, we suggest looking for short poems with a strong, obvious rhythm or rhyme pattern for the first weeks. Then as the school year progresses and your learners gain some proficiency, move on to poems with less obvious rhyme patterns or no rhyme at all, then on to longer poems with more imagery and deeper meaning. Just as emerging readers grow with the support of familiar, predictable, and repetitive texts, students will thrive on the support provided by poets who attend to the power of cadence and rhyme in poems for their youngest audiences. In short, select poems that fit the developing language of your learners.

We also recommend that you think through the ways you would like to weave poetry into the curriculum. As you search for poems to include in your class anthology, keep in mind the seasons, the milestones in children's development, the units of study you need to pursue across the curriculum and . . . well just think of all the ways poetry could be the avenue into deeper study.

If you are working with older learners, you may find that one poem each week is not sufficient to hold their interest. You may want to build an anthology that represents a broader range of poem types to demonstrate the potential poetry can have for a writer. One possibility for older students is to feature a new poem every second or third day. Instead of having the poems on charts that remain in view throughout the week, you could make a transparency of each poem to project when reading aloud. Here again, read it through once so the cadence and rhythm and meaning of the language can be heard. Stop to think aloud and let your students know how you make decisions about the sound of poetry when your read. Then project the poem for learners to read through silently while your voice still lingers in their ears. Follow this with a choral reading for which you remain the lead voice. Bring the poetry pause to a close by distributing a copy for each learner to add to a rapidly growing personal anthology.

On the second day, project the poem on the screen and read it alone to once again refresh the sound of it in their ears. Ask them to work in pairs or small groups, to open their anthologies to the selected poem, and to try reading it aloud within their groups with your cadence and stresses on their voices. Invite them to try reading it in alternate ways to find another oral rendition that fits the presentation of the print and matches the meaning of the poem. Because poetry is so dependent on phrasing, it is a natural for fluency work with readers of all ages. The playful exploration of reading poetry aloud will naturally lead readers to focus on phrasing and fluency in their search to find a meaningful sound.

For this pattern—one new poem every second or third day—we suggest that you pause after every five poems (about ten days) and encourage learners to find favorites to share through a poetry performance or in a poetry café setting. This may take two to three days of the poetry pause time. "Performance break" in the cycle offers an opportunity for you to select poetry in clusters—by theme, topic, or type.

Before we get to the books, here is one final plea from Kennedy and Kennedy (1999) for reading aloud: "People who wish their children to grow up liking poetry will do well, we believe, to start reading aloud to them as soon as they can sit up and help turn pages. Whether the text be Mother Goose or Dr. Seuss, there is nothing like a warm lap or an enclosing arm and a friendly voice to help a child learn to love words" (158).

## ■ Books for Continuing the Music with Poetry

For this third read-aloud opportunity of the day, the shelves are divided into the following seven categories:

- Moving Across the Year
- A Focus on the Natural World
- The Subject Is School
- Relationships
- Supporting the Curriculum
- It's All About the Game
- Collection Selections

### Continuing the Music with Poetry Bookshelf One: Moving Across the Year

Look to the calendar. One simple way to begin selecting poems for the classroom anthology is to think about the changing seasons and the flow of events marked by the passing months during a school year. Your personal anthology will be the source you draw from as you plan for a daily poetry pause. There are many poems and collections of poems devoted to the seasons and months of the year. Here's just a sampling for you to consider.

### Autumn: An Alphabet Acrostic

*Written by Steven Schnur*
*Illustrated by Leslie Evans*
Clarion Books 1997, ISBN 0–395–77043–2

> This book looks so simple at first glance. You flip through the pages and notice that every page begins with a word related to the autumn season. Each page features a word beginning with the next letter of the alphabet. OK, pretty simple, we could do that. Now each word is presented as an acrostic poem—yeah, we could do that. So what's the catch you might be thinking? Well, on a closer read we realize that each acrostic is not *just* a stand-alone poem, but that each one leads into the next so that all twenty-six can be read one after the other as one long poem. For others in this set, see our companion book, *Building Bridges Across the Curriculum with Picture Books and Read-Alouds* (2006, Heinemann).

### Brown Angels: An Album of Pictures and Verse

*Written by Walter Dean Myers*
HarperCollins 1993, ISBN 0–06–443455–9

> Walter Dean Myers collects long-forgotten turn-of-the-century pictures, which he used to inspire the poetry found in this collection. It was written in hopes that the reader will *celebrate the child in each of us as our most precious part.* The pictures are a treasure that you and your children will enjoy sharing. The verses that accompany the pictures are among our favorites of his work. No wonder this one feels like a celebration to him.

### Days to Celebrate: A Full Year of Poetry, People, Holidays, History, Fascinating Facts, and More

*Written and Edited by Lee Bennett Hopkins*
*Illustrated by Stephen Alcorn*
Greenwillow 2005, ISBN 0–06–000765–6

> *Days to Celebrate* can provide the foundation for poetry in your classroom for an entire year because it takes you through all twelve months filled with poems about people, holidays, history, facts, and more! At the beginning of

each month (before you get to all the poems), Hopkins gives us a calendar with important dates and facts that will enrich the reading of the selected poems. This treasure will become one of those books children will remember for years with fondness. If you hesitate to put poetry into the air, begin by using this book because it offers many types of poems that will encourage you to lift up your voice with a poem. You may want to purchase several to keep as gifts for new teachers.

### Pieces: A Year in Poems & Quilts

*Written and Illustrated by Anna Grossnickle Hines*
Greenwillow 2001, ISBN 0–688–16963–5

Twenty poems celebrating the changing seasons in beautiful language are paired with nineteen of the author's handmade quilts featuring her own original designs. These short poems can be shared throughout the year to mark the changing of the seasons.

### Summersaults

*Written and Illustrated by Douglas Florian*
Greenwillow 2002, ISBN 0–06–029267–9

Florian is at his best with this little book that spotlights the carefree summer activities of children. When words, such as *vaulting* and *tumbles,* are included, the letters are printed on the page in such a manner as to show the meaning of the word. The colorful pictures of children playing also demonstrate the meaning of less familiar words. Other poems feature many of the things children like best about summer while there is one to reveal those things that make some dislike summer. These are short and quick reads to share in those tight times.

## Continuing the Music with Poetry Bookshelf Two: A Focus on the Natural World

Children are fascinated with the world around them; every educator knows this as truth. Poets seem to know that as well. Or maybe poets are just keen observers who notice the little details and find efficient ways to capture them for us with words. In any case, we think you'll find a few poems for your collection in the sampling that follows.

### Animal Snackers

*Written and Illustrated by Betsy Lewin*
Henry Holt 2004, ISBN 0–8050–6748–5

Each of twelve animals is introduced in clever four-line rhymes that reveal both the animal's name and its "snack" of choice. The art is lively and supports each rhyme by portraying the featured animal enjoying a snack. Lewin includes details about every animal, including its natural habitat, at the back of the book.

### Farmer's Garden: Rhymes for Two Voices

*Written by David L. Harrison*
*Illustrated by Arden Johnson-Petrow*
Boyds Mill Press 2000, ISBN 1–56397–776–1

In this simple rhyme in bold print Harrison presents fifteen small poems that children will quickly be chanting. Each of them addresses what various animals and plants are doing on the farm. The two voices are those of the dog who poses the questions and of the animal or plant responding. The dog's voice, positioned to the left, is presented in normal type while the respondent's words are positioned to the right and presented in italics.

### If Not for the Cat

*Written Jack Prelutsky*
*Illustrated by Ted Rand*
Greenwillow 2004, ISBN 0–06–059677–5

Written in first person, each of these seventeen poems, presented in haiku, is actually a clue to the identity of the voice on each page. If you can't solve the riddle, don't worry because Ted Rand's beautiful illustrations will reveal the solution. And a key to the identities is provided on the final page in the form of an index. This is a treat to both the eye and ear.

### Silver Seeds

*Written by Paul Paolilli and Dan Brewer*
*Illustrated by Steve Johnson and Lou Fancher*
Viking 2001, ISBN 0–670–88941–5

This gorgeous book provides another example of acrostic poems. Each of the lovely poems describes things in nature, moving from *DAWN* to *SUN* to

*SHADOW* and continuing on to end with *NIGHT.* The text is thoughtful, but simple and within the reach of children. *Silver Seeds* could be a mentor text for those who want to create their own acrostic poems.

### Touch the Poem

*Written by Arnold Adoff*
*Illustrated by Lisa Desimini*
Blue Sky Press 2000, ISBN 0–590–47970–9

This delightful romp through the joys of childhood will surely ring true with the experiences of your students. Adoff's verse is crisp, precise, and direct with a clear focus on the senses. Each poem aptly captures a moment so clearly part of childhood you'll find connections popping like popcorn at the movies.

### Walk a Green Path

*Written and Illustrated by Betsy Lewin*
Lothrop, Lee & Shepard 1995, ISBN 0–688–13425–4

A unique book of short poetry about things in nature that are green. Every spread has a poem about the item featured in the illustration, then in italics Lewin tells the reader where she found that plant, tree, flower, or trail to paint. This book would be a good companion for a curriculum connection in science and to read alongside of *Here Is the Tropical Rain Forest.*

 *Continuing the Music with Poetry Bookshelf Three: The Subject Is School*

School is the subject of endless stories, songs, and yes, even poetry. This collection will ignite laughter, goose giggles, and have kids chanting. Who knows, with a subject so close at hand, these might even launch a few poems in the writers' notebooks of your learners. Take a peek at this sampling of school poems to see whether there are a few you might want to add to your anthology.

### Did You See What I Saw?: Poems About School

*Written by Kay Winters*
*Illustrated by Martha Weston*
Viking Juvenile 1996, ISBN 0–670–87118–4

In these twenty-four poems Winters captures the excitement of young children going to school. Every poem features the ordinary experiences of children in delightful verse, reminding young and old alike just how extraordinary little things are to youngsters and the young at heart. Remember the rumbling school bus, learning to read, that box of brand-new-never-before-used crayons, read-aloud time, chicken pox, snow days, and all those holidays. . . . Layer these in just for fun and to spark some interesting conversations about the routine events we take for granted.

### Lunch Money and Other Poems About School

*Written by Carol Diggory Shields*
*Illustrated by Paul Meisel*
Puffin Books 1995, 1998, ISBN 0–14–055890–X

This collection of twenty-four poems chronicles the events of school, so routine and so typical that children and even the teacher will nod in recognition. The poems included address a range of school day topics such as rushing to catch the bus, making lunch decisions, the morning pledge, classroom pets, recess, homework, and more. The quick pace and simple rhyme pattern will make these poems sure favorites for both reading aloud and poetry performance. Shields' humorous style will most certainly bring giggles and grins with every reading.

 *Continuing the Music with Poetry*
*Bookshelf Four: Relationships*

It is interesting that when Lester visits schools as an author of picture books he sometimes asks children whether they like poetry. The answer, of course, depends on what teachers have done with poetry in the lives of these young folks. The answers that ring like a fire alarm in Lester's head include: "Naaa, poetry is for girls." "That's for little kids, all that rhyming stuff like roses are red . . ." "Nuh uh, poetry is like all about love and junk like that."

Well poetry can focus on love. It can rhyme. But, it doesn't belong to one gender or age group. We believe that it is very important to include poems that focus on relationships to let children know that poetry is an avenue for expressing what too seldom is expressed out loud. Poetry can be a place where, as humans, we do explore our feelings about others and ourselves. Indeed, poetry can be a healthy way to launch conversations about our relationships with family and friends. So we invite you to read from this sampling to see whether you can find a few that might crack that door and invite those conversations into the thinking of your students.

## Becoming Joe DiMaggio

*Written by Maria Testa*
*Illustrations by Scott Hunt*
Candlewick 2002, ISBN 0–7636–1537–4

> This sparsely illustrated book contains twenty-four poems that flow one into the next telling a tender story. It is written in the first-person voice of a young boy who grows up during the era of Joe DiMaggio, the war, and V-J Day. We learn of his family's struggle to make ends meet while his father is in jail. We see the wisdom and strength of his maternal grandfather—Papa Angelo. We see the boy set his goals high to follow the lead of his new hero. If you should choose to read this one, you'll need to read it over time. It is an excellent example of using poetry to tell a story.

## Heartsongs

*Written and Illustrated by Mattie J. T. Stepanek*
Hyperion 2001, 2002, ISBN 0–7868–6947–X

> Mattie is an unusually gifted poet who sees all the possibilities in his world rather than any of the limitations. He has a rare form of muscular dystrophy. At a very young age he begins writing poetry as he lives with three of his siblings who are battling the same disease. In spite of the loss of all three, he continues to see hope where others see defeat. This is reason enough to make you want to buy his books, but we offer another reason—the poems are amazing. Those collected here have the potential to provide an uplifting moment as his words float out into the air of your classroom.

## Relatively Speaking: Poems About Family

*Written by Ralph Fletcher*
*Illustrated by Walter Lyon Krudop*
Scholastic 1999, ISBN 0–531–30141–9

> In this small text Ralph Fletcher brings us forty-two poems in the voice of an eleven-year-old boy, the youngest in his family. Through his voice we see our

own families and reflect on universal issues. Each poem can easily stand alone and will be certain fodder for thinking and talk and writing.

## Continuing the Music with Poetry Bookshelf Five: Supporting the Curriculum

Poetry can be the light that shines through all the dense language and concepts presented in the content areas. The collection here is a sampling of poems devoted to topics that could easily be found in the curriculum areas of many schools throughout the country. Browse through this shelf, pull a book and read through it; we are certain you will find a few for your own collection.

### Big Talk: Poems for Four Voices

*Written by Paul Fleischman*
*Illustrated by Beppe Giacobbe*
Candlewick 2000, ISBN 0–7636–0636–7

The three poems included in this book are not for you to read aloud. Instead, these are for your learners to gather around, try out in small groups, then to just have fun with. It will take a little rehearsal to get all four voices coming in on cue, learning to talk in sync, fade out, stand alone, speak with one or two or three others, and so on. But it will be such a hit. So when the poetry bug begins to nibble on your students, when they have it in their ears, when they have ridden on the rhythm of your voice, hand them this book and let them carry others on the journey.

### A City Is

*Written by Norman Rosten*
*Illustrated by Melanie Hope Greenberg*
Henry Holt 2004, ISBN 0–8050–6793–0

This group of fifteen poems celebrates life in the city. Although several describe the city in a generic sense and could be referring to any city, a few specifically mention well-known landmarks making it clear that the subject of these poems is New York City. And if there is any doubt after reading them aloud, just focus on the art. Every poem can stand alone and the collection could extend the final poem into *Home to Me: Poems Across America* selected by Lee Bennett Hopkins (see page 125).

## Creatures of Earth, Sea, and Sky

*Written by Georgia Heard*
*Illustrated by Jennifer Owings Dewey*
Boyds Mills Press 1992, 1997, ISBN 1–56397–635–8

> Hummingbirds sip from straws and dragonflies skim the surface of the water. Eagles glide on air, other birds migrate, and whales swim in the deep blue sea. This collection of eloquent poems celebrating seventeen creatures reveals the gentle nature of the poet and her love of the natural world. Every poem can stand alone or be woven into the science curriculum or into the writing workshop with ease and grace.

## Good Times, Good Books!

*Selected by Lee Bennett Hopkins*
*Illustrated by Harvey Stevenson*
HarperTrophy 2000, ISBN 0–06–446222–6

> This little book features more than a dozen poets and poems. The collection has as its focus the joys of books and reading. We can't think of anything we'd rather have children do than to fall in love with books and to embrace that joy of discovery. This jewel will help you expose children to this joy in small, bite-size installments. So think about filtering these into the poetry pause throughout the year just to keep that message alive in the minds of your students. And you could even select a few poems from this one for your newsletters to parents.

## Here in Harlem: Poems in Many Voices

*Written by Walter Dean Myers*
Holiday House 2004, ISBN 0–8234–1853–7

> In this fascinating study of voice Walter Dean Myers introduces forty-two of the folks living in the Harlem of his childhood. Myers says he adds photographs from his personal collection "to the text because I love the images, not to match the poems. The images and the voices race through my mind in a sustained triumph of place and community." The people you will meet here range from twelve-year-old students to eighty-plus-year-old veterans and

retirees, and they represent all walks of life—students, musicians, mail carriers, undertakers, janitors, nannies, educators, clergy, laborers, and more. Myers writes each of the poems, that's right one writer, forty-two voices. Read these as a study of voice, to gain a sense of place and the life of people in that place, to add depth of understanding to a study of a period in history . . . oh the possibilities.

### Home to Me: Poems Across America

*Selected by Lee Bennett Hopkins*
*Illustrated by Stephen Alcorn*
Orchard 2002, ISBN 0–439–34096–9

Lee Bennett Hopkins selects poems from many of the most noted poets of our time to provide readers with a lovely contrast of what *home* can mean. Each of the fifteen contributors writes a poem to celebrate the place he or she calls home. This could be a wonderful companion to *My America: A Poetry Atlas of the United States* (see page 126), another collection Hopkins also selected.

### Hour of Freedom: American History in Poetry

*Complied by Milton Meltzer*
*Illustrated by Marc Nadel*
Boyds Mills Press 2003, ISBN 1–59078–021–3

This one is a must to support any study of American history. At Reba's school the fifth-grade teachers made overheads and used the poems to support a study of American history and to help their children develop fluency and phrasing. The poems in this collection vary in length, allowing you to begin the year with the shorter ones and progress to the longer ones.

### In the Land of Words: New and Selected Poems

*Written by Eloise Greenfield*
*Illustrated by Jan Spivey Gilchrist*
HarperCollins 2004, ISBN 0–06–028993–7

This book of twenty-one poems is divided into two parts. Part one, The Poet/The Poem, features commentary from Greenfield giving readers a bit of insight into her thinking and the influences on her writing. Then in part two, In the Land, the poems focus on language—words, reading, writing, books, and poems. So here is another collection from which you might select poems to sprinkle throughout the year just to keep attention on the power of literacy in the lives of learners.

## A Lucky Thing

*Written by Alice Schertle*
*Illustrated by Wendell Minor*
Harcourt Children's 1999, ISBN 0–15–200541–2

Picture a young girl sitting at a table by an open window, pencil in hand poised on a notebook of paper. She is looking through the window out over the farm buildings and animals and surrounding land. Each poem in this collection of thirteen focuses on something within her vision. The first and last poems bring us back to her, searching, thinking, observing, wondering, and writing. This is a glimpse into the process of writing poetry, just look closely and listen to the metaphors she so carefully extends as our scaffolding. Oh and don't forget to look carefully at Wendell Minor's art. You'll notice fine detail in the farm images, but look past those to note the paper drifting through the scene or the pen or pencil tucked away.

## My America: A Poetry Atlas of the United States

*Selected by Lee Bennett Hopkins*
*Illustrated by Stephen Alcorn*
Simon & Schuster 2000, ISBN 0–689–81247–7

This collection of poems is organized by regions of the United States and represents the voices of thirty-nine poets. Each of the fifty poems features a landform, famous area, person, and so on associated with the region. Every section opens with a map of the region and a list of the states included. This is a rich resource to delve into again and again across the year.

## Sidewalk Chalk

*Written by Carole Boston Weatherford*
*Illustrated by Dimitrea Tokunbo*
Boyds Mills Press 2001, ISBN 1–56397–084–8

These poems reveal life in a city, a life that many children have never experienced. Take your learners on a visit down the city sidewalk where they will see men on the street polishing shoes in the poem *On the Corner*. Or move on down the block and see how city dwellers shop for food in the poem *The City Market.* By way of contrast, Weatherford also includes poems showing young people engaged in activities that children in many settings enjoy—jumping rope, eating out, writing with sidewalk chalk, and going swimming. Tokunbo's art is a visual treat to accompany the poems.

### Stone Bench in an Empty Park

*Selected by Paul B. Janeczko*
*Photographs by Henri Silberman*
Orchard 2000, ISBN 0–531–30259–8

This collection of haiku features the city as its subject. Every poem is paired with an accompanying black-and-white photograph that highlights the particular aspect of the city featured in it. The introduction provides the history of haiku and revisits the rules of writing haiku. Janeczko also tells us that the selections' poets followed the advice of haiku master Daisetz T. Suzukim who said that the haiku poet "gets inside an object, experiences the object's life, and feels its feelings."

### When Riddles Come Rumbling: Poems to Ponder

*Written by Rebecca Kai Dotlich*
*Illustrated by Karen Dugan*
Boyds Mills Press 2001, ISBN 1–56397–846–6

*When riddles come rumbling as no doubt they do, such poems are to ponder as clue after clue weaves words into puzzles then welcomes you in, when riddles come rumbling it's time to begin . . . ;* and with these words, Dotlich invites you into riddle after riddle. Don't show the children the illustrations until they guess the riddle because each one reveals the answer. What a wonderful way to get your children lined up for lunch every day! A riddle a day just may keep the boredom away!

### A Writing Kind of Day: Poems for Young Poets

*Written by Ralph Fletcher*
*Illustrated by April Ward*
Boyds Mills Press 2005, ISBN 1–59078–353–0

As readers we get an insider's look at the world through the poet's eyes and hear his thoughts pour onto his page. This collection of twenty-seven poems is a demonstration by a gifted writer of the ways that ordinary things and ordinary events in each of our lives can be the subject of poetry. Follow him along this journey and notice how ideas gather like rain clouds just before a poem sprinkles down. Go ahead, pause for poetry and share these out loud. Let them seep into the ears of your student writers.

## Continuing the Music with Poetry Bookshelf Six: It's All About the Game

Remember the boys who always say, "bleck, poetry is for girls. I don't want to write poetry." Well walk those boys over to this shelf, pull a few books and ask them to read the titles aloud. Sit with them a few moments and read one or two selections from a few of these. Flip through the pages and comment on the photography and how well it supports the poetry. Then lean in and whisper, "If you want to borrow one of these for a few days that would be all right." As you walk away grinning like a possum (that's southern for secretly gloating inside), just know that you are hooking another one for our side. Yeah, that always puts a smile on our faces too.

Now don't misunderstand us here. We are *not* saying that this shelf is for boys. Nooooo, that is not what we are saying. There are many, many girls who love sports and they will love these books as well. In fact, Reba is a big sports fan (especially when it comes to certain college football games) and Lester, well, let's just say he would rather write poetry than go to that game with Reba. But even Lester likes the books on this shelf. We are simply trying to add a little something here for those boys who have their minds made up that poetry just isn't a "guy thing."

### Diamond Life: Baseball Sights, Sounds, and Swings

*Written and Illustrated by Charles R. Smith Jr.*
Orchard 2004, ISBN 0–439–43180–8

This collection of fifteen poems paired with action photographs celebrates the game of baseball. Smith's characteristic style matches the fast pace of a game in progress as he spins clever wordplay and features various aspects of the game.

### Hoop Queens

*Written by Charles R. Smith Jr.*
*Illustrated by various photographers*
Candlewick 2003, ISBN 0–7636–1422–X

These twelve poems written in the staccato rap-style characteristic of Smith's earlier collections (*Short Takes* and *Rimshots*) profile a dozen professional women basketball players. The language is printed in white on the backdrop of photographs showing the featured player in action. The last two spreads include Smith's notes explaining the inspiration for each poem. Any reader interested in sports will enjoy the profiles, and the action-packed vocabulary of the language will have readers engaged from the first page. Be sure you rehearse these *out loud* before reading them to your learners or you will likely find yourself stumbling over the rapid rhythm. And if you score big with this one, you'll want to be sure to bring in his companion book, *Hoop Kings* (Candlewick 2004, ISBN 0-7636-1423-8).

### Rimshots: Basketball Pix, Rolls, and Rhythms

*Written and Illustrated by Charles R. Smith Jr.*
Dutton Children's 1999, ISBN 0-525-46099-3

Focused on the game of basketball, this collection of stories, personal reflections, and poems is paired with the author's photography. The poems are presented in a rapid-pace style that matches the fast pace of a basketball game. Smith plays with font, color, size, and placement of print that encourages readers to play with voice when reading these aloud. If you or your learners are fans of the game, you may fall in love with poetry. (See also these two written by Smith, *Short Takes: Fast-Break Basketball Poetry*—Dutton 2001, ISBN 0-525-46454-9, and *Tall Tales: Six Amazing Basketball Dreams*—Dutton 2000, ISBN 0-525-46172-8.)

## Continuing the Music with Poetry Bookshelf Seven: Collection Selections

We know that this entire book could be devoted to poetry—there is that much poetry available for children. However, here we simply wanted to provide you with a sampling, a jump-start of sorts, a little something to get you excited about the role poetry can play in daily life in your classroom. So on this last bookshelf for poetry we have included a few collections that contain dozens and dozens of poems representing a variety of styles and addressing a range of topics.

Almost any book on this shelf would be a tremendous resource for thinking through how you might want to organize your own anthology. But, more important, these collections represent the number of writers devoted to poetry, the number of topics poetry can zoom in on, and the assortment of ways that poems can be presented. So get a cup of coffee (or whatever it is you like to sip while reading poetry) and pull one of the books. Just read a while. You'll fall in; we have no doubt about that.

### Knock at a Star: A Child's Introduction to Poetry

*Selected by X. J. Kennedy and Dorothy M. Kennedy*
*Illustrated by Karen Lee Baker*
Little, Brown 1982, 1999, ISBN 0–316–48800–3

> This book contains dozens and dozens of poems, representing an array of topics and types, written by an outstanding list of poets. In addition to the excellent collection of poems there are suggestions for writing your own poems and an afterword to adults. The selections are clearly organized and targeted to children in grades three through six (roughly ages 8–12). Visit this collection as you build your personal anthology for a poetry pause every day. Then, set this one out for students to read independently. A few of them are very likely to begin an anthology of their own.

### Moon, Have You Met My Mother? The Collected Poems of Karla Kuskin

*Written by Karla Kuskin*
*Illustrated by Sergio Ruzzier*
Laura Geringer Books/HarperCollins 2003, ISBN 0–06–027173–6

> This comprehensive collection of poems by the winner of the NCTE Award for Excellence in Poetry for Children is organized by topic. There is an index that makes it easy to locate a favorite. Take a look at our favorite—"I Need to Read." This book will certainly be one to visit as your begin selecting poems for a personal anthology for the poetry pause.

# 5

## Supporting the Writing Workshop by Reading Aloud

THE PURPOSE of the fourth read-aloud is to offer support for the writing workshop by immersing writers in demonstrations of well-crafted written language. This in no way should be a substitute for an actual writing workshop. Rather, we view it as an opportunity to layer in examples of the writing moves we hope to see students make; that is, to feature moves made by other writers, to show potential, to extend invitations, to encourage exploration, and to lead the writers in our community toward new options within their own work. Material shared during this read-aloud will most likely feature selected segments from the second, third, and sometimes from the sixth read-aloud, as well as short pieces from newspapers, magazines, and other printed matter.

We envision this as a brief read-aloud, perhaps after lunch as a transition between the open-ended activity of returning from the cafeteria and a more focused period of instructional time or independent work. Again, we would use only those books that have been read in their entirety for a previous read-aloud. We make this suggestion because we carefully select only portions of one or two books to feature each day. For example, we can feature leads for one week. Every day we select two, maybe three, leads from books students are already familiar with. Before reading the selected segment (leads in this case) we fill the kids in on what we have decided to feature and explain why. So, it would go something like the following:

Writers, remember how we've been taking a close look at leads in our writing workshop? We've noticed that the lead does a job for the writer and the reader. We've noticed that a lead might introduce a main character or take us right into the action or put us right in the setting. And sometimes a lead does more than one of these things. Well today, and over the next several days, we are going to listen again to the leads from a few of our favorite read-alouds. We'll begin by revisiting books in which the lead introduces the main character. Listen now as I read just the lead to *The Recess Queen* by Alexis O'Neill. I would like you to notice how the author uses the lead to introduce us to Jean. OK, here we go . . .

After reading that lead, we ask the kids to turn and talk about what the lead reveals about Jean and to point to specific words or phrases or examples used in the text to make that revelation. Then we read a second lead to introduce another character. Perhaps this time it is the opening segment of *Frindle* by Andrew Clements and our focus would be on coming to know young Nicholas. After these two brief segments we remind students that leads have a job to do in any writing and we conclude with something like this:

So writers when you are back at work on your writing, think about how these two authors used the lead to introduce the main character in their stories. And tomorrow we'll listen to the leads from two other stories and think about how other authors use the lead.

Or, it may go more like the following:

So writers, think about the leads we read today. In each of the stories, one picture book and one chapter book, the author used the lead to introduce the main character. This makes sense for these two stories because each of them is really about a person and the things that person gets into. Tomorrow, at this time, we will listen to the leads from two other books, then we will take a look at the job those authors have the lead doing.

The point is to carefully select segments of writing that are examples of the type of writing you are trying to feature. Like all the other read-alouds in this book, this fourth one requires *thoughtful*, *"planful,"* and *reflective* teaching. As the teacher, you must note what your writers are doing, where they are growing, and where you might nudge a bit. As you notice and make note of these areas, *think* through the books you know well, the books you and your students have loved as read-alouds, the books that use language in ways you and your students admire.

From there, *plan* a week of carefully selected segments you can highlight by reading aloud (for example, the week of leads). As you feature them in a brief read-aloud, be sure to make specific connections linking back to work you are do-ing (or have done) in the writing workshop. Remember, the point of this fourth opportunity for reading aloud is to support the work of the writing workshop and to stretch your writers and their understanding of the work writers do.

Following your reading continue to observe their writing carefully and *reflect* on the influence this particular read-aloud is having on the insights your writers are developing and the writing they are producing. Remember that this thinking develops slowly with multiple opportunities for trying out moves as a writer and multiple opportunities for observing and listening and reading and talking about how writers do the work they do.

## ■ *Books for Supporting the Writing Workshop*

Now, with this in mind, we step back into our libraries and think about those books we have come to love. We look back through all the bookshelves assembled so far for this book and plan how to put selected segments of them to work for you and your students during this fourth read-aloud opportunity. So pour an-other cup of coffee and come on in, pull up a chair and browse through the books[1] we have pulled together as support for writing workshop.

### *Supporting the Writing Workshop Bookshelf: Literature*

The books here are presented in alphabetical order with the exception of the first one, which is one we both know very, very well. We have studied the craft in it carefully and used it in several writing workshops. We have carried it along with us when conferring with writers to show them what other writers do. And it is one we know almost by heart (maybe because Lester wrote it). We feature this one first to demonstrate what can be done with a single, thoroughly studied, well-loved book. Although we identify a variety of features in the books, we want to impress on you that knowing a few books really well can influence your teaching in amazing ways.

---

1. *Note:* All books used in writing workshop have been taken from other shelves for this opportunity to read aloud.

## Saturday and Teacakes

*Written by Lester L. Laminack*
*Illustrated by Chris Soentpiet*
Peachtree 2004 ISBN 1–56145–303-X

| | |
|---|---|
| **Strong lead that defines character** | *When I was nine or ten years old, I couldn't wait for Saturdays.* |
| **Uses a repeated phrase to establish a sense of routine and tradition** | *Every Saturday . . .* |
| **Repeated word used to show movement, distance, effort, and passage of time** | *Pedal, pedal, pedal . . .* |
| **Remembered sounds, including voices (indicated in italics)** | All speech from the boy, the mother, and the grandmother along with the sounds of the glider and zooming downhill on the bicycle are remembered by the adult narrator recalling a moment from childhood |
| **Use of ellipses to create a pause** | *In our little town everyone knew everybody . . . and told everything to anyone who would listen.* |
| **Use of ellipses and stretching out the print to show effort in climbing a hill** | *pedal . . . pedal . . . p-e-d-a-a-a-l-l-l* |
| **Uses spacing (print layout) and ellipses to show distance and time** | *One . . .*<br>*Two . . .*<br>*Three . . .* |
| **Use of specific place names and product names to create a sense of the physical setting and the time period** | *Thompson Street*<br>*Bells Mill Road*<br>*Mrs. Cofields's house*<br>*Chandler's Phillips 66*<br>*Golden Eagle Syrup*<br>*Red Diamond Coffee*<br>*Blue Bonnet* |
| **Repeated structure used as bookends to set out a segment of the story** | Upon arrival at the grandmother's house: *She was waiting for me. No one else. Just me.*<br>Upon departure from the grandmother's house: *She was waving to me. No one else. Just me.* |

| Intentional use of fragments to create emphasis and pace | *She was waiting for me. No one else. Just me.* |
| Richly descriptive language incorporating metaphor and simile to create an image for the reader | *. . . sending a shower of tiny pebbles into her flowers . . .*<br>*. . . sunlight poured through the windows like a waterfall and spilled over the countertops, pooling up on the checkerboard floor.* |
| Uses parentheses to turn aside and talk to the reader, layering in support and elaboration to clarify | *You go on ahead to the car house. (That's what Mammaw called the garage.)*<br>*Look in the Frigidaire (that's what she called her refrigerator) and find me two sticks of Blue Bonnet.* |
| Uses simile to contrast | *I gobbled mine down like a hungry dog, but she nibbled at hers like a bird.* |
| Uses specific direction within the story | *Put them in the oven to bake—375 degrees for fifteen minutes.* |

# All the Places to Love

*Written by Patricia MacLachlan*
*Illustrated by Mike Wimmer*
HarperCollins 1994, ISBN 0 06 021099 0

| Uses the lead to introduce the setting (time period and locale) as well as the narrator and one major character | *On the day I was born my grandmother wrapped me in a blanket made from the wool of her sheep. She held me up in the open window so that what I heard first was the wind. What I saw first were all the places to love: the valley, the river falling down over rocks, the hilltop where the blueberries grew.* |
| Use of dashes to insert an extra bit of information | *He carved my name—ELI—*<br>*on a rafter beside his name . . .* |
| Remembered speech indicated with italics rather than with quotation marks | *That sound, like a whisper,* she said; *. . .* |
| Rich descriptive language | *Where marsh hawks skimmed over the land,*<br>*And wild turkeys left footprints . . .*<br>*like messages.* |

| In the very next sentence the semicolon is used to show a contrast to the first statement. | *Grandfather once lived in the city,*<br>*And once lived by the sea;*<br>*But the barn is the place he loves most.* |

## Barn Owls

*Written by Tony Johnston*
*Illustrated by Deborah Kogan Ray*
Charlesbridge 2000, ISBN 0–88106–981–7

| Uses dashes to set off additional information | *. . . an owl awakes*<br>*to a shadow*<br>*—or nothing*<br>*at all—*<br>*and leaves . . .* |
| Contrasts with opposites | *Sometimes nothing*<br>*answers.*<br>*Sometimes something*<br>*does.* |
| Comparing inanimate objects with an animate object using repeated phrasing | *one by one stars . . .*<br>*and blink.*<br>*One by one owls*<br>*. . .*<br>*and blink.* |
| Repeats structure for effect to create a rhythm and lead the reader to anticipate | *Owls hunted . . .*<br>*spiders spun . . .*<br>*snakes sunned . . .*<br>*bees hummed . . .* |
| Repeated detail to establish the setting and draw attention to the enduring ritual of the owl | *one hundred years at least* |

## Before I Was Your Mother

*Written by Kathryn Lasky*
*Illustrated by LeUyen Pham*
Harcourt Children's 2003, ISBN 0–15–201464–0

| | |
|---|---|
| **Uses a repeating line to make a transition** | *I wasn't always your mother but* |
| **Repeated use of an enlarged word to make a transition** | *Once . . .* |

## Bob

*Written and Illustrated by Tracey Campbell Pearson*
Farrar, Straus Giroux 2002, ISBN 0–374–39957–3

| | |
|---|---|
| **Includes a cumulative pattern within the story and uses onomatopoeia** | Each time Bob meets a new animal and learns a new sound/action, all the previous ones are repeated<br>*MEOW-MEOW*<br>*WOOF-WAG*<br>*RIBBET-RIBBET-HOP-HOP*<br>*MOOOOOO*<br>*YUM-YUM-BUGS* |
| **Passage of time in only one sentence** | *He walked right out of the day and into the night, searching for a rooster to teach him how to crow.* |
| **Use of ellipses to slow down the reader and to provide suspense followed on the next page with an enlarged font to give more voice to text** | *And so it went all night long, over and over again. Until the first morning light, when Bob heard . . . [turn the page] . . . Cock-a-Doodle-do!* |

## Diary of a Worm

*Written by Doreen Cronin*
*Illustrated by Harry Bliss*
Joanna Cotler Books 2003, ISBN 0–06–000150–X

| | |
|---|---|
| **Personification** | The entire book is written from the perspective of the worm with aspects of life that overlap the lives of children. |
| **Uses a diary format** | Each new entry is marked by a date in the upper left corner of the page in all caps (e.g., APRIL 4). |

| Entries follow basic narrative | *Fishing season started today. We all dug deeper.* |
|---|---|
| Perspective | Each entry is written from the perspective of the worm who is commenting on his daily life. Humor is "worm humor." |

## Enemy Pie

*Written by Derek Munson*
*Illustrated by Tara Calahan King*
Chronicle Books 2000, ISBN 0–8118–2778-X

| Lead sets up the problem or tension from the start | *It should have been a perfect summer. My dad helped me build a tree house in our backyard. My sister was at camp for three whole weeks. And I was on the best baseball team in town. It should have been a perfect summer. But it wasn't.* |
|---|---|
| Writers never waste details | Details mentioned in the opening pages *(tree house, baseball, trampoline, enemy list)* and then later in the story *(basketball hoop, boomerang)* are used to weave the story together with events that bring closure. |

## The Hickory Chair

*Written by Lisa Rowe Fraustino*
*Illustrated by Benny Andrews*
Arthur A. Levine Books 2001, ISBN 0–590–52248–5

| Descriptive language | *. . . a good alive smell of lilacs with a whiff of bleach.*<br>*. . . I loved her molasses voice as she read . . .*<br>*. . . felt my father's shadow cold on my cheek.* |
|---|---|
| Made up words to describe | *. . . you got blind sight . . .*<br>*. . . favorite middlest grandchild.* |

# Home Run

*Written by Robert Burleigh*
*Illustrated by Mike Wimmer*
Silver Whistle/Harcourt Brace 1998, ISBN 0–15–200970–1

| | |
|---|---|
| **Use of authentic baseball cards throughout the book** | These are layered into the art and contain text that supports and extends the language of the story. |
| **Uses colon to set off a fact** | *But what he does not know yet is this: He will change this game he loves. Forever.* |
| **Uses a one-word sentence for emphasis** | *He will change this game he loves.* |
| **Text is written in the style of a poem, creating phase units and a rhythm that is heard when read aloud** | *But sometimes Babe's body and Babe's bat and the small white ball are completely one.* |
| **Use of dash to prolong the pause, to add silence between the thoughts** | *. . . the Babe just swung—and it was there.* |
| **Words are chosen and placed on separate lines to slow down the pace of the story.** | *But he waits for it. He wants it. Again and again.* |
| **Uses short, terse language to show the building tension and stretching out of the moment as if creating a slow-motion scene.** | *There. There it is. . . . The perfectness. The feeling. The boy-fire inside the body of a man. He moves down the line.* |

# Loki and Alex: Adventures of a Dog and His Best Friend

*Written and Photographs by Charles R. Smith Jr.*
Dutton Children's 2001, ISBN 0–52–546700–9

| | |
|---|---|
| **Point of view** | The photography for each spread reflects how the speaker views the world. When the boy is narrator, readers see the photographs in color. When the dog is narrator, readers see the photographs in black and white. |

## The Magic Hat

*Written by Mem Fox*
*Illustrated by Tricia Tusa*
Harcourt Children's 2002, ISBN 0–15–201025–4

| | |
|---|---|
| **Uses the lead to launch the action and create a setting** | *One fine day, from out of town and without any warning at all, there appeared a magic hat.* |
| **Repeated line signals transition to meeting the next character** | *Oh, the magic hat, the magic hat. It moved like this, it moved like that!* |
| **Use of a rhyming line that enables the reader to predict the next animal to be met** | *It spun through the air and over a road and sat on the head of a warty old . . .* |
| **Uses ellipses and spacing to encourage the reader to predict and to create a dramatic pause** | *. . . sat on the head of a . . .*<br>*(turn the page)*<br>*. . . TOAD!* |

## Miz Berlin Walks

*Written by Jane Yolen*
*Illustrated by Floyd Cooper*
Philomel 1997, ISBN 0–399–22938–8

| | |
|---|---|
| **Circular text structure; lead and ending use the same words to "wrap the story"** | *Well, child, I recall once upon a time an old woman lived on our street, oldest woman I'd ever seen.* |
| **Story within a story** | The stories of Miz Berlin's childhood are embedded and told within the story given to us through the narrator. |
| **Strong verbs** | *Lapped* |
| **Unusual adjectives** | *Pattering rain . . . whispering trees* |
| **Similes to help the reader connect the known to the new** | *Her hair was white and fine*<br>*like the fluff of a dandelion.*<br>*Her skin was the color*<br>*of milk agate, like some marbles.*<br>*Like wet tongues . . .*<br>*Trees were furled as tight as a baby's fist . . .* |

| Creates new words by combining known words with a dash | *silver-ribbed black umbrella*<br>*block-long tale*<br>*cotton-quiet* |
| --- | --- |
| Colons to separate a statement and supposition | *. . . I think I know why: even good habits are hard to break. Hearts break so much easier.* |

## Momma, Where Are You From?

*Written by Marie Bradby*
*Illustrated by Chris K. Soentpiet*
Orchard 2000, ISBN 0–531–30105–2

| Embeds specific examples within a sentence with dashes | *I am from beans—green, lima, and pea—picked, strung, snapped . . .* |
| --- | --- |
| Uses a question-and-answer format | *Momma, where are you from?*<br>*Where are you from, Momma?*<br>*I'm from Monday mornings, washing . . .* |
| Adds additional detail as an example at the end of a sentence | *. . . while my sister pressed with two flat irons—one to use, the other to heat up on the stove . . .* |

## Mr. George Baker

*Written by Amy Hest*
*Illustrated by Jon J Muth*
Candlewick 2004, ISBN 0–7636–1233–2

| The narrator speaks directly to the reader | *See this man? This one here, sitting on the porch? That's Mr. George Baker. . . .* |
| --- | --- |
| Creates a word by combining known words with dashes | *Mr. Harry-in-Charge* |
| Uses dashes to insert additional details | *When I'm crossing the lawns—his and mine—and he's always there first, waiting on the porch.* |
| Uses dash to add the answer to his own question | *What holds them up—suspenders!* |

| Specific details zoom in to give the reader a better image | Brown baggy pants with two side pockets, and two in back.<br>. . . his sweater, all hangy with three buttons. Little chocolate candies in twisty silver wrappers. |
| --- | --- |
| Choice of words and placement on the page slow the pace of the story and mark the passing of time<br>Notice the use of an extra space between the mention of the leaves and the description of them falling. | . . . And wait. We wait, watching leaves blow off trees.<br><br>They fly for a while; they float.<br>They tumble for a while; they swoop. |

## Night in the Country

*Written by Cynthia Rylant*
*Illustrated by Mary Szilagyi*
Aladdin 1986, 1991, ISBN 0–689–71473–4

| Uses a dash to add on specific examples (zooming in) | while outside–in the field, and by the river, and deep in the trees |
| --- | --- |
| Repeats a word to draw attention to the subject | There are owls. Great owls . . .<br>There are frogs. Night frogs . . . |
| Onomatopoeia | reek, reek, reek.<br>Pump! |
| Uses a colon and spacing to slow the pace | . . . hear an apple fall from the tree in the back yard.<br><div align="right">Listen:</div>[on the right side of the spread you see an apple tree and when you turn the page the entire spread is devoted to a close-up of an apple that has fallen and you see one word]<br><div align="right">Pump!</div> |

## In November

*Written by Cynthia Rylant*
*Illustrated by Jill Kastner*
Harcourt Children's 2000, ISBN 0–15–201076–9

| Personification to personalize the changing season and add a point of relevance for the reader | . . . the earth is growing quiet. It is making its bed . . . And the world has tucked her children in, with a kiss on their heads, till spring. |
|---|---|
| Use of simile to create a visual image | . . . how lovely they are, spreading their arms like dancers. |
| Uses a dash to add on specific examples (zooming in) | . . . give thanks for their many blessings—for the food on their tables and the babies in their arms. |
| Deliberate use of fragment to elaborate and extend idea from the previous sentence | The staying birds are serious, too, for cold times lie ahead. Hard times. |
| Repeated words used as a transition | In November, . . . |

## Piggie Pie!

*Written by Margie Palatini*
*Illustrated by Howard Fine*
Clarion 1995, ISBN 0–395–71691–8

| Selective use of enlarged font to signal the reader of shift in voice or mood | Piggie Pie!<br><br>Problem! |
|---|---|
| Art helps with the text (writing in the sky by the witch) | *SURRENDER PIGGIES!* |
| Onomatopoeia | *THUMP-P-P! THUMP-P-P! ERRRRCH-CH!* |
| Builds on the structure of a familiar text [*Old MacDonald Had a Farm*] | *The duck quack-quacked her. It quack-cracked there. Here it quacked. There it quacked. Everywhere it quack-quacked, "No piggies."* |

# The Relatives Came

*Written by Cynthia Rylant*
*Illustrated by Stephen Gammell*
Aladdin 1985, ISBN 0–689–71738–5

| | |
|---|---|
| **Lead establishes setting (time frame) and launches action** | *It was in the summer of the year when the relatives came . . .* |
| **Uses repeated detail to show the passage of time** | *. . . They left when their grapes were nearly purple enough to pick, but not quite.* (Note the two earlier mentions of the color of the grapes in relation to the timing of their travel and visit.) |
| **Compressing time with a few details *or* making a long story short** | *So they drank up all their pop and ate up all their crackers and traveled up all those miles until finally they pulled into our yard.* |
| **Unexpected use of words** | *. . . hugging time* <br> *. . . wrinkled Virginia clothes* <br> *. . . new breathing in the house* <br> *We were so busy hugging and eating and breathing together.* |

# Roller Coaster

*Written and Illustrated by Marla Frazee*
Harcourt 2003, ISBN 0–15–204554–6

| | |
|---|---|
| **Spacing signals the drop in voice and the sinking feeling experienced by the character** | *. . . never ridden on a roller coaster before,* <br><br> *ever.* |
| **Uses parentheses to add information for the reader, as if turning to tell you something aside from the story** | *(Lots of people change their minds . . . at the very last minute.)* <br> *(Now it is too late for anyone to change their minds.)* |
| **Dashes used to stretch out words and signal the reader to say them very slowly, to exaggerate the sound of them.** | *S-l-o-w-l-y the train . . . .* |

| | |
|---|---|
| Selective use of font size, color, capitalization, and placement to signal the changes in mood, action, and pacing | WHOOSH! THE TRAIN ZIPS. . . . AND GOES ALL-L-L-L-L-L-L-L- THE WAY AROUND WHEEEEEEEEEEE!<br><br>(All this text follows the action depicted in the art and in the storytelling.) |
| Small moment | The entire story is one small moment in time, waiting in line and riding the roller coaster for the first time. |

## Scarecrow

*Written by Cynthia Rylant*
*Illustrated by Lauren Stringer*
Harcourt Children's 1998, ISBN 0–15–201084-X

| | |
|---|---|
| Uses the lead to introduce the main character | *His hat is borrowed, his suit is borrowed, his hands are borrowed, even his head is borrowed. And his eyes probably came out of someone's drawer.* |
| Author zooms in on specifics as an example of the more general | *A friendliness toward birds. . . . Yes, birds . . . Crows, grackles, starlings, jays.* |
| Uses a colon to set off an example | *. . . the scarecrow's best gift: his gentleness.* |
| Personification | *He knows he isn't real. . . . He has seen the sun tremble and the moon lie still.* |
| The use of *and* connecting a series of events to show the passage of time | *The earth has rained and snowed and blossomed and wilted and yellowed and greened and vined itself all around him.* |

## School Picture Day

*Written by Lynn Plourde*
*Illustrated by Thor Wickstrom*
Dutton Juvenile 2002, ISBN 0–525–46886–2

| Uses a dash to zoom in and add specific examples<br><br>Plays with alliteration to make the read-aloud more fun | *Everyone was dressed in their best—bows and bow ties, sashes and suspenders, jewels and jackets.* (Phrases are repeated five more times.) |
|---|---|
| Uses ellipses to give additional information | *Now please, everyone, fill out the school picture form with your sharpest number-2 pencils. . . . And no fiddling.* |
| Repeated pattern of made-up words used to describe Josephina, the main character (repeated five times) | *highfalutin fidgeting, fiddling, fuddling, and foopling* |
| Connecting two known words with a dash to create a new, more descriptive word | *Super-fast*<br>*plush-deluxe* |

## Song and Dance Man

*Written by Karen Ackerman*
*Illustrated by Stephen Gammell*
Dragonfly 1988, ISBN 0–679–81995–9

| Descriptive details to create physical setting | *He moves some cardboard boxes and a rack of Grandma's winter dresses out of the way, and we see a dusty brown, leather-trimmed trunk* |
|---|---|
| Similes help the reader make connections between the known and the new | *His tap shoes make soft, slippery sounds like rain on a tin roof.*<br>*. . . does a new step that sounds like a woodpecker tapping on a tree.*<br>*. . . he begins to sing. His voice is as round and strong as a canyon echo . . .* |

## The Sunsets of Miss Olivia Wiggins

*Written by Lester L. Laminack*
*Illustrated by Constance R. Bergum*
Peachtree 1998, ISBN 1–56145–139–8

| Parallel stories | Contrast the story set in the present (Troy and Grandma Angel visit with Miss Olivia) with the story of the past (Miss Olivia's memories) |
|---|---|
| **Repeated phrase signals transition from present story to past story** | *She didn't move, she didn't even blink, but slowly and quietly she began to think . . .* |
| **Use of italics to signal past story** | All of Miss Olivia's flashbacks or memories are presented in italics. |
| **See-saw structure used to tell two stories in one** | Present story and past story alternate with each spread creating a see-saw effect |
| **Uses specific details to zero in on character** | *Sitting with her hands folded in her lap. Hands once strong, with nimble fingers that milked cows and gathered fresh eggs. Hands that shelled peas, shucked corn, and quilted bed covers. Hands that braided hair and soothed babies. Hands that loved.* |
| **Lead and ending closely match Uses the same words to "wrap the story"** | *Miss Olivia Wiggins sits and looks at nothing and at everything, all at the same time. . . . Miss Olivia Wiggins sat perfectly still, staring at nothing and at everything, all at the same time.* |

## Thank You, Grandpa

*Written by Lynn Plourde*
*Illustrated by Jason Cockcroft*
Dutton Children's 2003, ISBN 0–525–46992–3

| The lead introduces the two main characters and sets the quiet tone of the story | *They took their first walks together when the little girl was barely old enough to toddle.* |
|---|---|
| **Bookends—repeats a sentence (with only one word changing) to open and close a segment of the story.** | *Grandfather and granddaughter wobbled along, side by side, hand in hand, smile to smile.* <br> *Grandfather and granddaughter shuffled along, side by side, hand in hand, smile to smile.* |

| Metaphor | *That spiderweb is crying . . . Yes, child. Teardrops of dew.* |
| --- | --- |
| Making a long story short | *They took their last walks together when Grandpa was too old to walk by himself. . . . Until one day the girl walked alone.* |
| Repeated phrase (beginning and ending of the story) to slow the pace and set the mood | *Two steps and . . . . . . Three steps and . . .* |

## Tough Boris

*Written by Mem Fox*
*Illustrated by Kathryn Brown*
Harcourt Brace 1994, ISBN 0–15–289612–0

| Simple sentences give a see-saw or back and forth or contrast | *He was tough. All pirates are tough.* |
| --- | --- |
| Repeated structure throughout the book | *He was _____. All pirates are _____.* |
| Structure changes with simple contrasting sentence | *But when his parrot died, he cried and cried. All pirates cry. And so do I.* |

## Welcome to the Green House

*Written by Jane Yolen*
*Illustrated by Laura Regan*
Paper Star Books/Putnam 1993, ISBN 0–698–11445–0

| Author maintains a tight focus | *The rain forest as the "green house"* |
| --- | --- |
| Spacing helps the reader establish pace and rhythm | See the placement of text on the page |
| Descriptive and well-chosen language | *. . . fallen leaves, white rootlets . . . fungal threads . . . slow, green-coated sloth . . .* |
| Unusual word choice | *slow-quick . . . ever-new* |
| Eight ways to describe the shades of green | *. . . in the green house, dark green, light green, emerald green, bright green, copper green, blue green, ever-new green* |

| | |
|---|---|
| **Uses short sentences in a listlike poem to extend the description of the "green house"** | *This is a loud house.*<br>*A bright house.*<br>*A day house . . .*<br>*A fish and bird and*<br>*bee house.* |
| **Lead and ending closely match**<br>**Uses the same words to "wrap the story"** | *Welcome to the green house* |

# 6

## *Building Bridges Across the Curriculum by Reading Aloud*

**The world cannot be understood from a single point of view.**

—*Eleanor Roosevelt*

*I*MAGINE THIS SCENE . . . a group of fifth and sixth graders are engaged in a study of the civil rights movement in U.S. history. As a part of the study, they have been reading *The Watsons Go to Birmingham – 1963* (see Chapter 7 for annotation). Their teacher explains that the book is historical fiction; yet, in a conversation about the book, this question arises: "You know how in historical fiction the writer takes some stuff that is true and some stuff he makes up and puts it together to make the story work? Well, in the part where that church was bombed and those little girls got killed, was that part true or did he make that up?"

It is a scene like this one, playing out over and over again in classrooms throughout the country, that caused us to pause and wonder how we could help children *bring a deeper knowledge of truth and fiction to the curriculum*. The act of *bringing* knowledge to a topic is necessary if children are to *make sense of* what they are expected to learn and if they are to find answers to their own burning questions. In fact, it is the search for truth that will drive the desire to know more, to inquire independently and with guidance into topics of great interest. Learners of any age use what they know to make sense of what is new. We believe that textbooks, no matter how well researched or how well written, have so much content to *cover* that the depth of study on a specific topic within any text will be limited at best.

Given the time constraints we face as teachers and the curriculum we must cover, it would be fair to ask how anyone could be expected to do more. We are not suggesting more, we are asking you to consider the ways in which *thoughtfully* selected picture books can be *"planfully"* incorporated into the daily routine in the content areas. Think of it as a more efficient use of time. For example, if we could step into the preceding scenario and move the hands of time to the beginning of that study, we could plan for one read-aloud every day as a part of that social studies class. That single act of planning would allow us to place those thoughtfully selected picture books in a sequence that would layer in background day by day, enabling every student to bring more to the reading of any novel on the topic.

For a study of a topic like civil rights we would place the books in order by two criteria: chronology and complexity. For example, we recommend reading a few books that focus on slavery, the Underground Railroad, emancipation, and Jim Crow laws as a way to help contextualize the study. Then we'd layer in books on topics featuring events in the decades leading up to the enactment of civil rights legislation. There are many books to choose from on any one of the several topics we suggest, so we organize them chronologically, then within each topic we organize from the least complex to the most complex. When we select books to feature in a read-aloud, we consider the number of days that can be devoted to the unit of study. Then we consider the knowledge learners are bringing and choose picture books from each topic that will stretch existing understandings and lead learners toward new insights.

You may be wondering why we feature picture books as the chosen format. We find that picture books often contextualize information in small doses, supporting unfamiliar language and ideas with art to help youngsters visualize what they cannot even imagine as a result of their limited experiences. In addition, picture books often provide a level of support and elaboration in the writing that helps readers/listeners build a vocabulary essential for discussion. And *discussion*—an open interchange of insights—can lead to formulating new questions. And new questions can lead to new levels of engagement with the curriculum and that can lead to new learning.

In some ways we are doing what farmers do. To ensure a bountiful harvest farmers work the soil, layering in organic matter to enrich the nutrient levels to feed the crops that ultimately produce more abundantly. As teachers we realize that learners enter classrooms with varying degrees of background knowledge for the subject at hand. We recognize that a single textbook or course of study can adjust for such disparity in only very limited ways. That is why we believe that reading aloud from well-chosen picture books actually helps learners build the background understandings necessary to fully appreciate the information presented in most curriculum materials. In this way each read-aloud provides layers like the rings of an onion, one around the next. By the end of a unit of study learners are more grounded, having developed a more robust vocabulary to think about and discuss the topic. Learners have a pictorial repertoire to draw from as they try to envision the ideas being discussed. And they have a cache of story to help them make sense of it all.

Let's return to the scene we opened with. Imagine once again there is a group of students launching a study of the civil rights movement in U.S. history. Remember how the scenario began with everyone reading one novel focused on the events of the study? Suppose instead of beginning with that one novel, the teacher layered in all those picture books, one or two every day, and spun the fibers of those rich discussions into threads of thinking and then wove those threads back into the parameters of the curriculum. Imagine all that concluding with the launch of a literature study in the language arts class. Imagine in the language arts classroom small groups of four to six children clustered around books such as these: *Roll of Thunder Hear My Cry, The Well: David's Story, The Friendship, Mississippi Bridge, The Gold Cadillac, Let the Circle Be Unbroken, The Road to Memphis, The Land, The Watson's Go to Birmingham – 1963*. Just imagine the new vocabulary, the new images, the new insights, and the significantly increased knowledge being brought by these novels. Imagine the conversations. Imagine the interest in the lives of those characters who are living through what these children have just studied as *real* events in history. Imagine how the stories will filter into talk outside of class. Imagine the eager anticipation of getting to read a second novel in the set. Imagine the robust insights children will construct and nurture in their more-grounded minds as they read. Yes, let's imagine . . .

## ■ *Books for Building Bridges Across the Curriculum*

What follows is a carefully selected collection of books to support one topic. We deliberately focus on a single topic to help you imagine the immense possibilities read-aloud and picture books can have in most any inquiry or unit of study throughout the curriculum.

To continue this across the curriculum we have selected books for other topics in social studies, and several for English/language arts, science, and mathematics, which can be found in our companion book, *Building Bridges Across the Curriculum with Picture Books and Read-Alouds* (2006, Heinemann). Each list is presented as a starter set to assist you on a journey of your own as you *thoughtfully* select books and *planfully* design ways to make reading aloud a vital part of your curriculum.

## ■ *Building Background for a Civil Rights Unit*

Civil rights did not happen on a single day in the summer of 1964. Equal rights for all Americans regardless of the color of their skin did not take place because of one single event. Yet, many children read novels set in the tumultuous times surrounding the struggle and study the "topic" as if it were divorced from nearly two hundred years of history. On the shelves in this section we have placed the following five categories of books to help children (and teachers) establish a contextual framework for a unit of study about civil rights in the United States.

- In the Time of Slavery
- Escape from Slavery and the Underground Railroad
- Emancipation
- The Struggle for Civil Rights in the United States
- Honoring the Lives of African Americans Who Led the Way to Equal Rights

This collection could be used to enrich the social studies curriculum and to build much needed background knowledge, including visual images and vocabulary, for reading novels set during this period of history.

### *Civil Rights Bookshelf One: In the Time of Slavery*

To fully understand any study of the struggle for equal rights in the United States children need to be grounded in a broader view of the topic. Otherwise, when they read of specific events and isolated incidents, they have no contextual framework to help them make sense of any single piece of the puzzle. Therefore, we have included a collection of books on this shelf that will give readers a glimpse of life for African Americans long before the civil rights movement, long before Dr. King, long before Ruby Bridges and Rosa Parks, long, long before.

The books selected will help children build the understanding that Americans once captured human beings in another country, on another continent and took them away from all they had ever known, brought them across the ocean and sold them into slavery. Those human beings were among the first African Americans.

## Alec's Primer

*Written by Mildred Pitts Walter*
*Illustrated by Larry Johnson*
University Press of New England/Vermont Folklife Center 2005, ISBN 0–916718–20–4

> Education was not valued for people in the bondage of slavery. They were punished if they attempted to learn how to read. When the granddaughter of the plantation's owner wants to teach Alec to read, he becomes very frightened. However, the lure of being able to read, like his friend, is more than he can deny. Secretly, the lessons began until one day he is discovered with the primer. The owner punishes him by slashing his face and blood goes everywhere, even on his cherished book. The book stays with Alec when he escapes and stays with him as he himself becomes a landowner as a grown man. His granddaughter gives this blood-stained primer to the Vermont Folklife Center.

## A Strawbeater's Thanksgiving

*Written by Irene Smalls-Hector*
*Illustrated by Melodye Benson Rosales*
Little, Brown 1998, ISBN 0–316–79866–5

> In late November when the corn has been gathered, slaves hold a corn shucking—a contest to see who can shuck the most corn in a set amount of time. When the corn is shucked, a late night dinner is enjoyed along with singing and dancing. A fiddler plays for the dancers and a young boy is chosen to be the strawbeater. A strawbeater stands behind the fiddler to beat on the fiddle as if it were a drum while it is being played. This was an honor all young boys coveted. (Pair this book with *Christmas in the Big House, Christmas in the Quarters.*)

## A Voice of Her Own: The Story of Phillis Wheatley, Slave Poet

*Written by Kathryn Lasky*
*Illustrated by Paul Lee*
Candlewick 2003, ISBN 0–7636–0252–3

Phyllis Wheatley is a slave girl sold in 1761 to a family in Boston. Everything she has known in her homeland is taken away from her. But no one can take her zeal to learn. Despite the rule of that day, the Wheatley family encourages Phyllis rather than denies her the opportunity to become educated. She becomes the first black female poet in America. Although the text is long it is filled with the history of the life of slavery in the 1700s. While it isn't the sort of book you can read aloud in one sitting, it can be one of the sustained texts you select to read to integrate the curriculum content. Lee's art offers you full-page illustrations to support the text, making this story much more memorable and meaningful for students.

## Circle Unbroken: The Story of a Basket and Its People

*Written by Margot Theis Raven*
*Illustrated by E. B. Lewis*
Farrar, Straus and Giroux 2004, ISBN 0–374–31289–3

*Now, you've asked me, child, how I come to sew. Well put yourself in Grandma's arms, and listen to a circle tale, from long, long ago . . .* Then grandma tells the story of how her grandfather came from Africa as a slave and how he was taught the art of basket weaving before he came. He was sold to a plantation owner that owned land next to a long, curving river near Charleston, South Carolina. Even though he worked long hours in the rice fields by day, by night he sewed baskets as he'd been taught to do. Those weaving hours and the feel of the grasses brought him comfort. But the weaving and sewing of baskets did not end there. The art of sewing baskets has been passed from generation to generation and now as the grandmother finished her story, she tells her grandchild: *And time has come now, child, for you to learn the knot that ties us all together—The circle unbroken.*

## Daily Life on a Southern Plantation 1853

*Written by Paul Erickson*
*Photographs*
Puffin Books 2000, ISBN 0–14–056668–6

This picture book is presented in small chapters that highlight what life was like in 1853 on the Henderson's plantation in Louisiana. Once you begin reading picture books to develop the background for this unit of study, this book will provide different perspectives about various aspects of life on a plantation during this era. It offers much information complete with a timeline, glossary, and short segments supported by photographs. Your children will find it fascinating to pore over once their understanding begins to develop.

## Enemies of Slavery

*Written by David A. Adler*
*Illustrated by Donald A. Smith*
Holiday House 2004, ISBN 0–8234–1596–1

By 1861 when the Civil War began, there were four million slaves in the United States. This book provides a short profile on each of fourteen people who stood against slavery. Some of the fourteen will be familiar, but some profiles will introduce readers to brave citizens who stood with courage against what many just accepted. Adler gives readers a brief profile of each person and paired with that on the opposite page, Smith provides a portrait. We recommend that this be read in segments to support other books on the efforts of those who fought for the freedom of slaves.

## From Slave Ship to Freedom Road

*Written by Julius Lester*
*Illustrated by Rod Brown*
Puffin Books 1999, ISBN 0–140–56669–4

The author's note at the front of the book is an important part of understanding the intentions of this one. In it Julius Lester tells of his desire to give readers words to help them understand what it felt like to be a slave and why this is so important. He is *begging, pleading, imploring you not to be passive, but to invest soul and imagine yourself into the images. Art and literature ask us to step out of our skins and to put on the skins of others.* The story that follows is very graphic and terribly sad; and worse yet, it is the truth. It is a rather long text and should be divided into several sittings—not just because of the length but also because of the depth and intensity of the message. Students will need to linger with each segment and discuss the issues surrounding it. This may well be one of the more disturbing books on this shelf; but it will be one of the most important titles because it builds essential background necessary to understand all the history leading up to the need for a civil rights movement in the United States.

## Civil Rights Bookshelf Two: Escape from Slavery and the Underground Railroad

To follow a focus on slavery we selected books to help children build an understanding of the Underground Railroad, which may be one of the most frequently mentioned topics of this period in history. The books here will help children come to understand that many, many people were opposed to slavery and actually risked their own safety to help slaves escape to freedom. Through books on this shelf children will learn that the states were divided philosophically and geographically. They will learn that some states were free states and others were slave states. They will learn that even in slave states there were people who were opposed to slavery and openly assisted slaves in their quest for freedom.

### Almost to Freedom

*Written by Vaunda Micheaux Nelson*
*Illustrated by Colin Bootman*
Scholastic 2003, ISBN 0–439–63156–4

Nelson was inspired to write this story after a visit to a museum with an exhibit of black rag dolls. Some of the dolls had been discovered in the hideouts of the Underground Railroad. Nelson tells the story from the viewpoint of one of those little rag dolls whom she named Sally and put in the arms of a little slave girl, Lindy. Sally travels with Lindy from the cotton patch to the nights of storytelling around the fire to the time of the beating Lindy gets for asking the master's son to teach her how to spell her name. This is an irresistible read-aloud for building background about the struggle of this sad period of history.

### Escape!

*Written by Sharon Shavers Gayle*
*Illustrated by Eric Velasquez*
Scholastic/Soundprints 1999, ISBN 1–568–99622–5

The art in this one will have children sitting on the edge of their seats. The language will have readers traveling along with young children in their escape from slavery. Together we duck down into wells and hide out in dark cellars and in the dark of night we lie flat in the back of wagons. Gayle does an exceptional job of keeping readers in fear for the safety of the slaves. The book takes an unusual slant as the opening reveals a group of children on a field trip to the Smithsonian Institution. Young Emma is so captivated by the Underground Railroad exhibit that she quickly begins dreaming she is the young slave who is attempting to escape. The story ends with her friends coming back to wake her.

## Freedom River

*Written by Doreen Rappaport*
*Illustrated by Bryan Collier*
Hyperion/Jump at the Sun 2000, ISBN 0–786–80350–9

Before the Civil War, Kentucky was a slave state while right across the Ohio River the state of Ohio was a free state. In this story John Parker, a former slave, becomes one of the free men whose life is dedicated to leading others across that river into freedom. Rappaport writes with such heart and passion, you will be transported right into the story as time after time Parker crosses the river. Readers will likely feel breathless at times as they wait, listen, crawl, hide, and then run with the slaves.

## Liberty Street

*Written by Candice Ransom*
*Illustrated by Eric Velasquez*
Walker Books for Young Readers 2003, ISBN 0–8027–8869–6

Young Kezia is born a slave during the nineteenth century. Her family belongs to a widow in Virginia. Every day, except Sunday, they work from morning to night doing the chores assigned to them by Missus Grace, their owner. On Sundays, their only free day, they walk to town down a street that soon becomes known to them as Liberty Street. But one day all happiness is taken away from the family when Kezia's Papa is sold to another owner so that Missus Grace can pay off a debt left by her late husband. Soon after Papa is gone, Mama heard that Missus Grace is making arrangements to bond Kezia out to a sister in another place. That day Mama makes up her mind to somehow send her daughter to freedom. Mama is already using her clothesline to signal other slaves when it is safe to travel as they are making their way to freedom. As soon as there is enough money saved, Kezia joins a group traveling to Canada. This text adds a dimension to the collection not found in many other books about this period of time. In many books slaves are depicted as living on large plantations and working mostly in fields. But in this story Kezia and her family live in town and work in and around a home in the city of Fredericksburg, Virginia. Velasquez's art is bold and strong, just like the characters in this story. It is a visual mirror of the story's events.

### The Patchwork Path: A Quilt Map to Freedom

*Written by Bettye Stroud*
*Illustrated by Erin Susanne Bennett*
Candlewick 2005, ISBN 0–763–62423–3

Hannah's older sister is sold by the master and soon after, her mother dies. During the days before her death, Hannah's mother sews a quilt and she explains to Hannah what each of the squares mean. She knows one day this quilt will lead Hannah and her daddy to freedom. When they begin their journey, Hannah is so frightened but she has the gift her mother left her to comfort and guide her. Read this one as a companion text to *Under the Quilt of Night* and *Sweet Clara and the Freedom Quilt* to understand the dangers slaves faced and the courage they showed to even attempt a run for freedom.

### Under the Quilt of Night

*Written by Deborah Hopkinson*
*Illustrated by James E. Ransome*
Atheneum 2002, ISBN 0–689–82227–8

*RUNNING.*
*I'm young but my legs are strong. I can run.* These words begin the story of the Underground Railroad and the role quilts played in marking safe places for runaway slaves to sleep. The opening page is shrouded in deep purple night and the beams from the bright yellow moon highlight the slaves running for their lives. This page alone will have students leaning in and urging you to keep reading. Join the young girl featured in the story as she leads her people away from the master who is tracking them to bring them back. *But I'll make my steps quick whispers in the dark. I'll run where he won't find me, under the quilt of night.* Each step of their journey depends on their success in reading the quilts correctly. One mistake and their freedom may be lost and their lives could be over. Keep running with them night after night until you stand with them in the daylight of freedom.

## *Civil Rights Bookshelf Three: Emancipation*

This shelf's books focus on the period of history when slaves were freed. They show how life changed for many African Americans who moved to new places, claimed their own homesteads, and started new lives. Some books reveal how life for many changed very little even though they were legally freed from slavery.

### A Place Called Freedom

*Written by Scott Russell Sanders*
*Illustrated by Thomas B. Allen*
Atheneum 1997, ISBN 0–689–80470–9

> In the spring of 1832 after being set free by the master, the family of four leaves the plantation in Tennessee to travel to the land of the free in Indiana. Little Nettie *(a short drink of water because she was little)* and bigger brother *(long gulp of air because he was tall and full of talk)* are leaving with their Mama and Papa but they are leaving behind all their aunts and uncles who are still slaves. Papa tells them as they walk away that they will be following the drinking gourd to show them the way. When they reach the Wabash River, with help from a Quaker family, the family settles in to make their homestead. Everything they do has to be by hand because they can't bring any equipment so their survival depends on their work. Together they build a cabin and at night Mama begins teaching the family how to read and write. Over time, aunts and uncles join them in Indiana. As more and more people come, a church and a school are built. To celebrate they name their new town Freedom.

### I Have Heard of a Land

*Written by Joyce Carol Thomas*
*Illustrated by Floyd Cooper*
HarperTrophy 2000, ISBN 0–064–43617–9

> While many freed slaves moved north in the late 1800s, some families heard of the promises of land ownership in the West and joined the westward movement. There, they had the promise of a life of freedom and land owner-ship. They joined other black families and white settlers who were filled with hope and determination to make a new life in this new territory. Thomas' own family was one of those who sought the freedom of ownership, and this book was written in tribute to their courage and hope.

### Papa's Mark

*Written by Gwendolyn Battle-Lavert*
*Illustrated by Colin Bootman*
Holiday House 2003, ISBN 0–823–41650–X

Having the right to vote is both an honor and a privilege enjoyed by every U.S. citizen. But for years African Americans did not have that right. This sensitive story is about the struggle Simms went through hoping to help his Papa learn how to sign his name so that he wouldn't have to make an X on the bill of sale at the store. Every time Papa has to sign for supplies with the X, Simms grows more determined. Papa at first seems reluctant but Simms writes his name out and leaves it for Papa to practice. Many of the neighbors feel strong fear about seeking the right to vote but Papa reminds them that *freedom don't come easy.* By voting time Papa is able to sign his name to the ballot with great pride and he allows Simms to drop the ballot into the box. Bootman's art reveals the pride of this relationship between a young boy and his father. The author provides a detailed account of the history of voting rights in the United States, which makes this book an essential addition to your collection for this shelf.

## The Leaving

*Written by Bettye Stroud*
*Illustrated by Cedric Lucas*
Marshall Cavendish 2001, ISBN 0–761–45067–X

Even after slaves had been freed by President Abraham Lincoln, there were families still living on the plantations throughout the South. Many were paid paltry sums and, because of their circumstances, were forced to purchase their necessities from the plantation owners. This, of course, created more debt than they could ever earn, leaving them in virtual slavery still. In this story of the escape, Little Bit is determined to be free even though her parents aren't healthy enough to run with her. She knows of the risk and of the dangers. Readers will discover how the courage of a young girl helps provide a way to get her parents safely on the trail to freedom. Before you read this one contrast the image (on the first page) of the large plantation home where slaves were owned by a master with the small unpainted house (on the last page) where freedom lives. Those two pictures provide bookends to another powerful story of how slaves often risked everything, including their lives and the lives of their families, to gain freedom.

## The Wagon

*Written by Tony Johnston*
*Illustrated by James E. Ransome*
Tambourine Books 1996, ISBN 0–688–13457–2

This beautiful book opens with these words: *One Carolina morning, I was born. Everything was beautiful that day, Mama said, especially my skin like smooth, dark wood. But like all my family, birth to grave, my skin made me a slave.* The eloquent words on every page of this poignant book paint a sad, painful story of life as a slave. The text will still a room and leave readers/listeners wide-eyed and breathless. Johnston does a commendable job of pulling readers into the despair this young boy felt as he and others stay beaten down. Word of war and President Lincoln's efforts to free slaves will echo in the stillness that falls over the room. You must slow the pace as you approach the last page and let these words linger in the hearts of your students: *In my life, twelve plantings have come and gone. I was free. I could go where I please. I said, "I want to go to the funeral." So at dawn my family and I set out, creaking down the road toward Washington. Creaking along in a wooden wagon, to say good-bye to Mr. Lincoln.*

### Virgie Goes to School with Us Boys

*Written by Elizabeth Fitzgerald Howard*
*Illustrated by E. B. Lewis*
Simon & Schuster 2000, ISBN 0–689–80076–2

Once slaves were freed they faced many new barriers, not the least of which was access to education. During the Reconstruction period many groups around the country were forming schools to educate the freed slaves. One such group was the Quakers and often children had to travel many miles to attend a school. In this story Vergie and her brothers walk seven miles but stay at the school during the week. For many years everyone believed that girls didn't need to be able to read and write, but Vergie's parents, who were former slaves, felt differently. In the author's note, we find out that Vergie's brother was the grandfather of author Elizabeth Howard. We also discover that this story was passed down through her mother. Each of the brothers (pictured in the back) became successful citizens who made a difference in their world.

 ## Civil Rights Bookshelf Four: The Struggle for Civil Rights in the United States

Books on this shelf address the topics most people think of when they hear the words *civil rights*. The focus on segregation, separate schools and drinking fountains, refusal of service on the basis of race, and the prejudice that so defined the era. These stories, building on those from previous shelves, will help children build a framework, in concept and image and vocabulary, that is needed to understand the novels most often read as part of this study.

### A Dream of Freedom: The Civil Rights Movement from 1954 to 1968

*Written by Diane McWhorter*
*Illustrated with photographs*
Scholastic 2004, ISBN 0–439–57678–4

> This book provides a comprehensive history of the civil rights movement with powerful photos to explain and support the effective written descriptions of historic events. This one is not to be read cover to cover but rather in short segments to support the topic being explored. Between the covers of this 156-page book, you will find sections devoted to every aspect of the civil rights movement. This one is not to be missed.

### A Sweet Smell of Roses

*Written by Angela Johnson*
*Illustrated by Eric Velasquez*
Simon & Schuster 2005, ISBN 0–689–83252–4

> This sensitive book honors the thousands of young men and women whose names were never known and whose stories were never told, yet made significant contributions in the struggle for equal rights. Begin your introduction to this book with the author and illustrator's notes; the words offer additional insight into this turbulent time in history. The book features two little girls who slip out of their house to join a march led by Dr. King. Johnson tells the story through the eyes of a little girl using focused and precise language. Velasquez presents the images in black and white with a flash of scarlet red in several scenes—a teddy bear's ribbon, the stripes in the flag, and finally in the sweet red roses when the girls arrive back home following the march. We predict this book will become a "touchstone" book for everyone who is studying this period of history.

### Fishing Day

*Written by Andrea Davis Pinkney*
*Illustrated by Shane W. Evans*
Jump at the Sun/Hyperion 2003, ISBN 0–7868–0766–0

> Fishing day means a different thing to Reenie and her mama than it does to Peter Troop and his daddy. For Reenie it means a day of fun but for Peter the

success of catching fish means food that night. The problem is Reenie's mama knows a lot more about fishing than Peter's daddy. But Peter's dad refuses to have anything to do with Reenie and her mama because they are black. Even though Reenie and her mama have caught several fish, Peter's dad won't even look in their direction. When Peter's reel jams and his dad goes to the truck for tools, Reenie makes the first move to reach out to share the secret to successful fishing . . . the bait. The following day, Peter makes the first move to wave at Reenie. The author's note in the back of the book explains the symbolism of the river (Jim Crow River) to show the division that bigotry can cause. As with many books, we advise that you read the author's note before reading the book to children.

## Coming On Home Soon

*Written by Jacqueline Woodson*
*Illustrated by E. B. Lewis*
Putnam Juvenile 2004, ISBN 0–399–23748–8

During World War II, women in America had to take on new roles because the men were away. Mama leaves Ada Ruth with her grandmother so she can go work in Chicago—*They're hiring colored women in Chicago since all the men are away in the war.* Woodson tells a remarkable story in few words as she makes clear the scarceness of money and food. Letters go back and forth between Ada Ruth and her Mama. Woodson's language is finely crafted in this story and the art of Lewis is equally as spectacular.

## Freedom on the Menu: The Greensboro Sit-Ins

*Written by Carole Boston Weatherford*
*Illustrated by Jerome Lagarrigue*
Dial 2005, ISBN 0–8037–2860–3

*Just about every week, Mama and I went shopping downtown. I loved having her all to myself for the afternoon. Whenever it was hot or we got tired, we'd head over to the snack bar in the five-and-dime store. We'd stand as we sipped our Cokes because we weren't allowed to sit at the lunch counter. . . All over town, signs told Mama and me where we could and couldn't go. Signs on water fountains, swimming pools, movie theaters, and even bathrooms.* Just imagine if you were little and you went in for a Coke with your mother and weren't allowed to sit down. Just imagine how you would feel if you needed to go to the bathroom but you weren't allowed to go because the bathroom was reserved for others. Just imagine how you would feel if signs regulated your behaviors on the basis of nothing more than the color of your skin. The discrimination leveled against African American citizens and the struggles they endured just to be treated as equals in the human family is beyond the imagination of many people today. This moving story is about the courage of one group of young black men who dared to face the evils of discrimination and bigotry in North Carolina when they walked into a lunch counter, took a seat and refused to get up. By summer's end, that very lunch counter was serving *all* people. That lunch counter has now become an exhibit in the Smithsonian and can be seen by everyone who visits.

## Freedom School, Yes!

*Written by Amy Littlesugar*
*Illustrated by Floyd Cooper*
Philomel 2001, ISBN 0–399–23006–8

Littlesugar's language creates a rather disturbing but realistic image of the events of the 1964 Mississippi Summer Project when Freedom Schools were taught by young white volunteers from up North. This story takes place in a small segregated community called Chicken Creek. When a young white teacher moves in with a black family to teach black children about their heritage and the host of contributions made by heroes, such as Jacob Lawrence, Countee Cullen, and Benjamin Banneker, the host family is harassed by bigots who throw bricks through the windows of their home. But that doesn't stop the school. Then the church is burned down. But that doesn't stop the school either—the community joins together to rebuild and the school is held outdoors under a tree. This sensitive story is a tale of courage, hope, and determination and provides a lens to examine a part of history that is seldom included in books for children.

## Freedom Summer

*Written by Deborah Wiles*
*Illustrated by Jerome Lagarrigue*
Atheneum 2001, ISBN 0–689–83016–5

Want to know what life was like in 1964 in the South? This outstanding book transcends the evil of segregation, when Joe claims as his best friend young John Henry. These boys like so many of the same things, from wanting to be firemen when they grow up to swimming in the swimming hole. They also like to go to the store for a treat but John Henry can't go in with Joe. When the 1964 Civil Rights Act is passed *(Freedom Summer)* segregation becomes illegal. However, bigotry and hatred isn't something that can be legislated. Joe and John Henry realize this hard fact when they get up early and rush to town just to be the first in the town pool on the first day it is supposed to be open to all people—regardless of color. However, the town's solution to this new law was to fill the pool with asphalt. Through it all these two young boys remain steadfast friends.

## Going North

*Written by Janice N. Harrington*
*Illustrated by Jerome Lagarrigue*
Farrar, Straus and Giroux 2004, ISBN 0–374–32681–9

Begin this book with a look at the endpapers and take a moment to discuss the importance of them. Set in the 1960s this story is told through the eyes of Jesse, one of a family of five. Jesse doesn't understand why the family is moving north to Nebraska and leaving the only home she has ever known. She wonders why they have to leave Big Mama and Alabama where she feels safe and loved. She doesn't understand the adults and their notion of seeking a better life. As you read you will find that Harrington's language is meant to savor: *Going-North Day hurries to our door like it's tired of our slowpokey ways; tickle-twirled all over the place; looking at the world going by, red sand and cotton fields, pines marking the sky like black crayons* (because the family had to travel at night); *kudzu vines covering everything, kudzu leaves like big green hands clapping, clapping and waving to us.* The author's note at the back of the book tells you that this is a memoir of her family's actual journey from Alabama to Nebraska in 1964. Don't miss this one as you are building background for understanding this critical period of time in U.S. history.

## I've Seen the Promised Land: The Life of Dr. Martin Luther King, Jr.

*Written by Walter Dean Myers*
*Illustrated by Leonard Jenkins*
Harper Children's 2004, ISBN 0–06–027703–3

Beginning with the extraordinary front flap of the book jacket, you will re-visit all the major events of the civil rights movement as led by Dr. Martin Luther King Jr. The text is short and not difficult to follow but the work is focused and provides a concise timeline of Dr. King's powerful effort to lead all people to a life of peace and equality. *I've Seen the Promised Land* can be paired with a more difficult book on the life of Dr. King to help establish a more solid understanding of his work.

## Mississippi Morning

*Written by Ruth Vander Zee*
*Illustrated by Floyd Cooper*
Eerdmans Books 2004, ISBN 0–8028–5211–4

This story makes an excellent companion to *Freedom Summer,* a book that also works around the theme of friendship between a white boy and a black boy in the segregated South. However, *Mississippi Morning* is set earlier in the civil rights movement and introduces more graphic details, including stories about the Klan. A white boy named James Williams, who is secret friends with a black boy named LeRoy, learns many of the truths that underlie the fabric of his young life during a day of fishing. James doesn't want to believe much of what he has learned. But one early morning while walking in the woods, he discovers his dad coming home covered in a white robe with only the eyes cut out. For some reason his dad pulls the hood off and their eyes meet. Suddenly James knows that all he has learned about the white men in his community is true. His life, including his relationship with his father, changes forever.

## Remember: The Journey to School Integration

*Written by Toni Morrison*
*Illustrated with actual photographs*
Houghton Mifflin 2004, ISBN 0–618–39740–X

Even though 1954 was a landmark year with regard to the segregation of schools, it took many more years for things to truly change. The landscape of America began this change on May 17, 1954, when the U.S. Supreme Court declared segregated schools unconstitutional. Morrison's book *Remember* documents that journey in a sequence that is eloquent in its clear and simple presentation. The easy-to-understand text, alongside black-and-white photographs from those turbulent and painful years, will leave you speechless. Every American should take time to live through the pages of this book and be reminded of the impact of bigotry and racism. The photographs tell their story, but Toni Morrison's words speak the truth of life in a segregated society.

## Sister Anne's Hands

*Written by Marybeth Lorbiecki*
*Illustrated by K. Wendy Popp*
Puffin Books 1998, ISBN 0–14–056534–5

Readers will adore Sister Anne. She tells jokes, she reads aloud with voice, and she has the children doing math in the most delicious ways. But, Sister Anne is the first black person most of the children have ever seen. Before the first day of school is over, her color has become an issue. Some parents even pull their children from her class. Does it stop Sister Anne from teaching? How does she win the hearts and trust of children and adults and refocus their eyes from the color of her skin to the fiber of her character? This book will become one you will read every year to remind students that all people are more than the skin they are in. And to remind them that prejudice of any sort, on any basis, is short sighted. This book can be useful for several of the read-aloud opportunities we have outlined: Chapter 2, Building Community by Reading Aloud the First Thing Every Day, the It Happened at School bookshelf; and Chapter 5, Supporting the Writing Workshop by Reading Aloud. It is a must-read regardless of where you choose to use it.

## The Bus Ride

*Written by William Miller*
*Illustrated by John Ward*
Lee & Low 2001, ISBN 1–584–30026–4

From Rosa Parks: *I encourage all young people to believe in themselves and take a stand for what is right. It is my hope that reading this story will inspire you to learn about the past so you can help make the future better for all people.* In this book Sara's mother goes to work as a maid every morning on the same bus Sara takes to school. Sara doesn't like sitting in the back of the bus, but her mother tells her to be thankful for a seat. One morning after her mother has gotten off, Sara decides to find out what was so special about the front of the bus. The bus driver tells her he will put her off. But Sara refuses to get off or to go to the back. He calls a policeman and Sara is removed from the bus. From that day for many days to come they don't ride the bus and others join them by walking rather than riding.

## The Other Side

*Written by Jacqueline Woodson*
*Illustrated by E. B. Lewis*
Putnam Juvenile 2001, ISBN 0–399–23116–1

*See* description on page 51.

## Through My Eyes

*Written by Ruby Bridges*
*Articles and interviews compiled and edited by Margo Lundell*
*Illustrated with actual photographs*
Scholastic 1999, ISBN 0–590–18923–9

> This is not a book you will pick up and read aloud from cover to cover in one sitting. Rather, this important book will enable your older students to develop the conceptual frame, the vocabulary, and the images needed to understand the fear and anger experienced during the turbulent times of the late 1950s and early 1960s. Begin your shared journey with the "Dear Reader" letter written by singer Harry Belafonte included at the front of the book. In it Belafonte introduces you to the young Ruby, the first black child to walk into an all-white New Orleans public school in 1964. The text immerses readers in the history of this period through a narrative that will be irresistible to anyone curious about these events. This one is not a quick read. No, this one is like a southern porch; it will be a place to visit over and over. And on each visit readers will leave with a deeper understanding and greater insights.

 *Civil Rights Bookshelf Five: Honoring the Lives of African Americans Who Led the Way to Equal Rights*

The struggle for equal rights has many luminaries, heroes, and heroines. In this collection of books we feature those who broke ground and made historic steps forward for all people. We include books that profile those whose names are synonymous with the words *civil rights* and ones that will introduce little-known folks who played a role in establishing equal rights for all.

### Book of Black Heroes: Great Women in the Struggle

*Written by Toyomi Igus, Veronica Freeman Ellis, Diane Patrick, Valerie Wilson Wesley*
*Original photographs*
Just Us Books 1991, ISBN 0–940–97526–2

> They are educators and lawyers, writers and artists, athletes and entrepreneurs, but black women have struggled. Some have struggled in silence without recognition while others have achieved national acclaim. In this collection more than eighty black women are featured in stories and profiles that reveal how each of them worked to leave a legacy for all who come after them. Our suggestion for this book is to use it to support other read-alouds, to deepen your understanding. For example, turn to page 65 in this book when reading *Wilma, Unlimited* (see page 178) to your children and give them other pieces of interesting information. If this piques their interest, you will find four additional stories about black women athletes.

### Coming Home from the Life of Langston Hughes

*Written and Illustrated by Floyd Cooper*
Philomel/Putnam & Grosset 1994, ISBN 0–399–22682–6

> Langston Hughes grows up dreaming—dreaming of a home with a ma and pa instead of his grandma. But each time the train that runs alongside his grandma's two-room house keeps going along its tracks, his dream fades just as the train's whistle. Langston's grandma is very poor and seldom has enough money for food and clothes, but she feeds him stories and fills his life with the tales of heroes. There are times in his young life when he is allowed to visit his ma in the city and once they even ride the train to Mexico to see his pa. Each visit fills him with hope that they will make a home together. But each time, he ends up going home with his grandma. When she grows so old she can no longer care for him, he goes to live with another couple across town and for the first time in his life he has all the food he can eat. And for the first time in his life, he knows what home means. Once Langston begins school, he falls in love with writing and becomes popular with his classmates. (Read this along with the 2002 *Visiting Langston* and his 2004 *Langston's Train Ride*.)

### Duke Ellington

*Written by Andrea Davis Pinkney*
*Illustrated by Brian Pinkney*
Jump at the Sun 1998, ISBN 0–7868–0178–6

Duke Ellington was born in Washington, DC, in 1899. He is described as a *smooth-talkin', slick-steppin', piano-playin' kid!* A grateful nation fell under the spell of his ragtime music, loved to swing to the Duke's beat, and became enchanted with his melodies. The story very cleverly weaves together his efforts during the civil rights movement when all he wanted to do was play his beloved music. On January 23, 1943, Duke played at New York's Carnegie Hall to the applause of all citizens. In the end Pinkney gives you a detailed biography of the research she used to bring us this marvelous story about Ellington's life.

## Ella Fitzgerald

*Written by Andrea Davis Pinkney*
*Illustrated by Brian Pinkney*
Jump at the Sun 2002, ISBN 0 7868 0568 4

> *Determination was her teacher.*
> *The sidewalk was her stage.*
> *Imagination was her spotlight.*
> From a very early age Ella Fitzgerald is packed with talent that is recognized by all who watch her dance on street corners in Yonkers, New York. Soon she moves to Harlem where the spotlights freeze her feet but not her vocal cords. And it is on those velvet notes that her career takes off and she never has to look back. From Harlem's Apollo Theater, she sings at Yale then goes back to the Savoy where a radio show takes her voice across the country. In September 1947 Ella sings on the stage of Carnegie Hall where she brings the crowd to their feet with *her bebop to a high-and-mighty concert stage. . . . Ella put scat on the map. When she and Dizzy threw down their skippity-hop-doo-dee-bop, every soul in the place slipped into the jam.* Before her death in 1996, Ella Fitzgerald had been honored by both President Carter and President Reagan as one of the most talented American performers who had ever lived.

## Freedom Like Sunlight: Praisesongs for Black Americans

*Written by J. Patrick Lewis*
*Illustrated by John Thompson*
Creative Editions 2003, ISBN 0–898–12382–8

> In the exquisite language of J. Patrick Lewis, this collection honors black Americans who have made significant contributions throughout history. Lewis profiles notable figures such as Marian Anderson, Louis Armstrong,

Arthur Ashe, Billie Holiday, Langston Hughes, Martin Luther King Jr., Jesse Owens, Satchel Paige, Rosa Parks, Wilma Rudolph, Sojourner Truth, Harriet Tubman, and Malcolm X. The book is laid out so that each poem falls on the left page and is paired with a full-color picture of the featured person on the right. Lewis also provides biographical notes on each person at the back of the book. As with other books on this shelf, this one is not to be read all in one sitting. Rather we see it as a book to feature one person every day. As you read other books in this set, you might place the profiles from this collection in chronological order and feature them in history to coincide with the read-aloud of the day.

## George Washington Carver: The Peanut Wizard

*Written by Laura Driscoll*
*Illustrated by Jill Weber*
Grosset & Dunlap 2003, ISBN 0–448–43243–9

Your children will greet this little book with lots of enthusiasm and interest. The book begins with Ms. Brandt ending a unit of study by asking her class to complete a report on their favorite scientists. This clever book is written as a report from Annie Marcus on George Washington Carver. The text is very simple with lots of pictures and drawings to illustrate the information. Through Annie's report readers discover that George was born a slave in 1864 and belonged to a Missouri slave owner, Moses Carver. Therefore, his name became George Carver. Although slaves were freed shortly after his birth, George's mother was stolen by slave robbers who sold her. Moses Carver and his wife, even though they had once owned George and his brother, were kind people who raised them. George was very bright and the Carver family knew education was the key. Who would have thought that the little slave boy from Missouri would become the famous scientist who would invent the many wonderful ways peanuts could be used. This one is not to be missed and could be paired with *Carver, A Life in Poems* (2001).

## Hank Aaron: Brave in Every Way

*Written by Peter Golenbock*
*Illustrated by Paul Lee*
Gulliver Books 2001, ISBN 0–152–02093–4

Growing up in the South, Hank Aaron was a hero for many youngsters regardless of race or gender. The flap of the book jacket sums up this book so nicely: *On April 8, 1974, America watched as Hank Aaron stepped up to the plate. The pitch was low and down the middle. Hank swung—and hit home run number 715! With that hit, Hank Aaron surpassed Babe Ruth's legendary record and realized a lifelong dream.* Hank Aaron is born three years before Marian Anderson is allowed to sing on the steps of the Lincoln Memorial. And maybe his parents have not heard about this important happening in the life of another African American, but they dream that their boy will have the opportunity to make a difference in the world. They are in the middle of the Great Depression but the family surrounds little Hank with love and time to play ball. His mama's advice is always, *Set goals for yourself and always work to be your best!* Read this incredible story of a young man who did just that and became a hero to many. Lee's full-page illustrations extend the story and will serve to hold the attention of all those who take the time to peek inside.

### Knockin' on Wood

*Written and Illustrated by Lynne Barasch*
Lee & Low 2004, ISBN 1–584–30170–8

Despite racial prejudice, poverty, and a handicapping condition, Clayton Bates wants to be a dancer. He is born in 1912 on a sharecropper's farm in South Carolina. Without shoes and music, Clayton dances anyway. Wherever he goes he dances, which makes his Mama mad but even her anger can't stop Clayton. He hates farming, so at the young age of twelve he goes to work at the cottonseed mill to earn money. But on the third day, he has an accident that costs him his leg. With broomsticks as crutches, Clayton is soon up walking and before many days have passed he is dancing as well. His uncle makes him a peg leg and the rest is history. With that peg leg, Clayton became known as Peg Leg Bates and was a dancer that people around the world went to see. In 1951, Clayton opened his own club in New York. On the very last page, you'll find a photograph of Peg Leg Bates.

### Major Taylor: Champion Cyclist

*Written by Lesa Cline-Ransome*
*Illustrated by James E. Ransome*
Atheneum 2004, ISBN 0–689–83159–5

Lesa Cline-Ransome brings us the story behind the life of Marshall Taylor, the young man who became known as "Major Taylor" and "The Black

Whirlwind" because of his talent and speed on his bicycle. In the late 1800s, Marshall Taylor overcomes racial prejudice to become a champion cyclist. The facts of his struggle are embedded in this uplifting book that is sure to win the hearts and respect of readers. The art extends the story and helps makes the retelling of Marshall's success even more of a triumph.

### Minty: The Story of Young Harriet Tubman

*Written by Alan Schroeder*
*Illustrated by Jerry Pinkney*
Puffin Books 1996, ISBN 0–14–056196–X

The author's fictional account of Harriet's life is based on the known facts of the young slave who would one day show her great courage as she helped free hundreds of slaves. Minty is the nickname given Harriet who always finds it hard to be anything but difficult to her mistress as a youngster. Pinkney's irresistible art makes this surprising and joyful story of the very young Harriet Tubman even more engaging. This one will surely become a favorite of students. We predict they will ask for it again and again just to giggle at the feisty and headstrong Minty!

### Molly Bannaky

*Written by Alice McGill*
*Illustrated by Chris K. Soentpiet*
Houghton Mifflin 1999, ISBN 0–395–72287–X

Between the strikingly luminous paintings of Soentpiet and the superb storytelling skills of McGill, this book is one you don't want to miss as you build background for this area of the curriculum. The story begins during the 1600s in England with Molly, a chamber maid. When she spills milk one time too many, she is taken to court and cast out of England. Indentured as a servant to a man in America, Molly toils for seven years before earning her freedom. With the help of a slave she prospers on the land she lays claim to and eventually marries the slave who had been a prince in his homeland. Molly will easily win the respect of readers as the story unfolds to reveal her many remarkable characteristics. (Molly Bannaky was the grandmother of Benjamin Banneker.)

### My Brother Martin: A Sister Remembers

*Written by Christine King Farris*
*Illustrated Chris Soentpiet*
Simon & Schuster 2003, ISBN 0–689–84387–9

When we think of Martin Luther King Jr., we, like most Americans, think of him as a grown man leading marches or speaking to large groups of people. All this changes when his sister, Christine King Farris, takes out her pen to reveal a much younger boy who is full of mischief and laughter. She takes us into their home when this new baby arrives and later we play with them on the street pulling jokes on people. We even watch as he loosens the legs of the piano bench to keep from taking a piano lesson. But she doesn't stop there. She takes us forward to know him as the grown man who becomes the voice of the nonviolent movement to lead our world toward peace and equality for all, into a world that judges human beings by their works and behaviors, not by the color of their skin. Chris Soentpiet visited the King family home to photograph the setting and used members of the family as models for characters in this book.

## Powerful Words: More Than 200 Years of Extraordinary Writing by African Americans

*Written by Wade Hudson*
*Illustrated by Sean Qualls*
Scholastic 2004, ISBN 0–439–40969–1

The writings of thirty-six African Americans have been gathered in this one powerful book. Not only did Hudson gather their words but he also researched the responses to those words. Just to give you a sampling: On pages 4 and 5 you will find a letter from Benjamin Banneker (Molly Bannaky's grandson) to Thomas Jefferson asking for his help in eradicating the remaining bondages of slavery. Jefferson's response is given but unfortunately he did nothing to end slavery. Some of the other famous Americans whose writings appear include such notable figures as Fredrick Douglass, Mary McLeod Bethune, Langston Hughes, Toni Morrison, Sojourner Truth, and George Washington Carver.

## Promises to Keep: How Jackie Robinson Changed America

*Written by Sharon Robinson*
*Illustrated with actual family photographs*
Scholastic 2004, ISBN 0–439–42592–1

We believe any study of this topic must include stories about the lives of people such as Rosa Parks and Dr. Martin Luther King Jr. However, we also believe such a study must include stories about the lives of people who made significant contributions in other ways. Jackie Robinson is one such person. Robinson, the first black to play in previously all-white major league baseball, forged the way for black athletes to cross the color barriers of the day. The front flap reads: *On April 12, 1947, my father, Jack Roosevelt Robinson, stepped out of the Brooklyn Dodgers dugout, crossed first base, and assumed his position as first baseman. He paused, hands resting on bent knees, toes pointed in, then stood lifted his cap, and saluted the cheering fans. It was a defining moment for baseball . . . and for America.* Once this one gets in the hands of your baseball fans, you'll have a difficult time keeping track of where the book has gone; it won't stay on the shelf for any length of time. One additional hint: Remove the book jacket and take a peek at the cover; it alone deserves some turn and talk time.

## Talking About Bessie: The Story of Aviator Elizabeth Coleman

*Written by Nikki Grimes*
*Illustrated by E. B. Lewis*
Orchard 2002, ISBN 0–439–35243–6

Bessie Coleman is born during the late 1800s in Texas where segregation is a way of life. Because she is a girl and an African American, she is always being told she can't do things that she very much wants to do. When she is eleven, the Wright brothers make their famous flight and Bessie, like them, is destined to break some barriers of her own. This version of her life is noteworthy because it is told through the voices of multiple narrators. Each voice presents the perspective of one of several different people who knew her at various points during her life. While the story is fiction, it reads like truth when family and friends gather in Chicago to mourn the death of Bessie. As each of them reminisces about Bessie, the speaker's picture and memories are presented on the left page. And on the right, opposing the words, Lewis paints a vivid and memorable picture of that moment in Bessie's life.

## The Sound That Jazz Makes

*Written by Carole Boston Weatherford*
*Illustrated by Eric Velasquez*
Walker Books 2001, ISBN 0–8027–7674–4

Demonstrating her remarkable ability, Weatherford takes the African American story from the origin of native Africa through all the decades to modern-day America in only fifteen short pages. On every page she deftly weaves in the importance of music at each stage of the journey. The writing is exquisite because it details this comprehensive timeline. The art of Eric Velasquez surrounds the small amount of text filling the oversized pages to create a great book for a read-aloud.

## The Story of Ruby Bridges

*Written by Robert Coles*
*Illustrated by George Ford*
Scholastic 2004, ISBN 0–439–59844–3

The year is 1960 and six-year-old Ruby Bridges is the first black child to integrate the all-white schools in New Orleans. Ruby's daddy is a janitor and her mom scrubs floors in a bank and they want something better for their children. They believe the way to get that better life is through education. They are proud that their child is selected to be one of the children to integrate the all-white school but worry about her safety. The white parents who are called segregationists are extremely angry and pull their children out of the school. Young Ruby eventually becomes the only child in her classroom. To ensure her safe arrival at school, federal marshals have to escort her as she walks into the building every day. (For a firsthand version of the Ruby Bridges' story, including newspaper articles and black-and-white photographs of the events of that time, see *Through My Eyes;* a description of it is in this chapter's Bookshelf Four.)

## The Tuskegee Airmen Story

*Written by Lynn M. Homan and Thomas Reilly*
*Illustrated by Rosalie M. Shepherd*
Pelican 2002, ISBN 1–58980–005–2

In most wars prior to World War II, African Americans were cooks, janitors, or mechanics but all that changed in 1941 with the Tuskegee Airmen who became the first black pilots to fly combat missions. This is their story as told by one of those airmen to his grandchildren and their friends. The text is supported by full-color art that captures the essence of the times as the story moves from modern day back to the 1940s. His parting words to the children: *The Tuskegee Airmen proved that African Americans had the ability to be successful, not just as military pilots, but in all kinds of ways. They never gave up. They never stopped trying to be the best. That's what Grandma and I want you kids to do.*

## When Marian Sang

*Written by Pam Munoz Ryan*
*Illustrated by Brian Selznick*
Scholastic 2002, ISBN 0–439–26967–9

Before Dr. Martin Luther King Jr. and even before Rosa Parks, there were other amazing people who left huge footprints on the landscape of America. One such exceptional person was Marian Anderson, a singer whose voice could touch the very soul of anyone under the spell of it. This exquisite story about how Marian would not let the prejudices of others deter her from the goal of fulfilling her dreams could easily fit into the category of "believing in yourself." Readers will find it difficult to believe that this amazing talent was not permitted to sing for white Americans until Eleanor Roosevelt intervened and had her sing to an integrated crowd of 75,000 people on the steps of the Lincoln Memorial in 1939. Selznick's detailed drawings will pull you into the story as you are pulled along on the current of Ryan's language from page to page. No color appears until the very last page when the spotlight finally shines down on Marian at her debut with the Metropolitan Opera—her long-awaited dream had come true. This one is a must-read in this most important collection.

## Wilma Unlimited: How Wilma Rudolph Became the World's Fastest Woman

*Written by Kathleen Krull*
*Illustrated by David Diaz*
Harcourt Children's 1996, ISBN 0–15–201267–2

Wilma Rudolph is born in Tennessee as one of nineteen children of a family struggling to survive poverty. She is a tiny baby who experiences many health problems and there is only one doctor who will treat black families. When she is five, she develops polio and scarlet fever. The doctor says she will never walk again. However, there is one hospital in Nashville that will treat black children so she and her mom ride a bus to town where she can be treated. Wilma does her exercises even when she is tired and even when it hurts. The school refuses to let her attend until she can walk but that only makes her more determined. Not only does she learn to walk but she also learns to run. She earns a scholarship and is the first person in her family to go to college.

In 1960 she represents the United States in the Olympics as a runner. This is the first time the games are shown on television and there is Wilma . . . a poor little girl who couldn't walk at five but who can now run and will become the first person to win three gold medals in a single year. Following her experience at the Olympics, Wilma is honored by blacks and whites alike in her hometown of Clarksville. This gathering is the first event of the sixties in which the races join together as one community.

# 7

## *Closing the Day with a Chapter Book Read-Aloud*

*E*VERY DAY needs to be drawn to a close with some consistent routine. Mr. Rogers always reviewed the day as he untied his sneakers and put them away after stepping back into his loafers. And as he moved toward the door singing the parting song, he unzipped his sweater, placed it on a hanger, and returned it to the closet right where he had taken it from earlier that day—and every day before. Still singing he took the jacket he had placed there at the opening of the show and slipped in first one arm and then the other. Every day for thirty years of visits to the neighborhood, our trusted friend, Mr. Rogers, gave us peace and a sense of safety in knowing what was coming next. He did it through the use of simple, yet effective, structures and routines. His consistent behaviors and easy-going rhythms let us know the day was ending. But more important, we knew that tomorrow he would be there again—we knew what to expect. Likewise, Ralph Peterson (1992) reminds us of the following:

> When teachers use a touch of ceremony to make the day complete, the working rhythms of the day are slowed; loose ends are tied. Students [are] brought together to end on a harmonious note. . . . Regardless of how ceremony is incorporated, the intent is to establish a feeling of completeness before the students return to the everyday world beyond the classroom wall. (20)

So, we suggest that you establish a ritual and close the day with a gift. Offer something you believe will have a lasting impression, something you believe has the power to resonate in the minds of students and leave them longing for more. Let's pause a moment here and think of this final read-aloud as a parting gift; what better way to end a day? Katherine Paterson (1995) said in *A Sense of Wonder:* "[T]he best way to cultivate their tastes is to read to them, starting at birth and keeping on and on. 'Let me hear you read it' is a test. 'Let me read it to you' is a gift. So . . . read to them, read to them, read to them. For if we are careless in the matter of nourishing the imagination, the world will pay for it. The world already has" (282–83).

We share a growing concern that students are living in such a highly visual world and spend such large chunks of time engaged in video and computer games, the Internet, television, DVDs, and so on that there is little need for them to imagine. Many of the toys for children even come packaged as an extension of a game, TV program, or movie, filling the world of play with images created by someone else's mind. When children are so bombarded with preconceived images, little is left for them to do but take in the predigested "meal" like an infant bird who feeds on its parent's regurgitation.

To spend time listening to a story at the end of every day is powerful. The power to evoke images and ignite the imagination rests both on the skill and craft of the writer and on the passion and presentation of the reader (that would be you). The fact that novels have pages of print and no illustrations means that writers know they must use their most descriptive language to lead readers to a place where they begin doing the work of an illustrator. In this case, it isn't with brushes or clay or paper collage or with computer graphics—it is the human mind that creates the images, still or moving. It is the listener's power to imagine that will set the internal illustrator to work. It's appropriate to remember that Paterson (1995) said the following some ten years ago:

> The power of the imagination—the sound of the heart. What can we do? I think one thing we can do is to share with children works of the imagination—those sounds deepest in the human heart, often couched in symbol and metaphor. These don't give children packaged answers. They invite children to go within themselves to listen to the sounds of their own hearts. (172–73)

This final and closing read-aloud may hold more promise than you imagine. Consider what children are seeing in their minds when they listen to the most talented readers and storytellers weave the story of Cinderella. We are willing to wager that the majority of them will play out scenes from the Disney video that first introduced children to the character.

Lester recalls the first time he heard that story. It was at school and, of course, he had not seen the video (yeah, it's true, he is so old they didn't have videos back then). He clearly had not met a princess either (he isn't *that* old). His closest encounter was to see his Aunt Mickey in a red evening gown all dressed up for a local beauty pageant (you can imagine where this connection is headed). As the story was read aloud and Cinderella's transformation began to take place, the princess in his mind's eye was taking the form of Aunt Mickey. The images, like comprehension of the story, were constructions created through the interplay of his known world and the new one being woven by the story's words.

Isn't it important to actively engage the imagination? Isn't that worth the investment of our time? Is it not the active engagement of imagination that everyone needs to create poetry and fiction and fantasy and science fiction and to generate inventions and innovations? Clearly, we must purposefully and carefully design opportunities for students to use imagination. We must nourish it with the same sense of urgency felt by an ER team trying to revive a patient whose heart has stopped beating. We must revive and nourish, support and nurture children's imaginations and tell them that they must not forget how to pretend, for that is where fiction comes from. It is a vivid imagination that helps us see Cinderella for ourselves when she is stepping out of the coach and heading into the castle. It is a vivid and healthy imagination that can create images with only words, words powerful enough to take readers along with us. It is the healthy imagination that will find a solution to global warming and world hunger and find a cure for cancer and a vaccine for AIDS.

We must not slight this final daily opportunity for reading aloud to our students. For through this one ritual we can feed their imaginations, catch them up in the current of a well-written story, and whet their appetites for longer, sustained texts. While we have them longing for more, we are obligated to seize the opportunity to introduce other titles by a featured author and other related titles on the same topic and other related titles in the same genre. We are obligated to seize the opportunity to grow our listeners into the kinds of students who believe themselves capable of "living through" an entire novel on their own. We are obligated to seize the opportunity to broaden their horizons to include new authors and new topics and to explore new genres. We are also obligated to seize the opportunity to select examples of fine writing that we can revisit during writing workshops.

## ■ *Books for Closing the Day with a Chapter Book*

This final read-aloud isn't really final at all; in many, many ways it is only the beginning. . . . To that end this chapter presents a collection of novels that have become favorites of children we have worked with. In addition, we have invited some of the finest teachers we know to share a few titles they have found to be particularly effective.

 *Books That Beg to Be Read*

### Anna Casey's Place in the World

*Written by Adrian Fogelin*
Peachtree 2001, ISBN 1–56145–249–1

Like the swift currents of a river Fogelin will pull you right into the story before you finish the first chapter. Her richly developed characters are placed in a realistic setting and embedded in a plot that will have you turning the pages late into the night as you read this one before sharing it with your class. Anna Casey, a foster child, is so skillfully developed she will be alive in your mind. You will long to support and console and love her as you grow to respect her courage. As she reaches out to understand and support Eb, the other foster child in her home, you will be in awe of her understanding and maturity. You will laugh with Miss Johnette, the neighbor, as she literally absorbs what life has to offer and cares little for what society expects of her. Fogelin is a name that you are going to want to watch for because each of the books we've read by her are equally as well written as this one about Anna Casey. (We also recommend *Crossing Jordan,* written in 2000.)

### Because of Winn-Dixie

*Written by Kate DiCamillo*
Candlewick 2000, ISBN 0–763–60776–2

*My name is India Opal Buloni, and last summer my daddy, the preacher, sent me to the store for a box of macaroni and cheese, some white rice, and two tomatoes and I came back with a dog.* It is with those words that DiCamillo hooks children and teachers alike. When India Opal is in the Winn-Dixie to pick up groceries, an ugly stray dog runs into the store causing all kinds of havoc. The manager yells for someone to call the pound. India Opal knows if they come, the dog might be put to sleep, so she tells the manager the dog is hers. Since she doesn't have a name for the dog she names him Winn-Dixie. After all, she is named India because her daddy, the preacher, was once a missionary in India. Before she gets back to her trailer park, she already loves the dog with all her heart. Before the story ends, so does everyone else. *Because of Winn-Dixie* gives readers an bird's-eye view of a family that becomes complete because of the love of a stray dog.

## Bridge to Terabithia

*Written by Katherine Paterson*
*Illustrated by Donna Diamond*
HarperTrophy 1987, ISBN 0–064–40184–7

*Ba-room, ba-room, baripity, baripity, baripity, baripty—Good. His dad had the pickup going. He could get up now. Jess slid out of bed and into his overalls. He didn't worry about a shirt because once he began running he would be hot as popping grease even if the morning air was chill, or shoes because the bottom of his feet were by now as tough as his worn-out sneakers.* Jess, a young runner getting ready for fifth grade, is dedicated to practicing all summer because he wants to be the fastest runner in school by fall. Despite having to help his family on their farm, he slips away every day to practice in the fields around his house. Life changes for Jess when Leslie moves next door to him. Her family is so different from his, but Jess finds that Leslie's imagination only adds to their friendship. She creates a secret kingdom for them located across a stream deep in the woods far from their families and friends who either boss or bully them. In their magic kingdom, Terabithia, they are not fifth graders but a king and queen. Despite the severe hardships facing Jess's family and Leslie's overwhelming and desperate need for friends, their friendship continues to grow deeper and more important. In early spring, Jess goes to Washington with his teacher but purposely doesn't invite Leslie along. When he arrives home at the end of the day, he finds that Leslie has drowned trying to cross the creek to get to their beloved Terabithia. Sorrow and regret fill Jess. In the midst of his sadness, he wishes he'd never known Leslie. Paterson's writing is filled with such compassion and understanding. Her words are so strong and moving as she gets into the character of these young children and pulls the reader into their lives.

## Charlotte's Web

*Written by E. B. White*
*Illustrated by Garth Williams*
HarperCollins 1952, 1999, ISBN 0–06–028298–3

Every child should have *Charlotte's Web* read to him or her . . . and not just once. The book is a classic that has been loved and cherished by children and adults since 1952. But, just in case you are not familiar with it, a brief recap follows. *Where's Papa going with that ax? said Fern to her mother as they were setting the table for breakfast. Out to the hoghouse, replied Mrs. Arable. Some pigs were born last night.* These unforgettable words begin the adventure of Fern and her quest to save a little piglet from her father's ax. That pig grows up to be her beloved Wilbur. Wilbur is everyone's friend, but most of all he loves Charlotte, the spider who spends her day spinning webs in Wilbur's barn. But as with most piglets, Wilbur grows up into a rather large pig. He is such a fine pig that everyone knows he is destined to become something other than a pet. Like Fern before her, Charlotte becomes determined to save Wilbur from his destiny. With the assistance of a rat named Templeton, they make everyone think Wilbur is the smartest pig of all times. By the time they save Wilbur, Charlotte is near the end of her life; but before she dies, she lays a sac of eggs. All winter, the very sad Wilbur stands guard over Charlotte's sac. When the babies are born, Wilbur wants them all with him in the barn, but like all spiders they want to journey away. Many, however, stay and over the years raise their own babies in the farmyard. But none of Charlotte's children or grandchildren ever take the place in Wilbur's heart that Charlotte would forever hold.

## Fig Pudding

*Written by Ralph Fletcher*
Clarion Books 1995, ISBN 0–395–71125–8

Ralph Fletcher takes a family of six children through an entire year of their life together from December to December. Cliff, the oldest child, serves as the narrator. In the first few chapters, you get the typical view of family life with all the trials and tribulations of living inside the fishbowl called *family living*. But the seventh, eighth, and ninth chapters have such tenderness and insight that these three chapters alone are worth much more than the price of the book. When one of the young brothers gets killed while riding his bicycle,

Fletcher's words reveal how different people cope with the loss of a loved one. His words are filled with a sensitivity that seeps into the reader as he invites you to witness the core of that unbelievable grief. You can't help but notice how each member of the family faces the pain differently while providing support for each other despite the enormous energy that grief requires. In these chapters, Fletcher touches the heart and soul of every reader.

## The Great Gilly Hopkins

*Written by Katherine Paterson*

HarperTrophy 1978, 1987, ISBN 0-064-40201-0

Reba first read this one to a group of fifth graders in 1983. She and her students fell in love with Gilly and her ability to turn situations upside down, often creating havoc with disastrous results. To this day, long after she's been out of the classroom, Reba compares every chapter book to the fabulous job Paterson did in developing Gilly's character, creating a realistic and visually explicit setting within a strong plot that keeps a reader's eyes fixated on the page. Reba has never read *Gilly* to a class of upper-grade children who didn't grow to cherish the book as much as she does. In the story Gilly is a foster child who longs for her real mother to come and rescue her from all the foster homes. She imagines her mother to be *movie star* beautiful and just knows if this would happen, everything in her life would be perfect. When the agency places her with Maimie Trotter (a woman you simply have to meet in all her overweight glory) and her other slightly farsighted foster child, William Ernest (Gilly calls him retarded just to upset Ms. Trotter who loves everyone, especially William Ernest). By the time Gilly works through her anger to realize she does love Trotter and William Ernest, her grandmother arrives to take her to Virginia. Gilly realizes, far too late, that the grass is not greener on the other side. This is a very powerful story that is sure to have children talking about how Gilly covers her feelings with bad behavior simply to protect herself from rejection.

## Holes

*Written by Louis Sachar*

Dell Yearling 2000, ISBN 0-440-41480-6

*Sachar is masterful at bringing this realistic story and tall-tale motifs together. We haven't seen a book with this much plot, so suspensefully and expertly deployed, in too long a time (Kirkus Review).* The first page of this engrossing adventure will create such a strong visual image for children that they will moan when you stop reading the first day. The words will play around in their heads long after the last page has been read. As you read, the room will buzz with predictions about what is going to happen to Stanley Yelnats next. You will hear their frustration when they talk about Mr. Sir, the warden. *My name is Mr. Sir. Whenever you speak to me you must call me by my name, is that clear?* They will begin comparing the characteristics of the other boys at Camp Green Lake—Squid, X-Ray, Barf Bag, Zero, Magnet, Armpit, and Zigzag. Find out what Camp Green Lake actually is and why the boys were sent there. Why did all the boys have nicknames? Your students will be in for a real treat when you read this Newberry Award-winning book.

## Hope Was Here

*Written by Joan Bauer*
Putnam's Sons 2000, ISBN 0–399-23142-0

Hope is born prematurely to a woman who isn't ready for the responsibilities of being a mother. That woman names her Tulip, packs her up with a bag, and leaves her with her Aunt Addie before going off to live her own life. Baby Tulip finds love and acceptance with her vagabond aunt, a fabulous cook who goes from restaurant to restaurant. By age twelve, Tulip officially changes her name to Hope so that she will belong completely to Aunt Addie. Eventually, Hope becomes a waitress who leaves a note in each of her temporary homes to prove that *Hope Was Here.* Their family becomes complete when they meet the sheriff in their new town in Wisconsin. He longs to be the father Hope has never had and shortly after he marries Addie, he asks, *Hope, I was wondering if you'd consider letting me adopt you, because I'd like more than just about anything to do this father thing officially.* To show Hope how a new family can be made, he grafts a new tree limb onto the trunk of another tree. As they tie it to the graft, he tells Hope *that's what's going to happen to us. It's called grafting. Taking something from one place and fixing it to another until they grow together. We didn't start from the same tree, but we're going to grow together like we did.* The book is heartwarming as you learn that the human spirit can survive huge obstacles with determination and courage.

### In My Grandmother's House

*Complied and Illustrated by Bonnie Christensen*
*Vignettes by Award-Winning Authors*
HarperCollins 2003, ISBN 0–06–029109–5

This collection of vignettes written by twelve different authors is perfect for reading aloud. Grandmothers, the focus of each vignette, serve as the thread that weaves the collection together. For you upper-grade teachers who do author studies, this book will be a nice resource allowing you to also point out the power of voice. The authors have been very honest in sharing memories, which are sometimes rosy and sweet while others are tense and at times painful.

### Jazmin's Notebook

*Written by Nikki Grimes*
Puffin Books 1998, ISBN 0–8037–2224–9

The year is 1960 and Jazmin lives in a very small apartment with her older sister CeCe. Their building is between a laundromat and a bar and grill and Jazmin spends a lot of time on the stoop watching her world on Amsterdam Avenue. Her dad is dead and her mother is in a long-term care hospital. Jazmin's story is told as short journal entries about her daily life, her perceptions, and her concerns and celebrations. There are many poems sprinkled throughout the collection of short entries that are just right for a read-aloud. The children in your fifth and up classrooms will relate to Jazmin who never has what she wants since CeCe has to be very careful with money. Some of the entries are tender, others are filled with pain, while others reveal Jazmin's wonderful humor. One of the very best was written on September 7 where you find Jazmin beginning school as her typical *second-hand queen*. Since she doesn't have many new clothes, she is very jealous of the other girls at her school. After school, she goes to purchase a pair of black hose, which just happen to be in the department right next to the most expensive clothes for teens. *Looking was my first mistake. From that point on, my body was taken over by an alien. It was someone else who passed through the narrow entryway of 57th Street, someone else who drooled over clothes that smelled of money, someone else who floated into the dressing room to try on a dress so red, it burned her fingers. Once I was in front of the mirror, though, I had to admit, that someone was me.*

## The Landry News

*Written by Andrew Clements*
*Pictures by Salvatore Murdocca*
*Original Illustrated by Brian Selznick*
Simon & Schuster 1999, ISBN 0–689–81817–3

Cara Landry has to move to a new school where she is placed in Mr. Larson's classroom, the classroom that no one wants to be in. She dreads meeting all the new kids and she dreads being in Mr. Larson's classroom. She's hears all the rumors that he believes in an open classroom where children learn on their own while he drinks coffee and reads the paper. Cara is a very smart girl who bores easily, so within weeks she decides to give him a newspaper that would really entertain him—*The Landry News*. At first it entertains her and helps her pass the day. But soon the other kids want to write for the paper as well. Eventually, even Mr. Larson reads every copy of the paper and is quite excited about it. He even uses it to begin teaching the class again. All is well until the principal reads a copy of the paper that has an anonymously written true story about a sensitive subject. The principal knows he could use the paper as ammunition against Mr. Lawson. The paper has transformed Mr. Lawson and his teaching, yet at the same time he knows he has cheated all the children assigned to him for years. When the principal sends him notice that he is being brought before the board for a disciplinary hearing, he turns another corner in his teaching. The rest of the story will take readers from tears to cheers to puzzlement.

## Maniac Magee

*Written by Jerry Spinelli*
Little, Brown 1990, ISBN 0–316–80906-3

*They say Maniac Magee was born in a dump. They say his stomach was a cereal box and his heart a sofa spring. They say he kept an eight-inch cockroach on a leash and that rats stood guard over him while he slept. They say if you knew he was coming and you sprinkled salt on the ground and he ran over it, within two or three blocks he would be as slow as everybody else. They say.* This and more is part of the myth that surrounds a young homeless boy who gains the admiration of all the other children in town through his athletic abilities. Maniac has lost both his parents but is eventually taken in as a ragtag boy by another family who has a son around the same age. Maniac is white while his new family is black and lives on the opposite side of the tracks from most white families. But Maniac's attitude and character rub off on the kids from both parts of town and eventually pull them together. (Just a word of warning, occasionally one of the boys will use language that may offend some parents. However, we find it very authentic.)

## Missing May

*Written by Cynthia Rylant*

Orchard 1992, 2004, ISBN 0–531–05996–0

Summer's mother died when she was just a little girl. Her aunts and uncles pass her around for a long time before her Aunt May and Uncle Ob rescue her. For six years they live in a rusted old trailer in West Virginia where Summer witnesses what a family is supposed to be—people who support and love each other. When May dies, the world falls apart for Summer and Ob as they try to cope with the emptiness they both feel. This book allows readers to probe the depths of Summer's loss as they become witness to the steps she takes trying to cope with her sadness even though she lacks the support of an adult who could discuss her sense of loss and pain. One of the problems is that Ob believes in spirits and keeps telling Summer that May has come back to talk to him. Summer has never seen or heard any of May's visits. One day they try to locate someone that can help them communicate with May, but when they arrive, they find out the woman is dead. All their dreams and plans are dashed. They just stand on her porch . . . *dumbfounded. We were trying to outwit Death on this trip, rise above it, penetrate the blockades it put up between us and May. We were coming to Putnam Country to put Death in its place, and instead it had put us squarely back in ours.* Once they return home, Ob finally moves past grieving for May and begins making plans to honor her.

## Number the Stars

*Written by Lois Lowry*

Houghton Mifflin 1989, ISBN 0–395–51060–0

Living in Denmark in 1943 meant that families were under siege by the Nazi soldiers who had moved into all parts of Europe except for Sweden. The people had little food, nights meant blackout curtains, and Jewish people lived in fear for their lives every day. Young Annemarie's best friend, Ellen, is a Jew and lives in an upstairs apartment near her. They walk to school together, play together, and eventually their friendship proves to be the one constant that saves the lives of Ellen and her family. Lowry uses her best storytelling to reveal the personalities of each member of the family and the role each plays in saving their friends. From the innocence of Kirsti, the baby of the family, to the bravery of their mother as she helps Ellen and her family escape by boat under the disguise of a funeral. Your heart will speed up as you hear the sound of the soldiers' boots. Your mind will race as the trained dogs approach the boat and you fear what they will discover. You will grow to admire Annemarie as you watch a child who is brave and courageous beyond her young years. There are several wonderful picture books to read aloud to build background knowledge and vocabulary before reading this chapter book. For an extensive list of books on the Holocaust, see our companion book, *Building Bridges Across the Curriculum with Picture Books and Read-Alouds* (2006, Heinemann).

## Olive's Ocean

*Written by Kevin Henkes*
HarperTrophy 2003, 2005, ISBN 0–06–053545–8

When we think of Kevin Henkes, we most often think of Lily or Owen or Wemberly or Julius or Chester, but this chapter book reveals another dimension to his talents. Olive moves to Martha's school in February where she remains a stranger. Not once do Martha or her friends reach out to Olive or even invite her to sit with them at lunch. Shortly after school is out in June, Olive is riding her bicycle when she is hit by a car and killed. Not long after Olive's death while Martha and her family are packing for a summer vacation to visit her grandmother on the coast, Olive's mother visits to give Martha a page torn from Olive's journal. That page has a significant impact on Martha after many heart-to-heart conversations with her grandmother. Throughout the days of her visit with her grandmother, Martha learns several powerful and sometimes painful lessons about growing up. She also learns a lesson about moving beyond feeling sorry for yourself and reaching out with kindness and helpfulness to others in need.

## On My Honor

*Written by Marion Dane Bauer*
Yearling 1986, 1987, ISBN 0–440–46633–4

Starved Rock offers much temptation to the young boys, Tony and Joel, who will be going into the sixth grade when school starts. On this hot summer day, Tony dares Joel to ride with him out to the park to climb the rock bluffs. Finally, Joel decides to ask permission rather than to ride that far out without asking. With a lot of assurances from the boys, his dad finally allows Joel to go but tells his son he is going *On His Honor* to do all the responsible things. Joel promises. On the way to the park, however, they pass the dangerous Vermillion River where Joel dares Tony to swim out to the sandbar with him. Forgetting all that they had just promised, the boys jump in. But when Joel reaches the sandbar, he can't see Tony. He calls and searches but Tony has completely vanished. For the rest of the book, Joel tries to decide what to do and how to tell his dad and Tony's family the terrible truth. This is one all children in the upper grades need to hear and discuss.

## Pictures of Hollis Woods

*Written by Patricia Reilly Giff*
Wendy Lamb Books 2002, ISBN 0–385–32655–6

Hollis Woods is a foster child who is sent to a variety of families over the course of the story. As a means of protecting herself when the family no longer wants her, Hollis does everything within her power to keep those families off balance. But she finally feels accepted when she is sent to live with the Regans. After only weeks Hollis wants to become a member of their family. However, when she and Steven get into an accident, she blames herself and runs away. For once, her heart is broken because she had finally found a family who wants her. Giff does an incredible job of developing the character in this remarkable book. She reaches deep inside this frightened child to paint a picture that keeps us turning the pages to find out how the problem gets resolved.

## Poppy

*Written by Avi*
*Illustrated by Brian Floca*
HarperTrophy 1995, 2001, ISBN 0–380–72769–2

This book comes with a warning: Don't read this unless you are prepared to fall in love with a series of books about a deer mouse. After children became so passionate about Poppy, Avi gave us several sequels with *Poppy and Rye*

(1998), *Ragweed* (1999), and *Ereth's Birthday* (2000). Brian Floca illustrated each book in the series. Poppy falls in love with Ragweed and they plan to marry. Unfortunately Mr. Ocax, the owl who hunts deer mice every time he flies over Dimwood Forest where Poppy lives, kills Ragweed. Because Mr. Ocax thinks he owns the entire forest, he doesn't like the deer mice living there. All the books in the series are woven together when Poppy travels across the forest to visit Ragweed's family to tell them of his death. There she meets Rye, Ragweed's brother. They fall in love and eventually get married. Ereth is an adorable but grumpy porcupine who is Poppy's friend. In *Ereth's Birthday* when Poppy and Rye don't show up for his birthday celebration, he becomes angry and lumbers across the forest to find some salt as a gift to himself. His adventure brings about a change of heart when he befriends a pack of baby wolves left alone after their mother is killed. Ereth saves them before in the end they save him.

## Riding Freedom

*Written by Pam Munoz Ryan*
*Illustrated by Brian Selznick*
Scholastic 1998, ISBN 0–590–95766-X

*In the mid-Eighteen Hundreds, when the East was young and the West was yet to be settled, a baby was born, named Charlotte. When she was nothing more than a bundle, she surprised her parents and puzzled the doctor by surviving several fevers. Folks said that any other baby would have died, but Charlotte was already strong. She walked before most babies crawled. She talked before most babies babbled, and she never cried unless someone took something away from her.* Charlotte is blessed with all these traits because the trials she will face in her life will demand of her unbelievable courage and iron-will determination to survive. Just a few months after her second birthday, her parents are killed and Charlotte is sent to an orphanage where she becomes a servant. Her only joy is working in the stables and being near the horses, which is a talent that everyone recognizes and some are extremely jealous of. Even with these overwhelming beginnings, problems keep mounting for young Charlotte. When she can no longer endure the misery she feels, she disguises herself as a boy and flees the orphanage. She earns the right to become a driver, which is unusual for one so young. Eventually, she journeys even farther west to settle and purchase land where she plans to build a way station. The story will appeal to both boys and girls. The book is well written with all the elements you want in a great read-aloud: the characters are well developed, the changing setting is essential to the story line, and the plot is well laid out, building the tension until you find out whether Charlotte will ever meet up with the two people who have befriended her.

## Shiloh

*Written by Phyllis Reynolds Naylor*
Aladdin 2000, ISBN 0–689–31614–3

Shiloh is a beagle who has the misfortune to be owned by a cruel man named Judd Travers. He beats his dogs regularly if they fail to perform up to his standards when he takes them out hunting. One day Shiloh meets a young boy named Marty who falls in love with the abused dog that is too sick to hunt and has not been fed properly. Marty wants so badly to own this dog. He knows that Judd would never sell the dog to him and he doesn't have the money to buy it anyway. His heart wins out and he bargains with Judd for labor in exchange for the ownership of Shiloh. All you have to do is open the cover and let the story flow like a slow-moving river. The current will pull your students into the book as they learn how Marty earns the right to keep Shiloh.

## A Single Shard

*Written by Linda Sue Park*
*Illustrated by Jean and Mou-sien Tseng*
Clarion Books 2001, ISBN 0–395–97827–0

Don't let the setting of twelfth-century Korea turn you away from reading this fine book. If you don't read it, students will miss an unforgettable experience and the opportunity to learn about the Korean culture of that period of time. Four years after reading the book, the scenes are still memorable and strong. Park did a marvelous job of developing the images of the young orphan, Tree-ear. The traditions observed by the Korean people of this century will be strange, but intriguing, to your listeners and will spur lots of discussion. Your heart will ache as you watch Tree-ear yearn for stability and you will admire his tenacity when you read about the lengths he will go to earn it. Come along with Tree-ear as he secretly watchers Min, the best potter in the village from whom he so desperately wants to learn the trade. Work alongside Tree-ear as he labors under the impression that Min will teach him if he works hard helping in Min's shop. Fall into despair with Tree-ear when his first plan fails. His strength of character will amaze you and make you smile in respect for this young man. As you near the end, you will want to prolong those final few chapters just to make the book last longer. This winner of the Newbery Medal is too good to miss.

### The Watsons Go to Birmingham – 1963

*Written by Christopher Paul Curtis*
Delacorte 1995, ISBN 0–385–32175–9

When you read this one aloud you and your students will laugh at the antics of these three children, together you will cry with Kenny as he witnesses things no young child should ever have to see, and you will sit in awe at the wisdom of the parents. Once the reading begins, this one will be hard to put down. In this his first book, Curtis weaves magic as he develops the characters in the Watson family: Momma (who is ashamed of her teeth), Dad (who had rather drive all night than risk his family suffering any kind of discrimination), little sister Joetta, Byron (thirteen and full of himself), and Kenny whose eyes let us see the story of his family. The Watsons live in Michigan but are preparing for a trip to Birmingham to visit their grandmother. Once in Birmingham, Kenny witnesses the aftermath of the bombing of the church that kills four little girls (the book is dedicated to them) and he thinks little Joetta was hurt as well. His fears about what happened live with him for many weeks. Once again we recommend leading up to this novel with picture books selected from a civil rights shelf in Chapter 6.

### What Jamie Saw

*Written by Carolyn Coman*
Puffin Books 1995, ISBN 0–14–038335–2

The first two sentences of this slim chapter book will hook a reader so quickly that the pages won't turn fast enough. *When Jamie saw him throw the baby, saw Van throw the little baby, saw Van throw his little sister Nin, when Jamie saw Van throw his baby sister Nin, then they moved. That very night or was it early morning? Some time of day or night that felt like it had no hour at all, Jamie and his mother and Nin left the house where they'd been living with Van—Van's house—and they drove to Earl's apartment above Daggert's Sand on Gravel in Stark, New Hampshire, and from there they went on to the trailer.* And just so you know, Jamie's mother walks into the room where Jamie and Nin are sleeping just in time to catch the baby when Van throws her. These two sentences alone create a rather disturbing image of Jamie and his family. These images will generate plenty of predictions about this scene and where it will lead us as readers. The book is excellent to use with upper grades because the content is more mature and the story naturally calls on all the comprehension strategies that all good readers use. Lucy Calkins introduced this book to us in a workshop where she read only a few pages to demonstrate strategies for comprehension. You can imagine that, like your children will, we wanted her to keep reading. We were so intrigued by those opening lines that within the week both of us had purchased the book just to find out how Jamie's life would unfold.

## *Tried-and-True: Books Recommended by Friends*

The following chapter books are ones recommended by friends of ours, friends who, like us, *love* to read aloud to their students. The contributors to this collection represent educators working at all levels. Our friends are classroom teachers from the primary grades through the university level, principals and literacy coaches, reading recovery teachers, Title I teachers and reading coordinators, and district-level trainers and curriculum specialists. They come from Alabama, Florida, from Illinois and Indiana, Minnesota, New Mexico, and North Carolina, from Ohio, South Carolina, and Tennessee. They have read these books to children and received great responses. We hope you will trust their recommendations as we do.

### Behind the Bedroom Wall

*Written by Laura E. Williams*
*Illustrated by A. Nancy Goldstein*
Milkweed Editions 1996, 2005, ISBN 1-57131-606-X

**Target Audience:** Fourth grade through middle school

**Bumper Sticker for Book:** It takes courage to do what's right.

**Brief Summary:** Thirteen-year-old Korinna Rehme, who is in the Nazi Youth Movement, has been brainwashed to believe that the "Fatherland" comes before family. To help Germany she believes her country must deal with the *Jewish problem*. The youth movement has taught her that Jews deserve the treatment they are getting, and anyone who helps them deserves the same.

When she discovers that what she thought were mice behind her bedroom wall are really Jews, she is shocked. She believes she should reveal the refugees and their protectors, her parents, to the authorities. The longer she waits to reveal them, the better acquainted she becomes with the five-year-old child hiding in dark and frightening conditions under the eaves and behind the wall. She begins to question the actions of her friends and the leaders of the youth movement.

**Reason It Is a Good Read-Aloud:** This is a good read-aloud for character development, chapter endings, and to help paint a broader picture of the time period of the Holocaust. *Behind the Bedroom Wall* emphasizes the manipulation of the Germans who influenced the most vulnerable—the children.

**Connections:** Social studies (history) and character education

**Suggested by:** Trudy Nelson, Fifth-Grade Teacher, Wea Ridge Elementary (Tippecanoe School Corporation), Lafayette, IN

## The Best School Year Ever

*Written by Barbara Robinson*
HarperCollins 1994, ISBN 0-06-023039-8

**Target Audience:** Third graders and up

**Bumper Sticker for Book:** When you take the time to know others, you find everyone has unique qualities.

**Comments from Children:** My students always want to take the book home and share it with their parents. I always read this at the beginning of the year, and my students can't wait to hear *The Best Christmas Pageant Ever* during the Christmas season.

**Brief Summary:** Beth's class has a yearlong project to find compliments to share with their classmates at the end of the school year. Beth is assigned Imogene Herdman who is the worst student in the class. How will she ever find a compliment to share with Imogene?

**Reason It Is a Good Read-Aloud:** The book has a great beginning that really gets the students' attention. It is also a great example of character development. The ending leaves the reader with a lasting impression. Most important, it captures the students and they can't wait to hear the next chapter. They laugh out loud while listening to this book.

**Connections:** I, like Beth, have met others who outwardly had few qualities that made me want to get to know them. However, when given the chance to know them better, I found them to be very interesting and I was glad I had taken the time to get to know them.

**Suggested by:** Julia Tsitouris, Third-Grade Teacher, Western Union Elementary School, Waxhaw, NC

## The Circle of Gold

*Written by Candy Dawson Boyd*
Scholastic 1984, ISBN 0–590–43266–4

**Target Audience:** Intermediate grades

**Bumper Sticker for Book:** Family is important.

**Brief Summary:** Mattie's family is drastically changed after her father's death. Mattie works to bring her family together again with a special surprise for Mother's Day.

**Reason It Is a Good Read-Aloud:** Imagery from description; events lead to excellent class discussions about family dynamics.

**Connections:** Every year I have shared this book with students, we had rich discussions on family dynamics and challenges—bad times as well as good times. Very few children were unable to relate in some fashion to a "one-parent" home. The students grew together as a stronger community as they shared stories about their own families. And there are lots of springboards for writing workshops.

**Suggested by:** Suzanne Brockmeier, Principal, Ranchvale Elementary School, Clovis, NM

## A Dog Called Kitty

*Written by Bill Wallace*
Minstrel 1980, 1992, ISBN 0–671–77081–0

**Target Audience:** K–4

**Bumper Sticker for Book:** Boy saves dog and dog saves boy.

**Brief Summary:** When young Ricky was a baby, he was attacked by a dog. So, when a stray puppy takes a liking to Ricky, he tells it to get lost. The puppy is persistent . . . and starving. If Ricky doesn't confront his fears, the puppy may die. This is a story of a boy who must be courageous when he is scared, and how he finds a very best friend.

**Reason It Is a Good Read-Aloud:** Children have a special place in their hearts for animals, from Rolly-Poly to puppies. And, we all have fears we must face—being afraid of the dark, standing up to a bully, or being bit by a dog. Wallace's book immediately draws in his audience, for we can all relate to the love of animals and overcoming fears.

**Connections:** *Stone Fox, Where the Red Fern Grows, The Black Stallion*

**Suggested by:** Elizabeth Olsen, Reading Curriculum Specialist, CORE Center for Academic Excellence, Crystal Lake, IL

## Frightful's Mountain

*Written by Jean Craighead George*
*Illustrated by Sara Reynolds*
Dutton 1999, ISBN 0–525–46166–3

**Target Audience:** Upper elementary

**Bumper Sticker for Book:** Captive bird has a point of view.

**Brief Summary:** Frightful is confused in a world without Sam. She doesn't perceive her environment as a wild bird of prey, yet her instinct is strong to survive. The book is full of excellent description.

**Reason It Is a Good Read-Aloud:** The book can be used as an excellent lead for teaching writing. It is a great example of descriptive settings and for the development of empathy for the needs of animals.

**Suggested by:** Eric Sink, Fifth-Grade Basecamp Teacher, Summit Charter School, Cashiers, NC

## Frog and Toad Together

*Written and Illustrated by Arnold Lobel*
HarperTrophy 1971, 1979, ISBN 0-06-444021-4

**Target Audience:** Kindergartners

**Bumper Sticker for Book:** Friends play together and care for each other.

**Comments from Children:** They are good friends.

**Brief Summary:** Frog and Toad have everyday adventures that afford many opportunities to be caring and respectful to each other.

**Reason It Is a Good Read-Aloud:** The stories are short . . . important for kindergartners at the beginning of the year. The children identify with the circumstances and the emotions that are displayed by Frog and Toad who jump right in to discuss the issues.

**Suggested by:** Mary Myron, Kindergarten Teacher, University School, Johnson City, TN

## Gooney Bird Greene

*Written by Lois Lowry*
*Illustrated by Middy Thomas*
Houghton Mifflin 2002, ISBN 0–618–23848–4

**Target Audience:** Second and third graders

**Bumper Sticker for Book:** Your life is a story.

**Comments from Children:** This is a wonderful story to demonstrate how children can write what they experience, using their imagination and word choice.

**Brief Summary:** This is a story about a precocious second child who is blessed with a wonderful storytelling sense and shares what happens to her every day to tell what seems to be a tall tale, but it is just daily experiences. It is through Gooney's wonderful sense of word choice and way of telling a story that she captures her second-grade friends and the teacher, who sit on the edge of their seats waiting and anticipating her next life experience.

**Reason It Is a Good Read-Aloud:** To entice students to write about their daily lives and how we all have stories to share.

**Suggested by:** Lisa Morgan, Literacy Coach/Title I Assistant Coordinator/Second-Grade Teacher, Garfield Elementary, Brainerd, MN

## Henry Huggins

*Written by Beverly Cleary*
*Illustrated by Louis Darling*
HarperTrophy 1990, 2000, ISBN 0-380-70912-0

**Target Audience:** Elementary age

**Bumper Sticker for Book:** A humorous book of tales about a third-grade boy who always seems to be getting into a bind.

**Comments from Children:** Henry is just like me! He always tries to do everything right, but he always ends up doing everything wrong! I just *have* to read the next book about his paper route to see what he does next!—Chase, First Grade

**Brief Summary:** Henry Huggins is a third-grade boy who adopts a stray dog and begins his adventure trying to figure out how to get the dog home on the bus. Henry is an endearing character that boys and girls of all ages can relate to.

**Reason It Is a Good Read-Aloud:** The book is a wonderful example of personal narrative. Each adventure is a small moment that is carefully retold in a humorous way. Young writers can see their lives are filled with small stories that can be captured with their pens. *Henry Huggins* is an excellent resource for teaching the story structure. The story begins, a problem is posed, the tension builds, finally reaching a climax, the solution is presented, and the tension releases into the ending. The ending is always a life's lesson learned.

**Connections:** *Henry Huggins* and *Junie B. Jones* are similar books because they both develop a single character throughout a school year. *Henry Huggins* also reads like *Homer Price*—a compilation of small moments in a single character's life.

**Suggested by:** Beth Swenson, Literacy Collaborative District Trainer, Brainerd School District, Brainerd, MN

## Hoot

*Written by Carl Hiaasen*
Knopf/Random House 2002, ISBN 0–375–82181–3

**Target Audience:** Upper elementary and middle school

**Bumper Sticker for Book:** Everyone should give a *hoot* about each other and the world we live in!

**Brief Summary:** Roy Eberhart, the new kid in town, is bullied on the school bus when he catches a glimpse of a barefoot boy running through the neighborhood. His adventures when he attempts to find this boy get him wrapped up in a mystery involving a construction site and endangered burrowing owls.

**Reason It Is a Good Read-Aloud:** Haissen's tongue-in-cheek humor makes this book an excellent read-aloud choice for upper elementary and middle school students. His characters are truly brought to life through vivid descriptions, and students will be able to relate to Roy's vulnerability and his need to be accepted in a new town. There are several themes throughout the book that lead readers and listeners to make many inferences about real-world issues such as bullying and ecological concerns.

**Suggested by:** Leah Kinniburgh, Assistant Professor, Lynn University, Boca Raton, FL

## I'll Meet You at the Cucumbers

*Written by Lillian Moore*
*Illustrated by Sharon Wooding*
Atheneum 1988, ISBN 0–689–31243–1

**Target Audience:** K–2

**Bumper Sticker for Book:** Facing fears with courage.

**Brief Summary:** Adam Mouse faces his fear of leaving his home in the country to visit his pen pal, Amanda Mouse, in the city. He discovers that the letters he has written to her are poetry and that he is a poet.

**Reason It Is a Good Read-Aloud:** The book is filled with the poems of Adam Mouse, as well as a few well-known poems by Carl Sandburg and Langston Hughes. The action keeps younger readers' attention as Adam explores the city.

**Connections:** Genre study of poetry and letter writing

**Suggested by:** Ann Griffin, First-Grade Teacher, Mississippi Creative Arts School, St. Paul, MN

## Just Like Martin

*Written by Ossie Davis*
Puffin Books 1992, 1995, ISBN 0–140-37095-1

**Target Audience:** Fifth through eighth graders

**Bumper Sticker for Book:** Peace is won through using our hearts and minds—not arms!

**Comments from Children:** (1) This book made me think twice when I wanted to hit someone. (2) This book made me hear name-calling on the bus and not be afraid to stand up for the person being ragged on. (3) This book made me feel like I was there, like I was living inside Doresthena and Stone. (4) I could feel what they were feeling and that made me know what was coming up next. It was like "edge of your seat."

**Brief Summary:** The first novel by the late Ossie Davis is a historical fiction chapter book set in Alabama during the civil rights movement. The book opens as a church group is readying to leave for the March on Washington. It is set in a fictional town reminiscent of Birmingham, in a fictional church much like the 16th Street Baptist, with fictional characters. The events, how-ever, are most often ripped from the pages of history allowing students to live the events through characters much like themselves who have home, family, coming-of-age, romance, and identity issues that are as real today as they were during the 1960s. Each chapter ends with just enough foreshadowing and ten-sion to make students want the reader to keep reading. As a read-aloud, it is a jewel.

**Suggested by:** Louanne Jacobs, Professor and Professional Development Coor-dinator, Alabama A & M University, Normal, AL

## To Kill a Mockingbird

*Written by Harper Lee*

HarperCollins 1960, 1988, ISBN 0–06–019499-5

**Target Audience:** Grades 5 through 10

**Brief Summary:** Scout Finch, her brother Jem, and their father Atticus live in Maycomb, a small Alabama town. The children like to act out stories and be-come fascinated by a spooky house where Boo Radley lives. Atticus, a lawyer, defends Tom Robinson, a black man accused of raping a white woman, caus-ing Scout and Jem to be subjected to abuse by other children. At the local jail where a mob threatens to lynch Tom Robinson, Scout causes one of its leaders to disperse the mob by shaming him about his behavior through questions she asks him. Although Atticus proves Tom's innocence, the all-white jury convicts him anyway. Tom is shot to death as he attempts to escape from prison. Jem's faith in justice is tarnished. Boo Radley saves Jem and Scout from an attack by the father of the woman who claimed that she had been raped by Tom. Scout realizes that Boo is a human being, and she takes her fa-ther's continual advice of seeing life from another's perspective before making judgments. *To Kill a Mockingbird* is a story of the nature of human beings: in-nocence, prejudice, ignorance, justice, humanity, good, evil, and courage.

**Reason It Is a Good Read-Aloud:** This is a wonderful book to read aloud because of the rich characters and moral lessons.

**Connections:** Historical connections can be made to the Great Depression; and culturally, connections to life in the South and to the fact that good and evil can prevail relative to prejudice and courage.

**Suggested by:** Mary W. Spor, Professor of Reading/Literacy, Alabama A & M University, Normal, AL

## The Last of the Really Great Whangdoodles

*Written by Julie Andrews Edwards*

HarperCollins 1974, 1996, ISBN 0–06–021805–3

**Target Audience:** Elementary

**Bumper Sticker for Book:** Readers are encouraged to look beyond what meets the eye and use their imaginations.

**Comments from Children:** Former students who are now in high school still email to say that this is their favorite book.

**Brief Summary:** A professor and three children go on a quest to find Whangdoodleland, a perfect world of peace, love, and fun.

**Reason It Is a Good Read-Aloud:** The book provides wonderful opportunities for the reader's voice to take the listener on an adventure.

**Suggested by:** Nita Thompson, Assistant Principal, and Kathy Bickley, Teacher, at Vestavia Hills Elementary East, Vestavia Hills, AL

## Mr. Putter & Tabby Paint the Porch

*Written by Cynthia Rylant*

*Illustrated by Arthur Howard*

Harcourt 2000, 2001, ISBN 0–15–201787–9

**Target Audience:** Preschool and kindergarten

**Bumper Sticker for Book:** Painting and scampering animals don't mix!

**Comments from Children:** Tabby is just like my cat. He likes to curl on my mom's neck. Read it to us again! Why didn't Mr. Putter just put Tabby up?

**Brief Summary:** Mr. Putter loves his cat Tabby and they like to sit on the porch and read together. But on this spring day, he notices how badly his porch needs painting, so rather than reading he decides to paint. But when squirrels scamper across the porch, Tabby gives chase causing paint to fly everywhere. The next morning Mr. Putter tries again but this time his neighbor's dog causes another big spill. Finally, both animals are put up so the porch can finally be painted and this time instead of pink or blue, it was painted a lovely yellow.

**Reason It Is a Good Read-Aloud:** What we've grown to expect when we see Cynthia Rylant's name on any book proves to be true for her short chapter books as well. In the Mr. Putter and Tabby Series, she chooses to use many of the same crafting techniques we've grown to love in her other outstanding books.

**Connections:** The two series written by Cynthia Rylant—*Mr. Putter and Tabby* and *Poppleton*—would make a great author's study for first and second graders to compare and contrast her craft. Both are excellent examples of story structure with one having chapters that relate and tell a complete story *(Mr. Putter and Tabby)* while the other shows each chapter as a stand-alone story (*Poppleton*).

**Suggested by:** Christy W. Johnson, Reading Recovery and Writing Resource, Frances Nungester Elementary School, Decatur, AL

## Ramona Forever

*Written by Beverly Cleary*
*Illustrated by Alan Tiegreen*
Morrow Junior Books 1984, ISBN 0–688–03785–2

**Target Audience:** Primary ages

**Bumper Sticker for Book:** Growing up is hard work.

**Brief Summary:** Ramona Quimby is an average third grader with the world on her shoulders. The rich uncle of her best friend, Howie, is coming to town from Saudi Arabia with grown-up presents and a heart for her Aunt Bea. Ramona buries her beloved cat, Picky-picky, saves a wedding, and gets a new baby sister. Her family doesn't have the most money or the easiest life, but Ramona is always Ramona.

**Reason It Is a Good Read-Aloud:** Beverly Cleary develops her characters in a down-to-earth setting that excites the reader and keeps them wanting to read more. The illustrations create the opportunity for kids to visualize the story. The vocabulary is easily understood by most young children.

**Connections:** Most third graders deal with bossy siblings or adults who don't appear to understand them. Ramona's life connects with them and will provide students the opportunity to develop a positive self-esteem as well as a sense of pride.

**Suggested by:** Rachel Chapman, Austin High School Student, Woodmeade Elementary Office Aide, Decatur, AL

## Stone Fox

*Written by John Reynolds Gardiner*
*Illustrated by Marcia Sewall*
HarperCollins 1980, ISBN 0–690–03983–2

**Target Audience:** First and second graders

**Bumper Sticker for Book:** Hope, determination, and love prevail.

**Comments from Children:** (1) Little Willy made me cry. . . . (2) I never knew what a city slicker was before. (3) I am getting *Stone Fox* for my birthday.

**Brief Summary:** Ten-year-old Willy is determined to give his sick grandfather a reason to live. He hitches up his dog, Searchlight, to the plow and harvests the potato crop all by himself to keep the farm going. Now he needs money to pay off back taxes to save the farm. He enters a dogsled race against the best racers in the county. He is determined to beat the legendary Indian, Stone Fox, and get the $500 prize to save the farm. He reaches his goal in a gripping and memorable way.

**Reason It Is a Good Read-Aloud:** The language is masterfully used to grip the listener for a fast-paced story of farm life in Wyoming. The vocabulary is enriching, exposing students to words such as *strongbox, city slicker, moccasin, Samoyed, general store,* and *reservation.* The lead is so powerful that it hooks a young audience in just two sentences: *One day Grandfather wouldn't get out of bed. He just lay there and stared at the ceiling and looked sad.* Gardiner gives each character a distinct personality with his dialogue and the descriptive language he uses to bring each one to life.

**Suggested by:** Paulette Grady, Literacy Coordinator, Lakota Local Schools, Shawnee Elementary School, Cincinnati, OH

## The Tale of Despereaux

*Written by Kate DiCamillo*
*Illustrated by Timothy Basil Ering*
Candlewick 2003, ISBN 0763617229

**Target Audience:** Grades 9–12, but can be read aloud to children much younger

**Bumper Sticker for Book:** Love conquers all.

**Comments from Children:** WOW . . . just one more chapter, please!

**Brief Summary:** *Reader, it is your destiny to find out* (sentence from the book).

**Reason It Is a Good Read-Aloud:** The language is versed in fairy-tale prose. The entire book has a remarkable voice that just beckons to be read aloud. The characters are unforgettable. Flashbacks, foreshadowing, and narration abound . . . need I say more?

**Connections:** Since the main character is a mouse/rat, this book fits well with Avi's Poppy books or O'Brien's The Rats of NIMH Series. Despereaux also acts as a catalyst for several minilessons.

**Suggested by:** Josh Lynch, Third-Grade Teacher, Cowee Elementary School, Franklin, NC

## Tuck Everlasting

*Written by Natalie Babbitt*

Farrar, Straus and Giroux 1975, 1985, 2000, ISBN 0–374–48012-5

**Target Audience:** Fifth graders and up

**Bumper Sticker for Book:** If you could choose to live forever, would you?

**Comments from Children:** Children love this book—it is a classic. I have shared it with fourth- and fifth-grade students as well as with my second graders this last year. I was hesitant to share it with a younger crowd, but the timing seemed right. Sadly, death had been such a part of our year—one child's mother lost a baby, our superintendent died, our principal's mother died, Pope John Paul II died. The class devoured every minute of the book. Babbitt's rich words and lush description helped them understand, even at their young ages, that death is indeed a part of life.

**Brief Summary:** Suffocating from a life spent with her overbearing family, Winnie Foster meets the Tuck family. This meeting begins as a kidnapping and grows to a thunderous climax complete with a murder and a jailbreak. Follow Winnie as she embarks on her journey with the Tuck's and discover how they changed her life forever.

**Reason It Is a Good Read-Aloud:** The language is extraordinary, perfect for visualization as it is read aloud to younger children or read independently by older ones. From the murder scene on page 100: *But Mae's face was dark red. "Not Winnie!" she said between clenched teeth. "You ain't going to do a thing like that to Winnie. And you ain't going to give out our secret." Her strong arms swung the shotgun round her head, like a wheel. The man in the yellow suit jerked away, but it was too late. With a dull cracking sound, the stock of the shotgun smashed into the back of his skull. He dropped like a tree, his face surprised, his eyes wide open.* How can a reader *not* be at that scene? You can hear it happening . . . you can see it happening . . . you can feel it happening.

**Suggested by:** Clark Underbackke, Second-Grade Teacher, Trace Crossings Elementary, Hoover, AL

## Where the Red Fern Grows

*Written by Wilson Rawls*

Delacorte/Bantam 1974, 1996, ISBN 0–385–32330–1

**Target Audience:** Third graders and up

**Bumper Sticker for Book:** Boy loves dogs.

**Comments from Children:** Children plead with the reader to "stop" because it is so sad and to "keep going" because it is so gripping.

**Brief Summary:** A poor mountain boy yearns to have a pair of dogs. After much wishing and saving, he purchases two dogs. This is a family story of courage, sacrifice, love, and death.

**Reason It Is a Good Read-Aloud:** Students get very attached to the main character and are pulled into his life. Wonderful discussions take place about the character's hardships, about his love of family, and about how much he cherishes his dogs.

**Connections:** This book offers a good sense of time and place as well as an opportunity for students to make many connections to their own lives and their pets, as well as connections to other characters and stories.

**Suggested by:** Jan Scott, Principal, Jonesville Elementary in Union County, Union, SC

## Words of Stone

*Written by Kevin Henkes*

Puffin Books 1993, ISBN 0-140-36601-6

**Target Audience:** Fourth through sixth graders

**Bumper Sticker for Book:** Life can hurt and friends help heal.

**Comments from Children:** (1) I can identify with Blaze. (2) When I lost someone I loved, I found ways to cope that would not be understood by other people. (3) Joselle is really mean at first. You have to forgive her because she is hurting inside, just like Blaze. (4) Kevin Henkes knows how to write about "real things."

**Brief Summary:** Ten-year-old Blaze has had a ritual with imaginary friends on the anniversary of his mother's death for each of the past five years. He spends quiet summers with his grandmother until the *summer of Joselle*. Joselle torments Blaze by writing cruel messages in the stones around his mother's place of worship. He is disturbed and intrigued. The relationship grows to a trusting friendship that neither of them expected.

**Reason It Is a Good Read-Aloud:** Kevin Henkes provides descriptive writing in this book without going over the edge. The reader is introduced to the characters through their thoughts, conversations, and actions. Blaze and Joselle are developed in a way that the reader can almost think their thoughts. Henkes' writing in each of the chapters as they draw to a close makes the reader want to keep right on reading.

**Connections:** *Words of Stone* is real. Kids do see struggles in life, when adults tell them to *shake it off and keep going.* Readers will realize they are not alone, even if their situations are different from Blaze and Joselle's. This book offers hope. Its content offers a balance to the fast-paced life lived by many. It doesn't come with batteries, magic, remote controls, or computers. Henkes gives the reader powerful words, a realistic story line that can be pondered, and may even change the lens through which the reader views the world.

**Suggested by:** Patti Greene, Reading Coordinator, Prior Lake-Savage Area Schools, Prior Lake, MN

# A Closing Word

Wow, you made it all the way to the end and now you know our vision for what is possible. We recognize that simply finding appropriate books is one of the daunting tasks that keeps many teachers from reading aloud more than they do. We have done much of the initial work and have generated a good place to start for any teacher. We can only hope that you will now move from our shelves into your classroom and school and community libraries and begin pulling books to share with students.

Before you leave us, remember that we know time is a precious and often fleeting resource in the classroom. Please think about the six opportunities for reading aloud and consider those times during the day when minutes slip into space—those transition points between the various components of your day.

- Can one or more of those transition times be made to *work for you* with a read-aloud?
- Can you open the day with a short book and let that text *work for you* for classroom community-building and character education and conflict resolution and other issues that may arise in the format of a class?
- Can you begin a lesson or class with a read-aloud that can actually layer in content and vocabulary to extend your teaching point for the day and *work for you* in the curriculum?
- Can you give poetry a prominent place during the day and consistently immerse students in the rich and potent language of a poem?
- Can you feature carefully selected segments of texts to support writing workshop?
- Can you close the day with the gift of an ongoing story that will pull students in and have them living among the characters?
- Can you bear to let another day pass in which children miss the opportunity to learn from the authors you have grown to trust and admire?

• Can we afford the possibility of children who have never been pulled from the banks of onlooking into the swift currents of well-written texts flowing on the voices of passionate teachers like you?

We have shared our vision of what is possible. We can only hope that some of that will overlap with your vision and that by working together we will all see children learning under the influence of language and literature.

## Support for the Six Opportunities to Read-Aloud

## Support for the Six Opportunities to Read-Aloud, continued

| Read-Aloud Opportunity | Bookshelves |
|---|---|
| | *Holocaust Starter Set* |
| | *Immigration Starter Set* |
| | *America Starter Set* |
| | 1. Famous Americans |
| | 2. Historic Landmarks and Symbols |
| | 3. The U.S. Presidency and Voting in the United States |
| | *Living Through Conflict, Working Toward Peace* |
| | 1. Revolutionary War |
| | 2. Civil War |
| | 3. World War II |
| | 4. Japanese Internment Camps |
| | 5. Division of North Korea and South Korea |
| | 6. Vietnam War |
| | 7. Contemporary Events |
| *Language Arts* | 1. The Power of Talk |
| | 2. Taking Delight in the Sounds of Language and the Power of Words |
| | 3. Books that Feature Chunking Words |
| | 4. Books that Play with Compound Words |
| | 5. Books that Feature Idioms, Similes, Metaphors, Proverbs |
| | 6. Books that Play with Nouns |
| | 7. Books that Feature Oxymoron |
| | 8. Books that Play with Puns |
| | 9. Books that Feature Superlatives |
| | 10. Books that Feature Vowels and Consonants Wordplay |
| *Science* | Life Science Starter Set |
| | 1. Animals, Birds, Insects, and Fish |

Note: Starter sets can be found in our companion book *Building Bridges Across the Curriculum with Picture Books and Read-Alouds* (2006, Heinemann).

## Support for the Six Opportunities to Read-Aloud, continued

| Read-Aloud Opportunity | Bookshelves |
|---|---|
| | Earth Science Starter Set |
| | 1. Landforms and Bodies of Water |
| | 2. Plants |
| | 3. Rain Forest |
| | 4. Trees and Forests |
| | 5. Seasons and Weather |
| | Space Science Starter Set |
| | 1. Earth, Moon, Sun |
| | 2. Galaxies and Stars |
| | 5. Seasons and Weather |
| | Space Science Starter Set |
| | 1. Earth, Moon, Sun |
| | 2. Galaxies and Stars |
| *Mathematics* | |
| | 1. Addition |
| | 2. Algorithms |
| | 3. Calendars |
| | 4. Comparisons |
| | 5. Counting |
| | 6. Division |
| | 7. Fractions |
| | 8. Geometry |
| | 9. Graphing |
| | 10. Greater Than, Less Than |
| | 11. Measurement |
| | 12. Money |
| | 13. Multiplication |
| | 14. Patterns |
| | 15. Percentages |
| | 16. Shapes |
| | 17. Sorting |
| | 18. Subtraction |
| | 19. Time |
| | 20. Volume |
| | 21. Weights |

Note: Starter sets can be found in our companion book *Building Bridges Across the Curriculum with Picture Books and Read-Alouds* (2006, Heinemann).

# Works Cited

Calkins, Lucy. 1991. *Living Between the Lines.* Portsmouth, NH: Heinemann.

Kennedy, X. J., and Dorothy M. Kennedy. 1999. *Knock at a Star.* Boston: Little Brown and Company.

Laminack, Lester. 2000. "Living Language: The Art of Reading Aloud." *Teaching K–8* (September): 80–81.

———. Summer 2002. Hamline University Magalog. Professional Development for Educators, 56–57.

Paterson, Katherine. 1995. *A Sense of Wonder: On Reading and Writing Books for Children.* Calgary, Alberta Canada: Plume.

Peterson, Ralph. 1992. *Life in a Crowded Place: Making a Learning Community.* Portsmouth, NH: Heinemann.

Rogers, Fred. 2003. *The World According to Mister Rogers: Important Things to Remember.* New York: Hyperion.

Routman, Regie. 2003. *Reading Essentials.* Portsmouth, NH: Heinemann.

Rylant, Cynthia. 1990. "The Room in Which Van Gogh Lived." In *Workshop 2: Beyond the Basal,* edited by Nancie Atwell, 18–21. Portsmouth, NH: Heinemann.

# Index